# The Achievement Factors

# The
# Achievement
# Factors

*Candid Interviews With Some
of the Most Successful People
of Our Time*

## B. Eugene Griessman

Avant Books®
Slawson Communications, Inc.
San Marcos, California

Published by Avant Books®
Slawson Communications, Inc.
165 Vallecitos de Oro
San Marcos, CA 92069-1436
Cover design by Robert Antler

1  2  3  4  5  6  7  8  9  10


Library of Congress Cataloging-in-Publication Data

Griessman, B. Eugene
    The achievement factors: candid interviews with some of the most
successful people of our time / B. Eugene Griessman.
        p.      cm.
    Includes index.
    1. Success.    2. Celebrities—United States—Interviews
I. Title.
BJ1611.2.G75    1987
158'.1—dc19                                                90-53190
ISBN: 0-932238-53-X                                          CIP

Dedicated to Charles T. Briqueleur

# Contents

# Acknowledgments

Sid Pike provided the resources to begin this project, when he permitted me to do three interviews to help meet WTCG-TV's FCC public-service requirements. Vicki Rubensohn and Judy Henry assisted with its conceptualization and implementation. Auburn University provided a few hundred dollars to transcribe the material I was obtaining. A great boost for the project came when Lee Walburn, then editor of the *Atlanta Weekly*, gave me the opportunity to do a number of in-depth interviews for that magazine.

There have been other editors and television executives who have provided support: Billy Winn at *Atlanta* magazine and *Goodlife* magazine; Ted Turner, Bob Wussler, Jack Petrick, Jim Kitchell and Joe Rothenberger at Turner Broadcasting Corporation; Michelle Osborn, John Seigenthaler, and Peter Pritchard at *USA Today*; Joe Vecchione and Arthur Pincus at the *New York Times*; David Osier and Colleen Kelly at the *Atlanta Journal/Constitution*.

For assistance and valuable suggestions on this book,

I am profoundly grateful to Charles T. Briqueleur, Robin Bartlett, Mel Kanzberg, A.D. Van Nostrand, Joan Pettigrew, John Dunn, Ruth C. Hale, Regina Chaney, Andjela Kessler, Nick Scelsi, Melanie Belkin, Peter Grennan, Mark Bergeron, John Maloney, Robert Antler, Laura Stover, and Julia Glass, my editor. Others who helped with the interviews are Mark Ethridge, Randall Willis, Denise Jones, and Miriam Freeman.

My colleagues at Georgia Tech's News Bureau and in the School of Social Sciences—especially Charles Harmon, Dan Papp, Warren Heemann, and Cecil Phillips—provided a friendly and supportive climate in which to do my research and writing. My daughters—Katrina, Sharon, and Gloria—provided continual encouragement as well as thoughtful and valuable ideas. Finally, the interviewees themselves, who gave their time and risked their reputations—for that is what a person does whenever he or she grants an interview—deserve, and have, my deep gratitude. I know that their candid accounts of successes and failures will provide encouragement and guidance to many individuals who are not yet known as high achievers but someday will be.

# Introduction

High achievement is the American dream, perhaps *the* fundamental principle of our culture, the stuff of which novels and movies are made. High achievers score touchdowns, win elections, make key sales, and thereby gain fame, bonuses, corner offices with views, titles, and honors. Likely for everybody? No, but not an impossible dream. In our society, it happens often enough that people actually plan their success campaigns and take the spoils.

In the American dream, a person starts from scratch but makes it to the top, usually against difficult odds. Actually, most upwardly mobile individuals make only slow incremental moves, usually about a half-grade per generation—from upper-lower to lower-middle class, or from upper-middle to lower-upper class. Rarely does anyone move from lower-lower to the upper class. And no one moves from lower-lower to upper-upper, because upper-upper is, by definition, "old" money.

But occasionally people do take giant steps—from a dirt-floored mountain cabin to a penthouse lined with

Picassos. That happened to Xavier Roberts, producer of the Cabbage Patch Kids. And there are others: J. B. Fuqua, multimillionaire head of Fuqua Industries, who never went to college, yet has been so successful (and generous) that Duke University's school of business bears his name. And Senator Robert C. Byrd, longtime Democratic leader of the U.S. Senate, who finished law school part-time after he became a U.S. senator. All three started from scratch, without wealth or connections.

This is a book about Xavier Roberts, J. B. Fuqua, Robert C. Byrd, and scores of others like them—high achievers from different fields: business leaders, inventors, entrepreneurs, astronauts, composers, football coaches, scientists, entertainers, U.S. Senators, designers, ballplayers, writers, the President of the United States.

You will recognize many of the names. You have seen them in person or on television, worn clothes with their labels, bought their products, watched them perform, voted for or against them, read their books, seen their plays. This book tells what they did to reach their goals—often in their own words.

I began this study almost accidentally. During the mid-1970s, I began producing and hosting public-affairs programs for a television station in Atlanta, owned by a then relatively unknown entrepreneur named Ted Turner. I convinced Sid Pike, who was then Turner's station manager, that we should use television for historical purposes. We should record for future generations what major figures of our day were like, what they thought, and what they said about their lives. We agreed on the name "Up Close," and I began to interview leading figures in literature, art, music, politics, science, religion, business, and sports. People like David Rockefeller, Tennessee Williams, Hank Aaron, John Huston, Gloria Swanson, and Ronald Reagan. The television interviews led to further opportunities in newspapers and magazines, which gave the project even wider scope.

In 1982, I came to Georgia Tech, first as a visiting professor and subsequently as director of national media relations. Here I gained access to a remarkably successful and diverse group of alumni, plus a number of visiting luminaries, including Jacques Cousteau, B. F. Skinner, and Herbert A. Simon.

At first, I did not think about testing hypotheses, even hunches. I was trying to collect the raw data of history for future generations. But I soon began to be aware of similar answers to the questions I was asking. Could it be that great baseball players, serious composers, and the heads of major corporations have common experiences, similar qualities? I began to listen carefully for any mention of these factors, to look for them, to ask about them.

Several factors cropped up again and again—often enough for me to believe that they are central to high achievement in many, many fields. This is not to say that all high achievers are alike, or that all of them display all the characteristics in uniform amounts. Certainly not. The men and women I interviewed are anything but cookie cutouts. Some high achievers are very persistent—one of the factors—but are not overly concerned about time management, another of the factors. Some high achievers are highly focused, but they tend not to be very aggressive or claim to be courageous.

I eventually grouped the factors into nine clusters. This arrangement seems to capture many of the ideas that high achievers frequently mention when they or outside observers and biographers account for their success.

In this book, I define a high achiever as someone whose work and reputation is such that he or she cannot be ignored by people in their field. (Their peers do not have to approve of their work, but they must reckon with it.) This is a working definition—what social scientists sometimes call an "operational definition."

Peer evaluations are subjective, obviously. There is no universally accepted standard of excellence written somewhere on golden plates. Nor are evaluations about achievement timeless. Tastes, needs, and interests change. Knowledge increases. Today's success story may be forgotten tomorrow. And today's obscure scientist may be important tomorrow. Thus, Gregor Mendel is, by this definition, a high achiever because, even though his work on genetics went virtually unnoticed in his lifetime, all geneticists today take Mendel's work into account.

In addition to interviews, I have sought corroborative material from biographies, journalistic accounts, and autobiographies of high achievers. And, because much of the data is admittedly anecdotal, whenever possible I have sought explanations from the research material and theories of the social sciences.

High achievers tend to become wealthy, and wealthy individuals often hire wonderfully efficient gatekeepers, who keep interviewers like me at bay. Perhaps that is one reason social science knows so little about upper-class behavior. Interestingly, after I got past the gatekeepers, I usually found the high achievers to be friendly, cooperative and often quite candid. I cannot say as much for several of their functionaries.

Some achievement is beyond the reach of most humans. Mozarts and da Vincis are thrown up from time to time, for whom there is no accounting—prodigious talents beyond comparison. But many of the world's high achievers have not had extraordinary talent. Paul "Bear" Bryant, the legendary football coach, once told me what he did best was finding ordinary ballplayers and helping them become extraordinary. He produced achievers out of individuals who were only vaguely aware of their capabilities.

If pressed, most of us will admit that we too feel the tug of ambition—the desire to be really good at something. The goals may be crass or lofty: acquiring a bulging bank account, becoming head of the organization, owning a Rolls, gaining membership on the million-dollar roundtable, winning the Nobel Prize, producing a powerful novel, or creating a great painting. Even deeply religious people who eschew secular goals aspire to spiritual ones.

We are interested in the people who win races, individuals who triumph over difficulties. We like to see skill, bravery, and endurance pay off. We look to these people as role models, as leaders.

Leadership is an important and fascinating part of the phenomenon of high achievement—and this book discusses the achievement of several major leaders—but the leader is only one kind of high achiever.

Many world-renowned achievers have not been *leaders* in the basic sense of the word. They have not managed or controlled other people, and they have not had "schools" of followers. Some have been more or less solitary individuals.

Can the achievement factors be applied to an individual reader's situation? Why not? Not every factor will apply to every career, certainly, because some achievement factors are a matter of chance or social circumstance. But other factors *are* under the control of individual initiative.

For the individual who is willing to pay the price to be a high achiever—and make no mistake about it, there is a price to be paid—the achievement factors can be studied as a program of action.

Virtually everybody would like to get ahead, but many people simply don't know how. They may be working hard at the wrong job, or not using the telephone effectively, or spending quality time on minimum-wage tasks. Simple mistakes or omissions, perhaps, but enough to spell the difference between success and failure, between making the team and getting cut, between rejection slips and contracts, between being selected for promotion or watching somebody else get the plum job.

Often, what they need most is some straight, honest talk from someone who knows how to succeed—good advice—advice that is wise and honest. Not just any advice, though, because the old saying is true: advice is cheap. What is needed is advice from people who have succeeded, people who cleared the hurdles and broke out in front.

That's exactly what this book gives you. It asks high achievers how and why they cleared the hurdles, and gives their replies.

# 1

# Finding A Vocation and A Specialty

*I think the foremost quality—there's no success without it—is really loving what you do. If you love it, you do it well, and there's no success if you don't do well what you're working at.*

—Malcolm Forbes

*I guess the essence of life for me is finding something you enjoy doing that gives meaning to life, and then being in a situation where you can do it.*

—Isaac Asimov

*I love my work. Other people have hobbies—I just love my work. I adore it. Because of loving the work, I don't have any ambition at all. The job comes up and I do the job. I don't do the job to gain something else. I just like doing the job.*

—Bob Hoskins

## False Starts

Not many people know that Kris Kristofferson, the songwriter and actor, began his career as a military man. The son of an Army officer, Kristofferson majored in English literature at Pomona College, and—because he was an excellent student as well as a gifted athlete—was selected as a Rhodes scholar, eventually studying at Oxford University.

After college and the Rhodes-scholar days, Kristofferson enlisted in the Army, where he served as a helicopter pilot. If, at that point in his life, you had asked Kristofferson where his career was pointed, he might have replied, "West Point, where I intend to teach English literature."

But something was gnawing inside him. Years earlier, when he was studying in England, he had encountered the writings of William Blake, a writer who has held him in thrall ever since. One day, Kristofferson came upon a sentence in an obscure letter Blake had written in 1802. In it Blake had said: "If you who are organized by Divine Providence for spiritual communion refuse, and bury your talent in the earth, even if you should want natural bread, sorrow and desperation will pursue you through life, and after death shame and confusion of face to eternity."

"That was exactly what I wanted to hear," Kristofferson remembers that he told himself: "I'll be one [a creative person]... I gotta be one."

But time passed and Kristofferson did not keep his promise—although he tried. In Germany, where he was a pilot for the local general, Kristofferson organized a band that played at enlisted men's clubs. During those years, Kristofferson would write songs and mail them off, but nobody paid much attention to them.

Then, in 1965, when he was twenty-nine years old —over the opposition of friends and family, and, in particular, his father, whom he adored—Kristofferson made the plunge. Resigning his commission, he departed for Nashville, where he intended to become a full-time songwriter. In those days Nashville was *the* place to be, a thriving town full of energy, ready for a new breed of musician.

But Kristofferson was not greeted by instant applause, autograph seekers, or favorable reviews. He became the janitor at Columbia Records. "Bob Dylan was the first person I swept up after," Kristofferson recalls. There followed other tough, poor-paying jobs he took just to make ends meet. He took a job on an oil rig in the Gulf Coast, where he would work two weeks and then come back to Nashville, where he could write, learn, promote his work, and perfect his craft.

Meanwhile, his first marriage unraveled. "I lived in a slum tenement on $150 a month for booze, gasoline, cigarettes, food, rent—everything. I didn't have squat. One time I came back home and somebody had broken into my apartment and stolen my trash, and when the police told me they'd been in there, they said, 'They really trashed the place.' Well, I hadn't even known anybody had been in there ... it was such a shambles." Kristofferson laughed when we talked about it. "But the feeling was such that I had nothing left to lose, you know. It was really exhilarating, and that's where the line 'Freedom's just another word for nothing left to lose' came from."

The career of the celebrated science-fiction writer Isaac Asimov follows a similar pattern of hesitant starts. Asimov began his career as a researcher and college professor—he has an earned doctorate in chemistry from Columbia University—but his real love was writing science fiction and books and articles about science for the general public. Unfortunately, some administrators at Boston University School of Medicine felt an associate professor of biochemistry ought to be cranking out research articles instead of writing popular books. Things came to a head in 1957, when Asimov was thirty-seven years old. No more writing popular books on university time, his department head instructed him.

Asimov, in his defense, replied: "As a researcher, I can do a creditable job, but I am merely adequate—no more. As a science writer, on the other hand, I am one of the best in the world, and I intend to become *the best* ..." (Asimov 1980:111)

He already had tenure, so the young associate professor, who had published twenty-three books, told the obstinate and shortsighted school administrators that he would take a leave of absence without pay. That leave of absence has lasted three decades. In 1979, however, the Boston University School of Medicine, of its own accord, promoted Asimov to full professor.

In Asimov's case, the time came when he had to decide between a secure position doing what he knew he could do adequately, on the one hand, and an uncertain future doing what he felt he could do exceptionally well. Asimov chose the latter. At last count, Asimov had published 364 books, and was still going strong at the rate of about a book a month.

Kristofferson's and Asimov's early frustrations are not new or original experiences. In the early nineteenth century, Thomas Carlyle, the Scottish historian, philosopher, and essayist, first studied for the ministry but gave it up when he could no longer accept the narrowness of its creeds. He then tried teaching, but eventually gave that up too. Then he turned to writing, which, he said, was an "immense victory."

Later, in one of his essays, Carlyle wrote: "Blessed is he who has found his work; let him ask no other blessedness."

Vincent Van Gogh, the tragic, brilliant painter, also came to art after an unsuccessful stint in the ministry. Van Gogh's father was a clergyman, but his uncle, also named Vincent, was a successful art merchant, who had developed Goupil and Company into the largest chain of art stores in Europe. As a youngster, Vincent often visited his favorite uncle's home in the well-to-do suburb of Breda in the Netherlands, where he was exposed to his uncle's excellent art collection. Those early impressions in Breda never left him. (Lubin 1972:34)

When Van Gogh was twenty-six years old and still a lay preacher, his religious sponsors withdrew their support, saying that he had no talent as a public speaker and that his passion for self-denial bordered on the manic. They were right. He was no orator, by all accounts, and shortly before his firing, there was an episode in which Vincent gave almost all his personal possessions away, including nearly every article of his clothing, and slept in an outhouse on straw. The officials of the project felt that the young clergyman was taking Christian teachings a tad too seriously.

Then he turned to what all along had been something that gave him great pleasure—his drawing. Four years after the trauma of leaving the ministry, Van Gogh wrote his brother Theo: "In my opinion, I am often *rich as Croesus*—not in money, but (though it doesn't happen every day) rich—because I have found in my work something which I can devote myself to heart and soul, and which inspires me and gives a meaning to life." (Bernard 1985:43)

Blake and Carlyle and Van Gogh have described what writers sometimes speak of as "finding one's voice." Kristofferson, in fact, has taken Blake's words as a kind of personal watchword: "I really think that at least in this life, if you're set down to do something, and you don't, you'll be miserable. I've tried to live accordingly. I'll try to be a creative artist as long as I'm conscious."

James D. Watson, who with Francis Crick received the Nobel Prize for the discovery of the double helical model of DNA—the basic building block of all living things—has written about an early encounter that led to his more important work.

In 1951, Watson, who was then a young postdoctoral student in biochemistry, happened to attend a scientific meeting in Naples. There, Maurice Wilkins, an English physicist who had been working on DNA for several years, presented an X-ray diffraction photograph of DNA. Wilkins told a bored group of scientists that when the structure of DNA was known, we would more fully understand how genes work.

Watson was fascinated. He saw in that X-ray a solution to one of the most important questions in science. "Sometimes I daydreamed about discovering the secret of the gene," he later wrote in *The Double Helix*, "but not once did I have the faintest trace of a respectable idea."

Wilkins's presentation gave him that respectable idea. "Suddenly, I was excited about chemistry," Watson wrote. "Now, I knew that genes could crystallize; hence they must have a regular structure that could be solved in a straightforward fashion.... I proceeded to forget Maurice, but not his DNA photograph. A potential key to the secret of life was impossible to push out of my mind." (Watson 1968:32,35)

## How to Find Your Way

Some achievers find their way, seemingly guided more by intuition than anything else. An experience occurs, perhaps by accident, and they resonate with it. Something inside says, "Do it." Something clicks. A little light comes on.

Jack Lemmon was a nine-year-old student at the Rivers Country Day School in Chestnut Hill, Massachusetts, when an event occurred that gave him direction for the rest of his life. Young Jack, the son of the vice president of the Donut Corporation of America, became a last-minute replacement in the school play when the regular for the part became ill. Not knowing the lines, Jack had to step over to the wings every line or two. After a while, the routine became a comedy, and the audience began to laugh. Here is the way Lemmon recalls the experience: "Either I could have been horrendously embarrassed and never wanted to appear again on a stage; or, as it did happen, a little light went on, and I said, 'I think I like this.'

"So I started exaggerating it, you know. Even when I could remember a line, I'd begin, pull a blank, walk all the way over to the wings, tilt my body way over, obviously listening to get a cue. And they started to roar.

Also, the costume was for a kid who was about six inches taller than I was, the hat was falling down over my head, a cape that was to come to my ankles was dragging back like I was Marie Antoinette walking down toward the throne. The whole thing became funny, and that started me."

The first man ever to win Oscars as both best actor and as best supporting actor sums up the episode: "Obviously, I was getting appreciation from my peers, and I think that when that happens, you'll continue it."

As a child Aaron Copland liked to stand beside the piano, listening to his brother and sister play violin and piano duets, fascinated by the sound of the music. When his sister would say, "Aaron, why are you hanging around here; why don't you go out and play with the other kids?" Aaron refused. He had discovered something he loved more than playing games with the other kids.

Very early, Copland announced that he would become a composer of concert music. Nothing obvious had pushed young Copland in this direction. His father was not a musician—he owned a department store in Brooklyn, and in fact was astonished by his son's decision. The prevailing norms of the day did not push him this way. At the time, there was not a tradition in this country for people to make a career of composing classical music. What had happened was that Copland had heard a sound that caused sympathetic vibrations within himself.

Something similar happened to a poor black boy named Ray Charles in the hardscrabble backwoods of north Florida. Not far from the little frame house where Ray and his family resided, there lived a boogie-woogie pianist named Wylie Pitman—"Mr. Pit," Ray Charles called him. "Whenever Mr. Pit would begin to play," Ray Charles recalls, "I would stop what I was doing and run next door. I'd stand by the piano and pound on it with both hands." Wylie Pitman, the man Ray Charles says was the "beginning" of his career, willingly accepted the young-ster's presence and showed him how to play. He would lift him up on his lap and let the boy run his fingers up and down the keyboard. "He could have shooed me away. But he didn't," Ray Charles recalls. "Had it not been for him, there might not have been a beginning."

When Gloria Swanson was sixteen, after playing a few small parts in comedy films, the soon-to-be star was assigned to a serious picture. The director asked if she thought she would need any help producing tears. No, she replied. Swanson began to think about a humiliating experience she had with a director in a previous film, one in which she had been a failure. Swanson then burst into tears, eventually becoming almost hysterical. Every-one on the set was stunned. When the scene was over, and young Gloria was making her way to the dressing room, still sobbing and dabbing her eyes, Helen Dunbar, the grand old character actress, said: "Young lady, one day you'll be a good actress." Without hesitating, the unknown young actress replied: "Yes, I know. I'm going to be very famous."

Her reply, she told me years later, astonished and embarrassed her. "I don't know where the words came from.... I just said, 'I'm going to be very famous.'"

Swanson no doubt already knew she was good. Or perhaps she realized it that day. She "knew" it by reading it in the faces of the director and the other actors.

Dan Barry, who has written and drawn "Flash Gor-don" for more than three decades, discovered his vo-cation through a chance conversation. When Barry fin-ished art school, he found it almost impossible to sell his paintings and was casting about for something to do. "I had been interested in three things as a kid—art, writing, and theater. At that time I met George Mandel, who was doing comic book illustrations and was driving a big Cadillac. I think I was standing on the street corner pitching pennies when he drove by and somebody introduced me to him."

As a result of the conversation with Mandel, Barry realized he could do all three things he wanted to do. "In the comics, you're the writer, you're the actor, the director, you're the cameraman. You choose it all. It just seemed a natural. That summer, I found time to work up some comic book samples. At the end of the summer, I got a job with comic books, and I've stayed with comics ever since. I eventually got into doing educational comic books. King Features saw those books, called me, and asked me to do Flash."

Finding one's way is not an experience reserved only for writers or artists. It is a generic concept, appropriate for a wide range of careers. And, finding one's way to a successful career does not require some intuitive, highly subjective, mystical insight. Many high achievers, perhaps most, find their life work—their métier—much less dramatically.

An aptitude test in the hands of a caring and skillful guidance counselor helped Delta Airline's chairman Ronald W. Allen discover where his strengths lay. Allen grew up believing that one day he would become an engineer. In fact, he never considered anything else. Allen chose Georgia Tech upon graduating from high school, where he selected electrical engineering as his major. But Allen did not do well in electrical engineering. "I got into my first EE course and got lost very quickly," Allen remembers. "I'm not sure why. My high school grades had been excellent."

The crestfallen young student dropped the course and headed toward the dean of students' office. A counselor, whose name Allen can't remember, looked at Allen's scores on an aptitude test and asked Allen why he wanted to be an engineer. His test results clearly showed that he would do better in another area. They talked at great length about the decision: "I guess he saw my determination to be an engineer, so he encouraged me to shift into the *industrial* engineering field and become more of a generalist.... He really helped me turn the corner. After that, I had a new direction to take. When I got into my junior year, I felt the difference, and my grades blossomed."

The trick in finding your way is knowing what advice to take. Some achievers persist on a course, when seemingly everyone around them, including the experts, say no. And they do well. Other individuals persist in careers for which they are not suited—against advice—and fail.

Standardized aptitude tests, if interpreted by an experienced counselor, can give useful insights. So too can highly successful individuals in a targeted field.

## Specialties

Guidance counselors call them *aptitudes*. Helen Gurley Brown, the editor of *Cosmopolitan*, calls them *specialties*. She recommends working hard at a variety of jobs to find them, and, she counsels, we shouldn't be too concerned if such specialties don't surface strongly or quickly take shape as career possibilities. "Somewhere in the mélange of job and talent possibilities is *you*, with subtle little predilections that will keep cropping up until one day they become your *thing*," she writes in her book *Having It All*. (1983:13)

Brown didn't develop her specialty—her *thing*—until she was thirty-one years old—after holding seventeen secretarial jobs in thirteen years. She finally got a job writing copy, and realized she was good at it. Why was she good at this particular job? Because, she says, she had "feeling." She could *feel* a good letter, good copy.

She could *feel* what people wanted to hear. And she realized that this ability had been there a long time. She just hadn't recognized it as the asset it turned out to be.

Later, when Brown began editing *Cosmopolitan*, she could *feel* whether a story turned in by a writer would work or not. "I am still uneducated and not a heavy thinker," Brown writes. "It's such a *small* talent, really, 'feeling' one's way through a piece of writing, but it began when I was young. That specialty—feeling—isn't much, is it? But it was enough."

The specialty of Grammy Award winner Emmylou Harris is country music, something she discovered as a folk singer in the coffeehouses of Georgetown and Greenwich Village in the 1970s. At the time, Harris thought of music as a "really loving, intense hobby." Her goal was to be a dramatic actress, and she had a four-year scholarship to study drama. But as she began to examine what she really wanted to do, Harris realized that music was her real love. "The love that made me want to go that extra step beyond was music."

But it was not just any kind of music. It was *country* music that profoundly affected the city-reared singer. "I love the sound of it, the poetry of it, and what it does to me emotionally," she told me. "It just started something in me that was not there before. I shifted into another gear—the way I heard music, the way I approached music, the way I sang. Everything changed."

Here is what John Huston, the legendary director of films such as *The African Queen*, *The Night of the Iguana*, and *The Man Who Would Be King* answered when I asked him to tell me what qualities or characteristics had helped make him successful:

"I think I'm a talented person ... not just in motion pictures," said Huston, hesitating for a moment, looking for the right word, the right phrase, backing and filling, then rephrasing. "I could have been ... my first love was painting, and I had a degree of talent in that. I was, I would say, a gifted draftsman. I can draw what I see, and not with a primitive hand at all. It's an accomplished hand. I can draw with some style and distinction. . . . I recognize quality very quickly, instantly, I mean. And I recognize the absence of quality . . . in politics, as well as the arts. I think I recognize a charlatan when I see one, whether he's practicing his charlatanism in painting, in music, or in ideas. . . . I'm able, I believe, to see through to the heart of a matter rather more quickly than the average person. I can perceive falseness in a gesture, in a sentence, written or spoken—when an actor is acting instead of being, when a writer is writing instead of perceiving, observing. All these things have become instruments in my service."

After giving that account, Huston looked at me with roguish eyes, and in that deep, resonant voice of his asked: "Does that answer your question . . . at all?"

## Early Versus Late Choices

There are advantages for the individual who makes an early choice and stays with that choice. Those individuals who learn the vocabulary of a field can use it throughout their careers, adding knowledge as their chosen field develops and changes. More on that later.

Careers in traditional societies follow that model as a matter of course. In villages in India, even today, the son of a carpenter will inherit his father's trade as well as his father's customers. Obviously, there are disadvantages in such an arrangement: people are locked into jobs they may not be suited for and actually hate for their entire lives. But the level of craftsmanship one sometimes finds in societies with such systems is often astonishingly high—precisely because people begin to master the respective fields early in their lives.

Most of the high achievers I interviewed were well on their way in their chosen careers by their thirties, many by their twenties, and a surprising number had begun to make a mark in their teenage years. That was true of Isaac Asimov, who eventually made a career of what was at first his avocation—writing science fiction and popular articles about science. Even though Asimov's first article was rejected twelve times before acceptance, within a year the eighteen-year-old had sold two more. He was fortunate enough to find an editor who told the young man what he was doing wrong and gave him the opportunity to revise and resubmit. The young Asimov, to his credit and later success, was willing to keep working at it his craft until he got it right.

Aaron Copland published his first piece, "The Cat and the Mouse," subtitled "Scherzo Humoristique," when he was twenty years old. But he began writing seriously much earlier. When Copland was only seventeen, he set to music three poems written by a friend. (Those pieces were never published, and remained virtually unknown until they were discovered in 1986 among a collection of manuscripts in the archives at the University of Texas.)

While "Peanuts" creator Charles Schulz was still in high school, his mother showed him an advertisement that read: "Do you like to draw? Send in for our free talent test." The sponsor of the advertisement, the Art Instruction Schools, Inc., then known as Federal Schools, was located in Minneapolis, not far from the Schulz residence in St. Paul.

Schulz enrolled, and worked diligently at the instructions. Soon he was mailing out his creations to all the major magazines. For his trouble, however, Schulz accumulated a pile of rejection slips. Then World War II intervened.

When Schulz knew he was going into the armed services, he had a friend, who was a bookbinder, make up a special sketchbook that he took with him to camp. For three years, Schulz carried that sketchbook with him, drawing landscapes and people, developing his skill.

One of the world's leading architects is a quiet-talking, feisty man in his sixties by the name of John Portman. Portman's buildings are an important—and sometimes controversial—part of the landscape of many major cities of the world, including San Francisco (Embarcadero Center), New York (Broadway's Marriott Marquis Hotel), Brussels (the International Trade Mart), and Singapore (the Pavilion Inter-Continental Hotel). Some of the concepts Portman popularized, like open atriums and exposed bubble elevators, have become the clichés of recent hotel and mall construction.

Portman was an early bloomer. He knew what he wanted to become, and had developed a plan for attaining that goal, by the time he reached high school. During grammar school days, John was usually the student who was asked to do the designs for the carnivals. He built model airplanes of balsa wood, and he did murals and posters—all forms of art.

When Portman entered junior high, students were required to take various shop courses in order to expose them to different career options. They would take electric shop and build electric motors; woodworking, to see how things were made with wood; and print shop, where they learned how to set type. The school had a foundry and a metalworking shop and a mechanical drawing class. "I used to see kids sitting at the drawing board; I couldn't graduate until I took that course, so I left it till last. But when I got in there . . . I found I really loved it. It was just like a fish to water. . . . It was such a natural thing. . . . About the ninth grade, I came to the conclusion that I wanted to be an architect."

Portman then chose a high school where he could take introduction to architecture and architectural drawing. That particular high school was not the one his college-bound friends attended. In fact, it was the technical high school, with a curriculum designed for students who would not attend college. Portman asked the principal to let him devise a plan of study that would enable him to go on to college but take architectural drawing as well. The principal replied: "Young man, if you know what you want to do at this age, I'm not going to stand in your way. You got it." And so Portman studied architectural drawing three years in high school.

Portman, who is a developer as well as an architect, did his first "joint venture" as a youngster. He noticed that most of the theaters in town in those days didn't have candy counters. He also discovered that he could buy Beechnut chewing gum wholesale if he bought it by the box. Seizing the opportunity, the thirteen-year-old Portman purchased the gum, recruited a handful of kids, and stationed them at the box office of each of the major theaters. "When people bought their tickets, a little kid was standing there with a box of gum. We split the profits . . . I gave them fifty percent of the profits. . . . I had a bike and collected the money."

That early taste of success was never forgotten. Years later, after receiving his architecture degree, Portman decided he would not wait for clients to come to him. He raised the necessary capital himself and built parking decks and trade marts. He also entered into joint ventures with successful developers like Trammell Crow— a controversial approach that raised eyebrows and hackles in the profession.

Portman is undaunted by his critics "I am Leonardo to my own Medici. I am my own patron," he once told me. "I created it that way because I decide what I want to do, where I want to do it, when I want to do it, and how it ought to be done. I like that."

Portman and Copland both entered occupations that

are different from those of their parents. However, there are definite advantages for those individuals fortunate enough to grow up in situations where their parents want them to inherit the family business. One need not go to a village in India to find examples of this process or its benefits. Several of the high achievers I interviewed—David Rockefeller, Stanley Marcus, John Huston, Ted Turner, Richard Petty—followed the path of their fathers. But not quite in their footsteps, as we will see later in the book.

The other way toward high achievement is to start a bit later and then focus—really focus. Like Mark Twain. In 1874, when Twain was thirty-nine, he summarized his career thus: "In due course I got my license. I was a pilot now, full-fledged. . . . Time drifted slowly and prosperously on, and I supposed—and hoped—that I was going to follow the river for the rest of my days, and die at the wheel when my mission was ended. But by and by the war came, commerce was suspended, my occupation gone. I had to seek another livelihood. So I became a silver-miner in Nevada; next, a newspaper reporter; next, a gold-miner in California; next, a reporter in San Francisco; next, a special correspondent in the Sandwich Islands; next a roving correspondent in Europe and the East; next, an instructional torch-bearer on the lecture platform; and, finally I became a scribbler of books. . . ." (Clemens 1917:185)

Ideally, relatively late starters have a larger base of experiences upon which to build a career, because they have learned a little bit about a lot of subjects. This career route is in fact a preferred one in western societies. One gets a broad liberal arts education, goes on to a professional school, and then specializes. The ideal is for youngsters to cast about for a while, considering several conceivable options, broadening themselves mentally and emotionally, before settling into a career. The college years are looked upon as a time to look at options, where students encounter the world in microcosm, meeting engineers, accountants, scientists, historians, attorneys, physicians, theologians, writers—all prepared to teach courses about their respective fields.

James Michener is an ardent believer in this approach. The best-selling author of over thirty books (all written after age forty) urges that youngsters get a liberal education—that is, an early, relatively unfocused exposure to many broad aspects of knowledge, both academic and practical: "If you graduate in liberal arts, you will have a difficult time between the ages of 22 and 45, when nobody seems to want you," Michener wrote in an open letter to young people in 1984. "Your responsibility in those years will be to hang on, by your fingernails if necessary. But if you survive, and good people do, you will find that from age forty-five to the end of your life you will be increasingly valuable to society, for you will be running it. It will be you, and people like you, who will be editing the great newspapers, operating the television stations, directing the banks, guiding the universities and especially sitting in the higher seats of government. It's always been that way. It always will be." (Michener 1984:D1)

A few high achievers manage to make names for themselves in several fields. Nobel Laureate Francis Crick comes to mind. Crick has achieved renown in molecular biology, even though his early training was in physics. Currently Crick is becoming widely known in a new area seemingly far afield from his early work with DNA—dream research. Nobel Laureate Herbert A. Simon is another example. Simon is a major figure in economics, computer science, management science, and psychology.

Athletes occasionally achieve stardom in several different sports. Jim Thorpe was one. Thorpe is in the Football Hall of Fame, but he also won the pentathlon and the decathlon in the 1912 Olympics—the first man to win both—and subsequently played baseball as an out-fielder on three professional major-league teams.

One reason an individual may be successful in several different fields is that some fields have a common skill or knowledge base. This is true of the fields Herbert Simon has chosen—economics, psychology, and computer science share a number of knowledge elements. And it is true in the case of the Jim Thorpes of this world, where agility, power, and quick responses give one an edge in football and baseball.

Secondly, the talent, skill, and discipline needed to succeed in one field make it likely that an individual can succeed in another. Andy Rooney, America's favorite curmudgeon, has observed: "There is more chance that somebody who is good at one thing is going to be good at a second thing, than there is a chance that a man who has failed at one thing is going to be good at something else."

\*   \*   \*

High achievers *may* attain breadth of knowledge, but they *always* attain depth of knowledge in some one area. They may know a little about a lot of things, but they always know a lot about one thing. The only way to achieve depth, as we shall see, is through long-term focus. Long-term focus guarantees that all the small tasks and bits of knowledge add up and become a cumulative body of knowledge and skills. That is the way to competence, but it begins with an initial discovery—a discovery about what one can become very good at, and what one loves doing.

Actor Bob Hoskins delights in his work, and it has paid off. He received best-actor award in Cannes in 1986, the British Academy Award, as well as an Academy Award nomination for best actor in 1987. Says Hoskins: "I love my work. Other people have hobbies—I just love my work. I adore it. Because of loving the work, I don't have any ambition at all. The job comes up and I do the job. I don't do the job to gain something else. I just like doing the job."

I continually encountered that underlying relationship among love of work, competence, and high achievement. Malcolm Forbes sums it up thus: "I think the foremost quality—there's no success without it—is really loving what you do. If you love it, you do it well, and there's no success if you don't do well what you're working at."

To conclude this exploration of the way high achievers think about themselves and the work they do, I have saved for last an exceedingly wise observation by Isaac Asimov:

"I guess the essence of life for me is finding something you enjoy doing that gives meaning to life, and then being in a situation where you can do it. And I've reached that. To me, the writing I do, it gives sweetness to life, and I'm allowed to do it as much as I want to—so that life is sweet."

"How long has your life been sweet?" I asked.

"It's been sweet, really, all my life, because even when I was young—before I started writing, I was preparing to write, without even knowing it. I was reading all the books that I needed to have in my mind in order to be able to write properly. I belonged to the public library, and I had the time to read. My parents had no money. I had no money. We lived in very poor apartments and not very good neighborhoods. But I never knew that I was deprived, you see. I had the chance to read, and I enjoyed school, so that all through life, things have been very nice for me. And I've been aware of it. . . .

That's the important part. It's tragic if you're lying on your death bed and say, 'Gee, I've had such a good life and I never appreciated it.' But I always appreciated it. Every step of the way I knew I was lucky, and this is even more important than being lucky."

# 2

# Developing Competence

*Listen, I'm only just beginning to feel as if I've got anything under my belt at all. And I mean that.*

—Julie Andrews

*I don't think talent is as important as the work and the dedication necessary to become competent. . . . A lot of guys out there are more talented than I am, and through the years we've passed them by many times.*

—Jack Nicklaus

*He who knows not and knows not he knows not,*
*he is a fool—shun him.*
*He who knows not and knows he knows not,*
*he is ignorant—teach him.*
*He who knows and knows not he knows,*
*he is asleep—wake him.*
*He who knows and knows he knows,*
*He is wise—follow him.*

—Arabian proverb

No one is born competent. Jack Nicklaus—probably the closest to being a child prodigy of any of the individuals I interviewed—draws a sharp distinction between inherited ability and competence. "I don't think talent is as important as the work and the dedication necessary to become competent," says the man who has won more major golf competitions than any golfer in the history of the game. "Certainly talent needs to be above average, but I don't think it needs to be the top thing on the list."

Undeniably, unusual talent provide a tremendous advantage, particularly in fields such as sports and entertainment. But even modest talents, in association with other factors—passion, focus, decisiveness, time management, and the like—can be transformed into a force to be reckoned with. A kind of multiplier effect occurs when the achievement factors combine.

Asked if there are really talented golfers who never make it, Nicklaus replies: "Oh, hundreds of them. A lot of guys out there are more talented than I am, and through the years we've passed them by many times. You see guys and you say, 'Gosh, how did this guy not make it?' And then it's pretty easy to figure out why he didn't. He had a lot of talent, but didn't have much dedication, wasn't organized, didn't know how to learn, didn't know how to comprehend what he was doing, didn't try to learn how to get better." Competency, like so many of the factors that make for high achievement, has to be worked at and developed and polished. It is not something that drops into one's lap.

High achievement is a process. These individuals reached their present eminence by working at their craft, perfecting their skills, trying to overcome their weaknesses and fears, playing to their strengths. "I think the big thing about doing anything is striving to improve every day," Jack Nicklaus told me. "I'm learning new shots every day. I worked on a couple of new shots yesterday—ones that I didn't have in my game. I spent about two hours working on a specific shot yesterday that I didn't have. I got it today."

In golf, the body changes, and the champion golfer, who might have relied upon long, powerful shots when he was young, has to develop a different game as he ages. "You have to have more weapons and a bigger arsenal if you want to compete," says Nicklaus. "I know I'm not as talented as I was ten or fifteen years ago, 'cause I just don't have the physical ability. That's why I have to compete in another way. I have to compete with my mind—compete with a larger variety of shots and things."

Many of the high achievers mentioned points of weakness. But they refused to dwell upon them, and they avoided building a case against themselves. Instead, they confronted their weaknesses and tried to eliminate them. Or they sought ways to circumvent them, seeking situations or careers where they could capitalize upon their strengths.

Steve Allen—who has composed some five thousand songs, including "Impossible," "This Could Be the Start of Something Big," "Gravy Waltz," the lyrics to "South Rampart Street Parade," and ballads for several motion pictures, including *Picnic* and *On The Beach*—does not read music. That's right. Steve Allen does not read music. When I first learned this, I was astonished. "I started out the right way," Allen told me. "I took those old John M. Williams first-year piano lessons. But right from the start I had an ability to create my own things, and that ability soon outdistanced my halting ability to read, so I got impatient, and I didn't have a piano for a few years, so I lost the ability to read altogether."

How then does Steve Allen compose music? With a tape recorder. He always has one with him, and when he composes a song, he records it: "When there are ten or twelve songs on the tape," he explains, "I send it to someone who cannot compose a note of music but can put it down on paper, and for about twelve dollars a song puts it down on paper for me." In the early days, when there were no tape recorders, Allen would find people who would do his transcribing for him—perhaps a playmate who could read music but couldn't compose.

The point is that Steve Allen has found a way to capitalize on his strengths and overcome his limitations. Allen acknowledges that his inability to read is a formidable handicap: "It's a drag to me. . . . I wish I could, because not being able to read rules me out of playing the classics, which I would dearly love to be able to do. But that's how it is." He has accepted the limitation for what it is, without allowing it to destroy his career.

It is tempting to think of the legendary achievers of the past as being so gifted that they had little to overcome. Nothing could be further from the truth. Consider two examples from history: Benjamin Franklin and Abraham Lincoln. Benjamin Franklin, who became one of our nation's most skillful diplomats, was not born diplomatic. Quite the contrary. Diplomacy was something Franklin had to work at very hard.

In his autobiography, Franklin tells of a conversation he had with a Quaker friend, who told him that he was generally regarded as "proud," "overbearing," and "rather insolent." As a result of that conversation, the young Franklin, who had already devised a systematic self-improvement plan, took the following action: "I added Humility to my List. . . . I made it a Rule to forbear all direct Contradiction to the Sentiments of others, and all positive Assertion of my own. I even forbid [*sic*] myself. . . . the use of every Word or Expression in the Language that imported a fix'd Opinion; such as *certainly, undoubtedly*, etc. and I adopted instead of them, *I conceive, I apprehend, or I imagine a thing to be so or so*, or *it so appears to me at present*."

Franklin admits that at first his humility was more an appearance than reality. But his plan worked: "Conversations I engag'd in went on more pleasantly. The modest way in which I propos'd my Opinions procur'd them a readier Reception and less Contradition; I had less Mortification when I was found to be in the wrong, and I more easily prevail'd with others to give up their Mistakes and join with me when I happen'd to be in the right. And this Mode, which I at first put on, with some violence to my natural Inclination, became at length so easy and so habitual to me, that perhaps for these Fifty Years past no one has ever heard a dogmatical Expression escape me." (Franklin 1964:158, 159).

In the case of Abraham Lincoln, one of the President's severest critics during his lifetime—Horace Greeley—eventually conceded: "He was not a born king of men . . . but a child of the people, *who made himself a great persuader, therefore a leader, by dint of firm resolve, patient effort and dogged perseverance*. He slowly won his way to eminence and fame by doing the work that lay next to him—doing it with all his growing might—doing it as well as he could, and learning by his failure, when failure was encountered, how to do it better.... He was open to all impressions and influences, and gladly profited by the teachings of events and circumstances, no matter how adverse or unwelcome. There was probably no year of his life when he was not a wiser, cooler and better man than he had been the year preceding." (Italics mine) (Thomas 1952:497,498)

Talent is a gift. Competence is not. Competence is something one must *do*, one must work at—sometimes joyfully, always persistently and perceptively, realizing where one's strengths and weaknesses lie.

## Competence: The *Sine Qua Non*

"You almost always find that somebody who's gotten himself in a position of being known to a lot of people has some persistent quality," says Andy Rooney. "It's highly unlikely that somebody well known is going to turn out to be a complete cipher." The people whose interviews provide the basis of this book are anything but ciphers. Far from it. They are able to tell what they are good at and, often, what they're not good at. They know, and they know they know.

When taken out of context, their comments sound audacious, boastful, even arrogant. But if you could talk to these individuals in person, as I have, you would realize that they are making forthright self-evaluations, not brash boasts. For example, when I asked Kris Kristofferson to tell how he was different from other musicians, he replied: "I don't really consider myself a musician, because my musical background and my musical tools are fairly limited. I'm a writer, and I can carry a tune, and I can make up tunes, but my tunes are really the simplest part of the story."

That's the modest beginning of his answer, too modest, in fact, to be a complete answer. "But as a writer," Kristofferson continued after a long pause, "I think there are better craftsmen, maybe—like there are better rhymers, and there may be people who make better sense, but I think I rhyme and make sense maybe better than any of them.... I think I'm a good writer. I think I'm up there with the people I admire, like Bob Dylan and John Prine and Hank Williams—people like that. I think when it comes to just the writing part, I can hold my own with anybody."

There it is—finally. Self-deprecation at first, and then Kristofferson makes a statement about abilities he knows he has.

But Kristofferson would be the first to tell you that he was not a born rhymer or writer, and that he was not able to hold his own with the very best in his field when he began sending songs off to publishers, or even when he arrived in Nashville. That came much later.

Successful businessmen respond similarly. Take J. B. Fuqua, chief executive officer of Fuqua Industries, Inc., who, from a standing start on a poor Virginia tobacco farm has built a Fortune 500 company (ranked 324 in 1987) and a personal fortune of many millions of dollars: "I'm good at certain things, and the things I'm good at, I'm *real* good at.... I'm good at financial and business strategies—I'm real good at it, I think. I'm good at motivating people. There's something else I would give myself a ten on [the highest rating on the questionnaire], and that is—shall we call it persistence? I get determined to do something, and I don't give up. I just get it done."

What are you *not* good at? I asked Fuqua.

"Small details. I'm very poor at small details."

Mary Kay is another one of the Horatio Alger figures.

The subject of a cover story in the *Saturday Evening Post* and a guest on all the major talk shows, Mary Kay has built her business from a team composed of nine friends in 1963 to a company with 150,000 salespeople. And what does Mary Kay say about herself? "Whatever I start out to do, I make it a point to learn everything I can about that. I knew nothing about the cosmetics business. I had no prior knowledge of that when I started this company, but today I think I rank up there with Estée or anybody else as far as cosmetics are concerned. So I would say I am very competent from the standpoint of whatever it is I undertake."

Here's how Andy Rooney evaluates himself: "I'm quite creative. I do not tend toward clichés with words. I have a quick flair for occasional humor. I work quite hard . . . that's one of the things I didn't know about myself until later in life . . . because a lot of things I do, I don't have much ability to stick at and finish properly. But when it comes to writing, I work hard. I get in here early every morning and I stick at it."

And what is Rooney *not* good at? "I'm not as intellectual as I'd like to be. I think my brain capacity is limited. I'm better at starting something than finishing it. My hobby is woodworking. I'll get an idea for a piece of furniture and get some great wood and really work on the hard part of it, and get it almost done, and then not really bother to sand it properly."

Charles M. Schulz, the father of Charlie Brown and Snoopy and all their friends, responds to the question this way: "I don't know how *good* I am at drawing a comic strip, but I think I *know* as much about drawing comic strips, if not more, than anybody else. I think I'm really an expert on the comic strip as a medium. . . . I'm very proud of what I've done, and I think I've created some of the best comic-strip characters that have ever existed. But this does not mean that I'm the best. Nobody is best at anything. That's a foolish, modern thought that there has to be a number one in everything. But I think I really understand the comic-strip medium."

He who knows—and knows he knows . . .

Schulz, like so many other high achievers, knows his limitations: "I feel inferior in a lot of areas. I feel inferior that I can't draw better than I can, that I don't have a wider, broader knowledge, which I would love to have. I feel I don't have the extensive vocabulary I think it would be nice to have. I suppose this is why I'm able to function so well with Charlie Brown. I can caricature all of these faults, realizing as I've grown older that these are common feelings, and you'll meet almost no one who deep down really does not have feelings of inferiority. That is why, I guess, the readers can identify so completely with Charlie Brown."

The legendary guitarist Chet Atkins says: "You must have a certain intellect that tells you what your weak points are and what your strong points are, and work within those limitations."

If you look carefully at the self-evaluations of Kristofferson, Fuqua, Rooney, and Schulz, you will notice that their answers involve *acquired skills*, like knowing how to rhyme or plan financial strategies or understand the comic strip as a medium, and *native ability*, such as alertness, plus *habits*, like persistence.

That is what competence is—acquired skills and habits that result from refining and perfecting native abilities.


It probably sounds like a tautology to say that high achievers are competent. However, competence, by itself, does not necessarily lead to success. "There are lots of talented, competent people who never make it," Kristofferson reminds me, and he can give me the names of scores of superb writers and musicians who are un-knowns.

"Brains are cheap," Fuqua says. Fuqua should know. He has made several fortunes following the OPM and OPB principles—unabashedly using "other people's money" and "other people's brains."

Competence—to use the language of logic—is not a *necessary and sufficient* cause of high achievement. That is, competence by itself does not always lead to success. There are other very important factors that are essential to high achievement—timing, discovery, mentors, innovation.

But competence probably comes closer than any of the achievement factors to being a *necessary* cause. No one becomes a high achiever without becoming competent at something. Some individuals become high achievers without some of the other factors. Some are persistent but not very focused; other are highly motivated but not particularly good managers of their time. There even seems to be a kind of interchangeability of factors, so that an individual may fall back on determination or sheer grit when the joy of working begins to wane. But all the high achievers know something well, or they learn to *do* something well.

## The Nature of Competence

Nobel Laureate Herbert A. Simon and his colleagues have done fascinating research on two of the basic questions: What is competence? and How long does it usually take to become competent?

Simon says that humans are "symbol processors," in many respects like computers. By symbols, he means patterns of any kind—letters in an alphabet, dots and dashes from Morse code, a referee's signal of a foul in a ballgame, or pieces on a chess board. Very competent people—experts—are people who can recognize a lot of symbols. "There's no magic going on in the human head, "Simon says. "The expert has stored in memory a large number of *patterns*, which he recognizes when they occur in the situation around him. The grand master chess player, for example, has stored a large number of patterns, which he recognizes when they occur on a chess board before him."

Thus, experts are individuals who can recognize and make sense of more patterns than their peers. Sometimes, experts will "see" or recognize patterns that they may not be able to explain. They may even call it instinct or intuition.

How many patterns—or chunks of knowledge—does an expert have to have in memory? Tens of thousands, Simon and the late William Chase have found.

Here is the scientific statement: "Using simple probability models, as well as a computer simulation of the chess perception process, quantitative estimates were made of the "vocabulary" of familiar chunks in a master's memory. The estimates obtained by several different procedures all fall in the range of twenty-five thousand to one hundred thousand chunks—that is, a vocabulary of roughly the same size as the vocabulary of an educated adult in his native language." (Simon 1979:60)

How long does it take to attain mastery of a field?

A minimum of ten years. In a lecture in 1985, Simon stated: "Research done by my colleague John R. Hayes and I indicates that nobody reaches world class in less than ten years of diligent application. Bobby Fischer became a chess grand master in slightly less than ten years. It took a bit more than ten years for Mozart," Simon added facetiously. "Mozart was a slow learner." (Simon: 1985)

A major study recently conducted at the University of Chicago by Benjamin S. Bloom and his associates strongly supports this position. The study, called the Development of Talent Project, looked carefully at the careers of world-class concert pianists, sculptors, research mathematicians, research neurologists, Olympic swimmers, and tennis champions.

In the case of twenty-four world-class concert pianists, for example, the average amount of time that elapsed between the pianists' first lesson and the time they won a major international competition (such as the Chopin International Piano Competition, the Tchaikovsky International Competition, or the Van Cliburn International Quadrennial Piano Competition) was 17.14 years.

Research mathematicians and neurologists required even longer. World-class tennis players often started playing at age three or four, and then, many years later, made it into the top-ten rankings. The researchers concluded that natural gifts are not sufficient in and of themselves in explaining these extraordinary accomplishments. Unless there is a long and intensive process of encouragement, nurturance, education, and training, the individuals will not attain world class in their respective fields. (Bloom: 1985)

When I interviewed Jack Nicklaus, I wondered if perhaps he would be an exception to the ten-year rule. Nicklaus, after all, was sensational as a youngster. When he played his first nine holes at age ten, he carded a 51. At age thirteen, he won the Ohio State Junior Championship. At age fifteen, he qualified for the U.S. Amateur, and at age seventeen qualified for the U.S. Open, missing the cut.

However, my question was laid to rest when I came upon a definitive article on Nicklaus, written by Herbert Warren Wind for *The New Yorker*. Wind writes: "When old golf hands discuss when it was that it first occurred to them that Nicklaus might turn out to be not just a first-class golfer but a rare champion, more often than not they cite his performance in one or another of three events that took place early in his career: the 1960 World Amateur Team Championship, the 1960 U.S. Open at Cherry Hills, outside Denver, in which he was second, only two strokes behind Arnold Palmer, then the premier golfer in the world, and the 1962 U.S. Open at Oakmont, outside Pittsburgh, where he caught Palmer with an almost flawless last round of 69 and defeated him the next day in their playoff." (Wind 1983:67)

In 1960, Nicklaus was twenty years old—ten years older than when he played his first game.

## Attending to Details

The Smithsonian's National Museum of American History is filled with hundreds of fascinating artifacts, two of which are located side by side on the first floor, in the road and transportation room. One is the Brawner-Hawk racing car in which Mario Andretti won the Indianapolis 500 in 1969. Directly across the aisle is a red-and-blue Pontiac with a big number 43 painted on its side. This is the car in which Richard Petty won the Firecracker 400 race in Daytona Beach on July 4, 1984—Richard Petty's two hundredth victory.

I have had the opportunity to interview both of these men. At first glance, they could not be more different. Petty—a tall and lean, slow-talking man from North Carolina. Andretti—a short, wiry man with an accent brought over from his native Italy. But both men are legends in an unforgiving occupation, where a momentary lapse of concentration or the failure to tighten a bolt can result in sudden death.

It is a business of inches, Petty says, that begins long before the starting flag falls. The race actually starts in the design rooms and the mechanics' sheds, where skilled, intense men add horsepower and shave inches and pounds from sleek, powerful missiles, knowing that the same activity is taking place in the competitors' shops and sheds.

If you go to Indy or Daytona and visit the racing stalls just before the race, you will see these men tinkering and testing, hour after hour—adjusting and fine-tuning, adding and subtracting—right up to the final seconds before the race. Nothing is left to chance. Meanwhile, the teams that change tires and add fuel are practicing, trying to shave fractions of seconds from their orchestrated performance.

There is a pecking order among the racing teams. In fact, some of the best teams—the most competent ones—choose the drivers.

As for the racers—men like Andretti and Petty—competence involves knowing how to push the engine to its very limit; how to drive within an inch or two of the wall on the curves and not crash; how to hang over the edge and not fall off. My cameraman shot Andretti's wheels, going almost two hundred miles per hour, coming within inches of the corner wall.

Details really count at that speed, that close to the wall.

Details count in every field, though perhaps not as spectacularly as on the race track. Ninety-one-year-old Arthur Murray told me in 1986 that he was so attentive to details that he almost never delegated responsibility: "I never left anything of importance to other people, and if I did, I directed them very closely."

However, not every high achiever claims to be good at details. In fact, many big-picture people delegate to others—whom they feel they can trust—much of the detail work, plus work in areas where they do not feel competent. Andrew Carnegie used to say that he made it a point to assemble around him people who knew far more about making steel than he did. He left the technical details to them.

Mary Kay, who says she pays a lot of attention to details, does so only in the area of her competence. Her son Richard handles the financial side of the business: "I don't pay any attention to his figures," she says. "At the end of the month, he sends me the financial report, and I look at it, and if it's good—wonderful. If it's not—well, we'll have to work a little harder. But I'm not really informed at all as to what's going on from a financial standpoint till the end of every month."

These high achievers recognize that it is a mistake to spread themselves too thin, to fret over details that can be readily delegated. They think in terms of a kind of "economy" of attention. Cabbage Patch creator Xavier Roberts says, "You can worry about making fifty dollars or fifty million. It takes the same amount of worry. Really."

Isaac Asimov says he doesn't worry much about small details. "I'm not a perfectionist," says the author of 364 books and thousands of articles. "I sometimes describe myself as an *imperfectionist*. . . . Let's give me a five [on the ten-point scale] on that."

So, should would-be high achievers concern themselves with small details? Yes, certainly at the beginning of the career. But as one advances up the organizational hierarchy, the details that really matter may be of a different order from those at entry-level positions.

When I asked Admiral Thomas J. Moorer, former chairman of the Joint Chiefs of Staff, to talk about how good he was at details, he responded: "It depends on what level you are, and how old you are. When you are young, you must know the details about your particular job. As you go up the ladder, you must significantly broaden your general knowledge, while at the same time you surround yourself with people who have the details. In other words, you can't have a very broad knowledge and all the details too, because there are not enough hours in the day. . . . As you get older, it becomes a fault to spend too much time on details."

The disagreement about the importance of details also seems to turn on definitions, on what is a critical detail and what is not. J. B. Fuqua says he isn't good at small details, but people who have observed Fuqua at work say he has an amazing facility for remembering numbers and recalling the specifics of deals he has been involved in.

"Fuqua reads annual reports like some people read a novel," a colleague says. "The numbers, for him, are converted into a vision of corporate worth. He has the most unusual talent I've ever seen for doing this. Extensive experience has taught Fuqua what to look for. During a given year, he will read hundreds of annual reports and then watch those conversions be tested in the actual marketplace—whether they are his own transactions or those he reads about that someone else has executed. He knows exactly where to look in an annual report. He will read the chairman's report, which most people will read, and he will glance at the income statement and balance sheet, and he's got the patience to read the footnotes—which most people don't read. It's in the footnotes that you find what's going on in a company."

Fuqua reading an annual report is a grand master looking at a board. So is Richard Petty reading a race-track. "An experienced driver will beat a young driver sometimes just because he's got the experience," says Petty. "He's been there before; he understands what's going on. He won't drive into a wreck or something on the track and then figure out how to get out of it. Before he gets there, he knows what's going on, and he knows how to take care of it." Petty realizes that as a man gets older in the racing business, he does not have the reflexes of the younger man. But Petty believes the older man gets smarter: "He learns to anticipate so much more of what's going to happen . . . he just knows it . . . it's built-in radar, or it just comes from experience."

Home-run king Hank Aaron told me about an almost uncanny feeling he sometimes experienced at the plate. "Somehow my baseball knowledge just took over and I could see some things that other players did not see. For example, I could tell before a pitcher released the ball whether it was going to be a curve ball or a fast ball. The average player could not do that." Sometimes it was the way the pitcher curled his arm or the way he gripped the ball or some other cue or combination of cues that told him in advance what was about to happen. Such attention to detail spells the difference between major- and minor-league play.

From the beginning David was the quietest and least flamboyant of the Rockefeller brothers. David stayed in the shadows. Even after he became head of the Chase Manhattan Bank, Rockefeller meant Nelson—"Rocky," the governor of New York and subsequently United States vice-president. Even his Arkansas-governor brother, Winthrop, often received more media attention than David.

The comparative obscurity was partly by choice— he rarely gave interviews. But he made up for his reticence about publicity by seeking out and cultivating people who became useful to him in his business and philanthropic endeavors.

David Rockefeller joined the Chase Manhattan Bank as an assistant manager in the foreign office in 1946. But he obviously was no mere novice working his way up the ladder. His maternal grandfather, Nelson Aldrich, had been president of the bank before him, and the name Rockefeller was not exactly unknown in financial circles.

After fourteen years' experience at various levels in the bank, David Rockefeller, at the age of forty-five, became its president. It would be easy to assume that his achievement occurred simply because of the name and family connections. But there is more to David Rockefeller's story than that. He quietly, steadily perfected certain skills that served him well throughout his career.

As a youngster, his scientific inclination was stimulated by an extensive trip through the West, where he studied geological formations and wild life. He was especially fascinated by insects and began an extensive collection. He subsequently studied economics, earning a doctorate in that field from the University of Chicago.

When Rockefeller began his career at the bank, he began another collection, a collection of names of people he met. At the time of my interview, that collection contained close to fifty thousand names: "When I first joined the bank, I started keeping a record of the people I met, and put them on little cards, and I would indicate on the cards when I met them, and under what circumstances, and with whom, and sometimes I put on the card a little notation which would help me remember a conversation or something of that sort. And then I extended that, and did it in addition to alphabetically— geographically, and by company, so that if I know I'm going to call on a company, I will take out the cards of that company and look at the names of the people that I've met there before which will help me remember if I see them again." Rockefeller added, "People are always pleased if they think you remember having seen them. And my memory isn't that good—it needs a few props. So, it's been a very valuable thing for me."

For David Rockefeller, attention to detail means being able to recall the names of his customers and the particulars of their lives.

Thomas J. Peters and Robert H. Waterman report in *In Search of Excellence* that the really good companies —the excellent ones—typically have executives who manage by walking around—looking, studying, noticing details. IBM's Thomas Watson, Jr., Hewlett-Packard's William Hewlett, and Polaroid's William Land all created legends walking the plant floors. McDonald's Ray Kroc regularly visited the outlets, assessing them on four main factors—quality, service, cleanliness, and value.

When I asked Helen Gurley Brown, editor of *Cosmopolitan*, to rank herself on small details, Brown replied: "I'd probably say nine or ten [the highest score], but that's too high a score, because if you want to be a good executive, you shouldn't be that good at small details. You should be good at the overall concept, and delegating. So, if you're into the nine category in small details, that's too high. But I think that's where I am."

Mary Kay says she's "tremendously" good at certain kinds of small details. "I write little thank-you notes. I'm very, very detail oriented. Every single letter that comes in here must be answered as quickly as possible. We get out about seven thousand letters a month. . . . I figure that most people don't like to write letters, they put it off till the last dog has died, shall we say, and if somebody cares enough to sit down and write me a letter, they deserve an immediate answer. So, whatever it takes to get an answer off to that person as quickly as possible, we do it. I have seven secretaries to do that."

"The retail business," says Stanley Marcus, "is a business of details—a business of minutiae." With that philosophy, Marcus took a regional department store and transformed it into an international institution. He adopted the practice of carrying a notebook so that he could jot down observations and clues customers dropped by chance. He even took the notebook with him to social occasions.

One evening, during the intermission at a symphony concert, a man told him he had bitten through the stem of a pipe he had bought, and had been advised that there would be a three-month delay getting a replacement. First thing next morning, Marcus was on the phone to his buyer, who informed him that they had received a new shipment of stems. "The salesman must not have known," the buyer said. "Give me the man's number, and I'll call him." When the customer arrived at his office later in the morning, there was a message on his desk that Neiman-Marcus was delivering the replacement before noon.

That same customer called Stanley Marcus to tell him he didn't know that kind of service still existed. A month later, he came to the store and made a purchase of a fifty-thousand-dollar ring. "Perhaps the two incidents had no relationship," Marcus writes in *Quest for the Best*. "I like to think they did."

Marcus insisted that all complaints be answered within forty-eight hours. (Marcus believes that the speed with which a complaint is answered is as important as the final settlement.) He also saw to it that complaints from customers with special qualifications to complain get special management consideration. "If we could satisfy the most critical of our customers, it would be easy to please the balance," Marcus says. "Conversely, we believed that if we didn't satisfy the 'bell ringers,' they would drift away from us and would lead the flock of less discriminating customers with them."

Marcus not only learned to listen to criticism, but turned the use of criticism into a philosophy and a science, institutionalized the practice in his store, and made it profitable. He says that making a policy was easy, but enforcing the forty-eight-hour response rule required hard-nosed management that refused to accept excuses. "Reputations, like plaster walls, require constant maintenance," he says. (Marcus 1979:44,147,148)

## Passing Tests

Woe to the individual in any field who somehow manages to rise to a position of high visibility without being competent. Their fate is often trial by ordeal. For example, musicians in the top orchestras of the world —who tend to be skeptical of conductors generally— have clever ways of finding out if a visiting conductor is competent. Harold Schonberg, formerly chief music critic of the *New York Times*, describes the sly examination: The flute will play a phrase an octave up, or a violinist may purposely go slightly off pitch, or the first and third horns may interchange parts. "If the conductor does not realize what is going on, the orchestra *knows* who and what he is." (Schonberg 1986:127)

The same kind of informal but deadly serious examinations take place among jazz musicians. Ray Charles tells how musicians in jam sessions will sometimes call for a song, and then do it chromatically, which means that they play it in all the keys, one by one. "All kinds of dudes be throwing knives at your head," he recalls from early experiences. "If you didn't know your stuff, you'd be laughed right out of the place." (Charles and Ritz 1978:79,80)

Admiral Thomas J. Moorer says: "I always felt that the key to leadership was knowledge." Moorer, who was commander-in-chief of the Pacific fleet, commander-in-chief of the Atlantic fleet, and chief of naval operations, observes: "It's difficult to deal with people and get people to work together to achieve a common goal unless you know as much about it, or more than they do."

## The Hunger for Learning

Art Buchwald never graduated from college. In fact, when he was sixteen years old, he dropped out of high school, ran away, lied about his age, and joined the Marines. Today, this high school dropout has a wall full of honorary degrees, many of them from the most prestigious universities of the nation.

One reason Art Buchwald has become the foremost practitioner of his craft is that he has learned how to learn. "There are too many people who think they're educated because they have a diploma," Buchwald says. "They aren't. You don't get educated; you prepare yourself for an education. You prepare yourself to know how to look up things, to know how to use books, how to think."

Buchwald speaks at scores of universities he never attended, to people with far more formal education than he, for very handsome honoraria. But Buchwald regards the visits he makes to campuses and conventions as a part of his continuing education. "I'm learning every day, all the time," he told me. "When I make speeches to doctors, lawyers, chambers of commerce—I am learning."

Dean Rusk, who served as secretary of state under Presidents Kennedy and Johnson, and as assistant secretary of state under President Truman, told me that President Truman drew upon his in-depth reading about the American presidents for guidance in his own administration: "It was fortunate for all of us that he had a lifelong avocation of reading about American presidents. As a little haberdasher in Kansas City, he read about American presidents, and he knew more about the former American presidents and the precedents of the office than anyone I ever encountered."

"Give me a top score on that. . . . I'm teachable," Fuqua said when I asked him to rank himself on teachability. "I've been in more different businesses than anybody you ever met, and I've tried to learn something about all of them."

One way Fuqua learns is by reading. "I can't pass a

bookstore," he says. "Everything that man has learned, he has written down someplace. So, all previous learning is available to us, and the practical way to obtain that today is to read.... I've read a tremendous amount."

Many of the high achievers I interviewed are voracious readers, an appetite they typically acquired in their youth. Patricia Roberts Harris was one of them. Of the high achievers I have interviewed, Harris, who died in March 1985, was among the most remarkable. The daughter of a dining-car waiter, Harris went on to become the associate dean of Howard University School of Law, ambassador to Luxembourg, secretary of Housing and Urban Development, and later the secretary of Health, Education, and Welfare (later Health and Human Services)—the highest-ranking black woman in the federal government.

One of her childhood memories was coming home from the library laden with the maximum number of books she could check out at any one time—five. "I read *Hamlet* at a very young age. One of my favorite Shakespearean plays was *Antony and Cleopatra*, which I had read before age eleven about three times."

Ted Turner has been an avid reader from grade school days. He desperately wanted to be an athlete, and tried out for all the team sports—football, basketball, baseball, and swimming. But he lacked sufficient talent to be a star in any of them. "I was no good," he told the writer Christian Williams. "I was on all the teams, every one, but I couldn't make a contribution." So, while other kids played organized sports, Ted turned to books. He particularly loved biographies of heroes. He had a great curiosity about why people behaved as they did. Alexander the Great, in particular, fascinated him: "He decided to go farther than anyone had ever tried to go; there were no limits to his imagination." (Williams 1981:23,27)

Actress Janet Leigh says of her early days at MGM, "I was like a sponge, sucking in and absorbing the knowledge and craft that was developed. You have to be open for that to permeate you."

Nobel Laureate Paul A. Samuelson told journalist Tom Walker, "When I started in economics, I used to read every journal in the profession, and every article in every journal."

The 1966 edition of *Current Biography* states: "If the art of choral singing has at last achieved the standing it deserves in the United States, the man most responsible for its elevated status is Robert Shaw. . . ." And how did Shaw attain his competence in the field? Through long, diligent study.

In the early 1940s, Shaw—who had never taken a formal course in music in high school or college—received a $2,500 grant from the Guggenheim Foundation to write a book. Shaw asked if he could use the money to study. The foundation agreed, and Shaw gave the money to a German-Jewish musician named Julius Herford. (Herford had headed analytical studies at the state school of music in Berlin.) "I said, 'Here, teach me.' At the time, I was preparing choruses for Toscanini and Stokowski. But I spent forty to sixty hours a week with him. I lived at his house for three or four years, and the association went on for fifteen to twenty years. For three or four years, I was the pupil who took most of his time. . . . I would go to sleep studying on the couch in his front room, and we would start in again the next morning."

## Practice, Practice, Practice

A policeman on his beat at Times Square was approached by a young man with a violin case under his arm: "How do you get to Carnegie Hall?" the young man asked.

"You have to practice, and practice, and practice," replied the policeman, without batting an eye.

The amount of time that really great performers, whether musicians or athletes, devote to practice is mind-boggling. "You gotta know your instrument. You leave it [the guitar] in the case three days," Chet Atkins says, "and it doesn't know you anymore. . . . You can't play it. You don't know the positions. . . . It's easy if you just strum chords, but if you play solos, it's very, very difficult."

In the early 1950s, Hank Aaron was playing ball for the Jacksonville Tars, in the South Atlantic League, under the great manager and disciplinarian Ben Geraghty. The Tars were loaded with talent then, and in 1953, Aaron recalls, they were about to clinch the division lead. He remembers one game in particular in which he and the right fielder Horace Garner converged on a fly ball that was hit into short right field. The bases were loaded. Somehow, they let the ball drop between them for a base hit, and everybody scored. After the game, the manager came up to them and said: "Now, boys, one thing about it. I don't mind errors, but somebody should have caught that ball. Henry, you and Horace are going to stay out here and learn how to holler, 'I got it,' or 'You take it.' We stayed out there two hours trying to learn how to catch fly balls."

Did Aaron resent that humiliating practice? Perhaps at the time, but today Aaron says Geraghty was one of the greatest managers he ever played for.

Very often in business and in universities, individuals will be promoted to a top management position primarily because they are competent in a technical or scientific field—the Peter Principle at work. But for many of those same individuals, such a move means virtually starting all over. There are thousands of new patterns that they must store in memory, patterns that have little or nothing to do with technical competence. Those cues tell whether subordinates are motivated and superiors are happy, whether subordinates should be fired or transferred, prodded gently or reprimanded sharply.

Practice, for the manager, means improving social abilities, making an art out of communicating, knowing how to give an order without giving offense, learning to lead. "It's personality that counts—the ability to interact with those above, below, and with peers," says Roberto C. Goizueta, the man who heads Coca-Cola. "You can go around crying, 'I am good. I am good', but somebody else has to say it. A leader has to have followers, or he isn't a leader." Goizueta advises young people, especially those with freshly minted MBAs, to approach their first job with humility. "You can learn to be good," he says.

Practice, for writers, means writing and rewriting. Albert Payson Terhune used to say that an aspiring writer should write one million words and throw them into the wastebasket. Only after a million words is an aspirant qualified to make a beginning in the art of authorship. The message is that any writer who manages to become successful prior to writing a million words is well ahead of the game.

On-the-job training is required in many fields. The newcomer must become apprentice to the master. The research assistant does the bidding of the powerful full professor, pledging fealty for succor and an eventual recommendation. The cub reporter must submit to the demands of the editor.

Jacques Barzun, longtime Columbia University professor and one of the foremost practitioners of the craft of writing, maintains: "Only an apprenticeship under a vigilant critic will gradually teach a would-be writer how to find and correct all the blunders and obscurities that bespangle every first draft." (Barzun and Graff 1962:249)

In the case of Charles Schulz, his hard work did not pay off immediately. After he returned from World War II, he called on every art department in town and heard a chorus of noes. Schulz even considered taking a job lettering tombstones, but the owner never called back. Schulz confesses that he was relieved when he didn't: "I had already begun to worry what my friends might say about my new job."

But he eventually found two jobs. One involved doing the lettering for a series of comic magazines. They gave Schulz the comic-book pages that had been drawn by others, but with the balloons left blank, and he filled in the dialogue. The other job was at the art correspondence school, where he corrected lessons sent in by others. There Schulz came in contact with bright, talented people who, he says, taught him a great deal. The head of the department was a famous magazine illustrator. Directly in front of the young Schulz sat Frank Wing, a highly talented artist who was a perfectionist at drawing things as they appeared. "He taught me the importance of drawing accurately," Schulz says. "Almost nothing I draw now, in what is sometimes an extreme style, is not based on a real knowledge of how to draw that object, whether it be a shoe, a doghouse, or a child's hand." (Schulz 1976:26)

Ray Charles, who began his musical career on the lap of the piano man Wylie Pitman, has been able to do what few musicians are able to do—create music that appeals to young and old, black and white, rich and poor. Because of his ability to successfully cross major boundaries, other musicians ungrudgingly use words like "genius" to describe him.

His career is straight out of the storybook, one that began in abject poverty mingled with tragedy. He lost both parents and a brother before he was grown, and grew up in a school for the blind, where he learned to play and sing. By his late teens, Ray had become something of a sensation in central and north Florida. His friends were telling him that he was the greatest talent they had ever heard or seen. And Ray believed them.

In 1946, when Ray Charles heard that Lucky Millinder's band was coming to Orlando for a gig, he managed to get an audition. It was his first chance at the big time. This was the band that made records that Ray loved. At the appointed hour, Ray walked in, seated himself at the piano, and began to perform, singing and playing with all his might. Millinder sat quietly listening. At the end of the audition, the young musician confidently waited for the praise he knew would be forthcoming. Instead, silence. Then the chilling words: "Ain't good enough, kid."

Ray Charles could not believe he was hearing correctly, and asked Millinder what he had just said, hoping he had heard wrong. "You heard me. You don't got what it takes."

Years later, when he told me that story, he still could remember the pain he felt when he heard those words. "I went back to my room and cried for days," he recalled.

And what was the effect of that body blow to the blind musician's career? "It was the best thing that ever happened to me," Ray Charles told me between two sold-out shows at a posh club. "After I got over feeling sorry for myself, I went back and started practicing, so nobody would ever say that about me again."

Even after they make it to the top, high achievers have another task—guarding against complacency. Chet Atkins says, "As you get older, it's so tough to keep mediocrity from coming in. You get so you perform and you're predictable and people know what you're going to do before you do it. That's what you have to fight as you get to be successful. You make money; you go home and watch TV. You don't have to go downstairs and practice anymore."

Many of the high achievers expressed the idea that they did not want their best efforts to be in the past, and were still committed to trying to improve their work. "I'm always trying to make the strip better," Charles Schulz told me. "My big worry has always been that my work would flatten out and cease to have any real spark to it."

# The Habit of Excellence

It is a long way from the O'Connor ranch in a remote part of Arizona and New Mexico to Sandra Day O'Connor's chambers on the first floor of the U.S. Supreme Court Building. From those high-ceilinged offices, formerly occupied by Chief Justice William H. Rehnquist, she has an excellent view of the Capitol building where the laws are enacted that she and her colleagues will interpret. No woman in the history of the republic has ever had an office here.

When asked what qualities have served her well, Justice O'Connor replies: "I just tried to make it a habit to do the best I could with whatever little problem I had or any client regardless of the means to pay.... I did that in school; I did it in the practice of law, and I did it in every job I've ever had. I still have that desire."

Mel Kranzberg—longtime editor of *Technology and Culture* and principal founder of the Society for the History of Technology—echoes the same theme: "You get into a *habit of excellence*.... You don't let yourself say, 'This isn't very important, so I won't do it very well.' "

Kranzberg, who has given literally thousands of lectures on the history of technology all over the world, was preparing to give a speech at a little-known college in a rural area when I conducted the interview. "I won't benefit monetarily from this particular talk, and it will certainly do nothing for me professionally, but I will do the very best job I know how. . . . You have to set standards for yourself."

When I asked Admiral Thomas H. Moorer what qualities had served him well in his career, he replied: "First, every assignment I was given, I tried to do it as best I could." Moorer added: "I always tried to reach for perfection."

Moorer says he has tried to follow some advice his father once gave him. "He told me two things: 'I don't care what you do. You can be a circus tightrope walker, but never do anything you don't enjoy, and try to do it better than anyone else.' "

Charles Schulz says he recommends to beginning cartoonists: "Just try to draw a good strip every day." He says there's a tendency for amateurs and beginners to think that once they're established, then they will do great things. That's a big mistake, Schulz says: "You should start doing your great things right away. I think this is the secret in any sort of performing art—not trying to save yourself for the great day when you become famous, but just do the best you can each day."

## Nature/Nurture

How much of talent is inherited? Frankly, science has no conclusive answer. One of the most bitterly fought debates in this century has centered on just how much of the variance in IQ tests is explained by inheritance. The educational psychologist Arthur R. Jensen created a furor in the late 1960s when he concluded that eighty percent or more of the variance in IQ scores is explained by inheritance. Most social scientists hold to a much lower figure.

The high achievers are not "Jensenites," but many of them believe native ability to be critical to high achievement. Guitarist Chet Atkins told me, "I can't pat myself on the back and say, 'Look at me and what I did.' What I did was select my parents carefully." But Atkins sees his achievement as a blending of nature and nurture: "They [my parents] gave me that desire to be somebody."

Arthur Ashe—the first American black to achieve international ranking in men's tennis—believes inherited ability is absolutely essential in his field. "You're born with certain abilities, be they physical or mental or a combination. Not all of us are gifted in equal shares in these departments, and I guess I was just blessed with physical ability, and the mental ability to go with it. . . . But there's no doubt that you have to be persistent and determined to succeed."

When I asked Isaac Asimov to pick three qualities or characteristics that had served him well in his career, he replied: "I guess one is persistence, and the second is industry. The third one is a quick mind, if you want the truth."

*Cosmopolitan* editor Helen Gurley Brown says "brain power" is essential to success: "It's never discussed, because it's an elitist concept," Brown told me, "but somebody with an 89 IQ cannot possibly achieve as much as somebody with a higher intelligence quotient, although the 89-IQ people can make up for quite a lot with ambition and working hard. As I say, it's never discussed. People act as though it doesn't exist, but you just cannot do as well if you don't have a good intelligence."

If Brown's assumption is a valid one—and I believe that it is—the essential question is: What besides intelligence is needed for high achievement?

## The Dream and the Reality

Ours is a land of optimistic dreamers. Youngsters grow up believing that it is really possible to become the nation's President or a big-league ballplayer or a famous actress or a general, admiral, or chairman of the board of IBM. Unfortunately, too many good dreamers never ask themselves the questions How? and Doing what?

The blunt truth is that unless you learn to do at least one thing very well, perhaps a bit better than the other people who have the same dreams, there is little chance of actually attaining lofty goals.

What does this mean to you? It means that if you wish to make a mark as an achiever, you must recognize what you enjoy doing *and* what you have a reasonable chance of doing very, very well. That decision involves gaining personal insights about your preferences, decisions about what you really enjoy, plus feedback from others, and trial-and-error as you experiment to see if the fit is good.

In the final analysis, however, there is no magic formula and there are no guarantees. Aptitude tests, guidance counselors, experts, the inner voice—they are all indicators, clues. But not final answers. Even the most skillful psychologists, sociologists, and guidance counselors cannot completely explain the process or provide an error-free formula for choosing.

Choosing can be painful. Søren Kierkegaard, the Danish existentialist philosopher, made choice one of his fundamental concepts. In Kierkegaard's view, people are just faces in the crowd until they make a choice. Someone becomes an individual only by choosing—a mate, a religion, a political philosophy, a career. You make choices by saying no to something or some things, and that often can be painful.

Fortunately, our society—unlike traditional societies with rigid caste systems—permits choosing and making changes, sometimes several changes during a lifetime. Our society is also relatively forgiving of people who try and fail, particularly if the failures come fairly early in life.

After you have found your voice—your "specialty," as Helen Gurley Brown puts it—then there is the road toward mastery. The cliché—It's not *what* you know but *who* you know that counts—is misleading. Who you know *is* important, as Chapter 8 makes abundantly clear. Having knowledgeable friends and influential contacts is a decided advantage. But unless you are competent, you will only embarrass them if they put you into a place of major responsibility. The idea of being discovered, after all, suggests that there is something to discover—some talent, some ability.

Turning an area of interest into an area of excellence always involves years of diligent focused work. To travel the road toward mastery, you must be able to absorb relevant knowledge from books and professors and coaches and from chance encounters as well as from formal training.

Competence involves learning through diligent application until one has stored in memory literally thousands of patterns. And it involves practice—not just repeating mistakes (thereby converting errors into habits), but getting feedback from the best people available.

If you do all this, you will become competent. And that is a very significant reward in itself. You will know, and you will know that you know. Striving for and attaining skill and knowledge is one of life's very satisfying experiences. It is an aspect of a process that the psychologist Abraham Maslow called self-actualization, an important phenomenon that will be explored in Chapter 5.

Such an achievement provides no automatic guarantee that you will receive international acclaim or riches. There are other factors that determine when and how well competence is rewarded. But because relatively few individuals are willing to pay the high price of attaining competence—real mastery of some field—you will have greatly improved the odds in your favor.

# 3

# Time on Your Hands

*I've wasted an enormous amount of time, and time is life. Time is all there is.*

—Gloria Steinem

*I always know what time it is and what I've got to do next, and I'm always very punctual. I would say that I'm almost time conscious to a fault.*

—Thomas Moorer

*I live by the clock. As a judge, you always do.*

—Sandra Day O'Connor

*I'm often asked, "Is there anything you wish you had that you don't?" and I always say, "More time." That is one thing that people really don't appreciate enough until they begin to run out of it.*

—Malcolm Forbes

# Time Consciousness

The year is 1977. *Courageous* has just won the America's Cup.

Champagne corks are popping in Newport, Rhode Island; crew members are throwing one another into the water, and turning the dockside into a twentieth-century version of Bedlam. America has once again beaten off the upstart Aussie challengers. The "100 Guinea Cup," first won by the Yacht America in 1851 at the Royal Yacht Squadron Regatta, can remain on its pedestal in the New York Yacht Club for another three years. (The Cup, as almost everyone knows, was won by the boys down under in 1983 and recaptured in 1987.)

But where is Ted Turner, the triumphant skipper? In a phone booth. Striding ashore as soon as *Courageous* was safely docked, Turner made for the nearest phone. What for? To talk about the race? No. To nail down a business deal.

Some months later, I am conducting an interview

with that same successful skipper—by then known as Captain Outrageous—for his own television station. As usual, Turner has other things on his mind, and he is barking orders nonstop to secretaries, assistants, directors, cameramen, and functionaries, as the audio director mikes him for the taping.

The cameras' red lights glow, and Ted is off and running, offering heartfelt opinions on everything from currency fluctuations to the Apocalypse—all singular insights.

After about twenty minutes of good, exciting television material, he decides he has had enough. Other matters he considers more important beckon urgently. The problem is that a thirty-minute television show requires about twenty-three to twenty-four minutes of material, depending upon the advertising spots used. Even if all the interview is usable without a single edit, we still need at least four more minutes of material. It is point-of-no-return time for this particular interview.

"How much longer is this thing going to take, Doc?" he asks impatiently.

"Ten minutes," I reply, hoping for the luxury of being able to use only the best material.

"No way," he answers. "Five."

"Seven," I reply, hoping for the best.

"Deal."

He gives me seven more high-energy minutes, and then with a crisp but friendly good-bye, the owner of the Atlanta Braves and Hawks and superstation WTBS and, subsequently, founder of Cable News Network is off and away, waving at buddies, giving orders to subordinates.

Three years later, I am in New York City in the executive suite of the Chase Manhattan Plaza, waiting to begin an interview with David Rockefeller. A vice president of the bank has already informed me that Rockefeller has only once before agreed to do a full-length television interview. "One hour is the absolute limit," the vice president insists. "From ten till eleven."

Precisely at ten o'clock—you could have set your clock radio by the event—in walks David Rockefeller, at the time chairman of Chase Manhattan Bank and one of the world's most influential figures. A quiet, smallish, understated, almost shy man, Rockefeller answers my questions steadily and carefully. But when eleven o'clock comes, he says softly, "It's been very pleasant talking with you, and now I really must go." An audio man unclasps the lavalier mike from his lapel, and Rockefeller nods to the crew and disappears within the confines of his handsome office suite.

Ted Turner and David Rockefeller are opposites in many respects. One is brash, noisy, and off-the-cuff; the other polished, cautious, urbane. What they have in common, in addition to wealth and power, is time consciousness. For them, time is a commodity to be carefully guarded, inventoried periodically, and dispensed carefully.

Malcolm Forbes told me that he is often asked, "Is there anything that you wish you had that you don't?" And what is the reply of the owner of a South Sea island, a Tangier palace, a French chateau, presidential letters, toy soldiers, toy boats, hot air balloons, and twelve Fabergé Imperial Eggs? *More time.* "That is the thing people really don't appreciate enough until they begin to run out of it."

Stanley Marcus, the man who nurtured Neiman-Marcus to its present status as an internationally recognized arbiter of taste and fashion, stated that he is "extremely" time conscious: "Time is probably the most precious asset I have, and which I have in the least supply."

Marcus, who has spent his career dealing with wealthy, powerful, and famous people, is a respected authority on their preferences and life-styles. It is Marcus's opinion that high achievers are almost uniformly time conscious. "They pretty well have to be," Marcus says. "The world has expanded in almost all directions, but we still have a twenty-four-hour day.

Historian Mel Kranzberg says: "I try to fill every minute. I'm a professor, so there's always a backlog of books and journals. When I have a free moment, my question is not, 'What do I do now,' but 'what do I do next?' I don't ever remember not having something to do."

Kranzberg continues, "I set aside time for certain tasks—to get out ten letters a day, another ten items of internal stuff. As for priorities, my students come first, then items with deadlines. I use a dictating machine; that saves time. I take work along on my trips so that I can get things done while I'm waiting in airports.

"There is a constant tension, and I don't know what I would do without that tension. I've discovered lots of other people who are very busy—they would be very unhappy if they weren't all wrought up about something."

"Are the high achievers you know time conscious?" I ask.

"Yes, in the sense that they try to use every moment of time."

One of my early interviews was with Gloria Steinem, a leading figure of the women's movement and a founder of *Ms.* magazine. Steinem told me that many women never reach their goals because they keep waiting for someone to take charge of their lives and tell them what to do, instead of seizing the initiative themselves. I was thinking quietly that not just women, but men as well, need to understand that lesson. Then Steinem said, "I've wasted an enormous amount of time, and time is life. Time is all there is."

What Steinem stated so poignantly is an old idea. At the beginning of the Christian era, Seneca, the Roman statesman, wrote: "Nothing is ours except time." (*Epistulae ad Lucilius*, Epis. i, section 3)

Goethe called time an "element," one of the basic building blocks of the universe. The poet Longfellow, writing about time, sounded remarkably like a modern physicist: "What is time? The shadow on the dial, the striking of the clock, the running of the sand, day and night, summer and winter, months, years, centuries— these are but arbitrary and outward signs, the measure of Time, not Time itself" (*Hyperion*, Book ii, ch. 6). In fact, one of the basic ideas of quantum theory is that time, space, and energy are essentially one—a concept that has attracted the attention of leading figures from physics, theology, philosophy, and art.

The "outward sign" of an individual's time on earth—to use Longfellow's words—are the seconds, minutes, hours, days, and years that we live. If you live seventy years, for example, your inventory at birth comes to about 25,550 days, or 613,200 hours, or almost 37 million minutes. When time is thought of this way, it can be dealt with rationally—managed, inventoried, parceled out, and invested.

I hasten to add that some high achievers are repelled by such an idea. They do not like to think of life in terms of discrete segments, with beginnings, middles, and endings—like novels. They lean toward non-Western modes of thought that emphasize the continuous nature of existence. Many high achievers in fact deliberately try to create blocks of nonlinear experiences.

However, most of us function in the Western world of deadlines, contracts, interest payments, hourly wages, appointments, and reservations. The next section deals with how high achievers cope with those constraints.

# Time Management

"I live by the clock. As a judge, you always do," says U.S. Supreme Court Justice Sandra Day O'Connor. She explains how critical time is to the ongoing of the nation's highest tribunal. The justices have to be absolutely on time when they go to court. They have to meet certain deadlines in getting their work out. They impose deadlines on others, and they must live by them as well. "I am absolutely governed by a need to meet time deadlines," concludes O'Connor.

The people who know super agent Mark H. McCormack best say the one thing that stands out in his career is his ability to manage his time efficiently. He describes that skill in his best-selling *What They Don't Teach You At Harvard Business School*.

McCormack manages his time by viewing a week as 168 hours and then scheduling time for relaxation and rest as well as work. He schedules time to play tennis, to read the morning paper, to take a nap in the office, or simply to do nothing—to free his mind from any sort of work-oriented thoughts or decisions.

McCormack says he constantly challenges himself to fit needed activities—like making phone calls or getting aboard a plane—into shorter and shorter time segments so that he can obtain "moments of empty space —a minute an hour, or a weekend in which to enjoy having nothing to do." He regards those moments as the carrots at the end of the stick (1984:210).

Those carrots are very important to McCormack. "I think my leisure time is something that's more inviolate to me than anything else." He told me that if he plans to be away on a vacation or plans to take an afternoon off, he gives those plans high priority. "People tend to quickly give those things up for things that really aren't that important."

It is important for people who deal with successful people to recognize that they are time conscious and often have short attention spans. "Get to the point," McCormack recommends. "Don't start with your life story; don't drag out a presentation.... All you'll succeed in doing is irritating people, or worse, making their minds wander" (1984:106,107).

The celebrated author Isaac Asimov is so jealous of his time that when asked what he resents most in life, he answers: "Having to give time to other people. I resent that very much." He confessed that dealing with that attitude has required more effort on his part than any other.

Dennis Hayes, at age thirty-seven, is one of America's most successful entrepreneurs. His company, Hayes Microcomputer Products, is consistently ranked among the very top companies in the computer industry, both in terms of its growth and sales and the quality of its management.

Not born to wealth, Hayes literally started his business on his kitchen table, with five thousand dollars— at age twenty-seven. His boss told him he would be lucky to sell twelve units of modems. Last year, his company produced 65 percent of the PC modems in the world.

Hayes attended Georgia Tech, a technological university that has always prided itself on its Marine bootcamp approach to education—pushing students to their limits of endurance.

Looking back on what prepared him for business success, Hayes states: "In college I learned how to manage more tasks than anyone could possibly finish. Literally. We learned how to keep a lot of balls in the air at the same time. You couldn't study for every class every day, so you had to decide what could be put off till later. The experience taught us to set priorities.

"That was a tough and a toughening experience. Learning how to deal with that kind of pressure is important later on. I often stayed up all night and walked into the classroom to take a test with no sleep. Business requires that same kind of stamina. There are times when you get involved in a marathon session, and your ability to deal with people long-term is critical."

Many high achievers hone that attitude to a sharp edge. J. B. Fuqua is one of them. Fuqua is the driving force behind a conglomorate that owns American Seating Company, Snapper Power Equipment, photo finishing and sports equipment companies, and a major bank.

Listen to J. B. Fuqua talk about using the phone, an instrument he regards as a moneymaking tool: "The ability to talk on the telephone should be taught in school. A lot of people get on the phone and spend three or four minutes talking about the weather or last night's football game, and then finally get around to discussing the subject they called about. That's a great waste of time. People ought to learn how to use their time—because time is all we've got."

There's that theme again—the same idea that Gloria Steinem and Seneca expressed, almost word for word.

"How do *you* use the phone?" I asked Fuqua.

"I make simple notes before I call," he replied. "When I get on the phone, I get to the point—I don't talk about the weather—I get the phone call over with, and that's that. And when I talk with people in my office, I try to carry in my mind a reasonable agenda, and if I go to see somebody else, I do the same thing. . . . Get it over with. I don't spend a lot of time socializing."

I asked him if there were times when small talk helped gain his objective: "Seldom. Not in my experience.

For that reason, I'm not strong on lunches. You may accomplish something in a luncheon conversation—if you plan to accomplish something—but generally I think there are a lot of lunchtimes wasted in this country. I'm impatient. I can accomplish a lot more if a person will come to my office or if I can go to their office."

Many of the high achievers take precautions against letting any significant amount of time slip by unused. Malcolm Forbes says that he can't sit in a car or go to bed without pad and a pencil or loaded with reading material. Like Stanley Marcus, if Forbes finds himself somewhere without part of the backlog of "reading stuff," he feels that he has lost time. He also begins the day with "to see," "to call," and "to do" lists. Forbes calls it an elementary system, one in which he runs a red line through what he's done and carries over what isn't completed to tomorrow's list.

Whenever Stanley Marcus travels, he always has a paperback book in his pocket. "That way I don't get ulcers when I get caught in a traffic jam. If I have a book with me, when I go to the doctor's office, I can read it instead of his worn-out magazines. I always travel with a book."

Marcus, like Fuqua, says he tries to avoid small talk. "That doesn't make you very popular," Marcus says, "because lots of people like to waste your time with small talk. You can waste an awful lot of time just talking about nothing.

"I am always punctual," Marcus says, "because my time is important and the other guy's time is important. If I find that people aren't going to reciprocate, then I find a way of doing business with somebody else."

Actor Bob Hoskins claims to be "awful" at time management, but his reputation for being punctual on the set is legendary. When asked why he manages to be punctual, yet is a professedly poor time manager, Hoskins replies: "I just don't like bad manners.... It doesn't have anything to do with time."

It is good manners and good sense. Whether motivated by good manners or time consciousness, the net effect is the same. In a craft where high-priced technical people and actors must work in concert, producers and directors are happiest when everyone is ready to work at the appointed hour. Anyone who is habitually tardy had better have awesome talent or power to compensate for the defect.

Hank Aaron admits that he has been late for appointments, but not when it came to baseball: "I don't know of any manager who can ever say that I was late getting out on the baseball field in twenty-three years."

Lillian Vernon Katz, head of the nation's largest mail-order gift business, told me: "I manage my time very well. I really do! You give me a job. It gets done. If they give me a ream of copy [for the *Lillian Vernon Catalog*] tonight, they'll have it back tomorrow morning.... I'm never late. That's like a disease, you know."

## Keeping Long Hours

In 1959, Osborn Elliott published *Men at the Top*, one of the classic studies of chief executive officers. After conducting over two hundred interviews with top businessmen, Elliott concluded that these men were "among the hardest-working men in the world."

Charles B. Thornton, then head of Litton Industries, got up at four A.M. so he could be in the office by five. "You live it, eat it, sleep it, breathe it," Thornton told Elliott. The head of General Electric arose at 5:15 and returned home, usually around seven o'clock in the evening. Robert Gross, the chairman of Lockheed Aircraft, told Elliott: "Damn right it wears me out. I'm tired as hell. I suppose I average four or five hours' sleep a night."

But when Elliott's interviewees were asked how they felt about their heavy time investment, they overwhelmingly reported that they enjoyed their work: "I would not change it for a million dollars a day," Wayne Johnston, then head of the Illinois Central, stated (1959:17,18).

The names of many of the executives in Elliott's study are not well known today, but the pattern of activity seems virtually unchanged. A 1986 report of the characteristics of chief executive officers of hi-tech firms—based on 1,399 responses nationwide—depicted the typical CEO as working sixty hours or more per week.

Joyce Dannon Miller, vice president of the Amalgamated Clothing and Textile Workers Union—and the first woman ever to be a member of the AFL-CIO Executive Council—told me in a 1987 interview: "I have always put in long hours. I never would take a vacation because I always felt that my work came first. It's only in the past few years that I started realizing that I should take time off."

Many high achievers learn to use off-peak time effectively. One of the best practitioners of that art was the late Sid Rubensohn, who, from scratch, built one of the largest advertising agencies in Australia. Rubensohn made it a practice to be in his office by six in the morning, often much earlier. That gave him time to catch up on correspondence, reading, and odds and ends, hours before anyone else showed up, or phoned. By two or three o'clock in the afternoon, Rubensohn had invested eight hours of quality time at the office, and was off to the golf course or the racetrack with buddies and clients.

Mary Kay has created what she calls the Five O'Clock Club for the people in her company. "I try to get everybody to get up at five o'clock in the morning and do all those things that women particularly don't like to do, like bookkeeping and writing notes and doing newsletters and things that are important in our business. To do all those things before the family gets up, before all of the intrusions begin–phones and dogs and children and husbands and whatnot." Mary Kay says she has found that she can get more done in those three hours before eight o'clock than she can do in six hours after eight o'clock.

She also puts out a form—which her people are asked to fill out each evening—entitled "The Six Most Important Things I Must Do Tomorrow." "Everyone is to fill this out every single night before they go to bed, to keep them on track the next day, to keep them from running off on tangents. Then I say, 'After you have finished those six important things, then you may take the rest of the day off with my blessing.' And you know, what happens is that they really do have a day of accomplishment by doing that. And it also keeps you very time conscious. . . . I am very conscious of the fact that every day is precious. I would give myself a nine, maybe even a ten, on time consciousness and time management."

# Flexibility

Some high achievers purposely keep a flexible agenda, because they want to be free to seize new opportunities, learn new information. "Do you plan your day?" I asked J. B. Fuqua. "Not as well as I should," he answered. "I'm not a detail planner. Some people have everything in a slot. I'm not a clean-desk operator. That indicates I'm not a very good planner."

"A lot of good things that happened to you weren't planned for?" I commented.

"Right."

"Are you willing to abandon any agenda to pursue a new opportunity?"

"Absolutely," Fuqua replied.

When Stanley Marcus was still running Neiman-Marcus, every evening he would write out an agenda of things he planned to do the next day. But that agenda was flexible. "A retail store is very difficult to manage, if you are customer conscious, because a customer's demands transcend all others. If a customer wants you to see a wedding gown on her, or a fur coat on her, you have to interrupt a planned meeting or something else to go see the customer. You have to fit in your correspondence and other appointments as best you can."

Bob Hoskins says, "I try to manage today well. But who knows? Something might turn up. You take it as it comes."

High achievers are usually careful not to confuse effective time management with busyness. Busyness may, in fact, be counterproductive. "It is necessary to be slightly underemployed if you are to do something significant," is the way Nobel Laureate James Watson puts it (Judson 1979:20).

You can be so busy with little activities that grind you down that there is no time left for big thoughts or deeds. You can be consumed by busyness. Edith W. Martin, who heads The Boeing Company's High-Technology Center, states that she tries to strike a balance in the use of time, a balance that she is continually reviewing. "I'm someone who says, 'You must have time for yourself.' So I make that time, and I'm always reflecting to see if, in fact, I'm using that time I have as effectively as I should be. That doesn't mean that it's all work. That means there's a good balance."

What emerges from these observations is a variation on the standard version of the Six Days Shalt Thou Labor work-ethic imperative. The common denominator is time consciousness. But there is considerable variation in the way high achievers actually use the time. Some wait till the last minute to begin the project; others start early. Some work by agendas, others do not.

Why this variation? Part of the explanation is the temperament of the individual. Part is the nature of the high achiever's work. For example, the constraints of a comic-strip artist, who must produce a strip every day, or a bond trader who must be at his or her desk every day the stock market is open—their constraints are not the same as those of a clothes designer, whose major deadlines are seasonal showings, or those of an actor, who may work eighteen-hour days for a three-week stretch and then have a slack period between pictures.

## Taking Time Off

Nobel Laureate Francis Crick told me that he immerses himself in research for days, sometimes weeks or months. But Crick also alternates leisure with these immersions. Crick doesn't think big breakthroughs come from people who are just everlastingly plodding along.

"The brain works by associations—seeing similarities between patterns," Crick says. "It's well documented that the best way to have ideas is first of all to immerse yourself in a subject for longish periods—like months or more—in which you study intensely, and then step away and do something else—go for a holiday, go out dancing, or something like that. Very often ideas come in this sort of incubation period."

Linus Pauling, a two-time Nobel Laureate, says much the same thing: The good insights come "after long immersion." Pauling says he has "flashes of inspiration" that usually come "after long periods of preparation."

Some achievers openly admit to what seems to be goofing off, to being less than rigorous in managing their time.

Oscar de la Renta stated that he waits until the deadline is almost upon him before he begins to work on a project in earnest. "I'm a procrastinator," he confessed. "I work well only under pressure. I do my best at the point of no return."

"Are you tightly strung?" I asked.

"Yes," he answered quickly. "I look cool, very calm, but in fact I am not."

That kind of behavior is not uncommon, especially among creative people. For example, Beethoven seems to have been a procrastinator. He did not complete the manuscript for his first piano concerto for piano and orchestra until hours before the concert. During the last two days before the event—his first before a public audience in Vienna—the brilliant young musician, who was at that time known only in the salons, worked furiously, handing each new page of the manuscript, with the ink still wet, to four copyists who prepared the individual players' parts in an adjoining room.

Perhaps this seeming procrastination on the part of high achievers is not due to their lack of discipline or their failure to appreciate the importance of time, as much as it is that they realize that they are not ready yet. Ideas are germinating, perhaps in the subconscious, but are not well enough formed for expression or public scrutiny.

Hugh Stubbins, the architect who designed the Citicorp Center in New York City and whose firm is now designing the Ronald Reagan Library, rated himself a ten on time consciousness but only a five on time management. Asked to explain the difference in scores, Stubbins replies: "Ideas don't come like turning a water faucet on, you know. Sometimes it takes time to get ideas. I run behind schedule a little bit, but I'm still conscious of time."

Listen to Ernest Hemingway describe the dilemma

that Stubbins mentioned—when the faucet is turned on, and the ideas won't flow: "Sometimes when I was starting a new story and I could not get it going, I would sit in front of the fire and squeeze the peel of the little oranges into the edge of the flame and watch the sputter of blue that they made. I would stand and look out over the roofs of Paris and think, 'Do not worry. You have always written before and you will write now. All you have to do is write one true sentence. Write the truest sentence that you know.' So finally I would write one true sentence, and then go on from there." (1984:17)

Hemingway observed a routine to help him overcome writer's block. He would sit and write at a regular time—in the mornings—and when the session was over, he would not write again on that subject until the next morning came. In fact, he would avoid even consciously thinking about the subject until the next morning.

". . . I learned not to think about anything that I was writing from the time I stopped writing until I started again the next day. That way my subconscious would be working on it and at the same time I would be listening to other people and noticing everything, I hoped; learning, I hoped; and I would read so that I would not think about my work and make myself impotent to do it" (1984:17).

There are levels of thought and emotion that we may be unaware of—levels below the threshold of awareness. Recent work in psychotechnology shows that when we relax, the brain waves are often measurably changed. Electroencephalographs (EEGs) taken of individuals with a great deal of experience in meditation show alpha waves slowing from the usual frequency of nine to twelve cycles per second to seven or eight cycles per second, and rhythmical theta waves appearing at six to seven cycles per second.

Researchers have suggested that in these more relaxed states—known as alpha and theta—a higher level of mental organization may occur. The balancing of intense work with relaxation that many high achievers mention may be a technique they have discovered to more fully exploit their mental abilities. Seen that way, relaxation is not a waste of time.

\*    \*    \*

High achievers develop the ability to reconcile the demands of deadlines with the desire to write a perfect sonata or design a flawless building. When the ideas don't come, they find ways to tease ideas out of the subconscious. They work longer, or they find a compromise. Engineers and architects do what is called "freezing the design." They will go with a *good* solution, instead of waiting for the perfect one.

If even the mighty Beethoven had to learn to focus in on projects, meet deadlines, and learn to work within the constraints of time, people of lesser talent can do no less. There are exceptions, to be sure, but in a world where talent is probably recognized more quickly than at any time in history, the people who make and break careers—agents, editors, impresarios, producers—often will abandon those who do not deliver on time in favor of others who will cause them less grief.

If you have noticed that many of the comments by high achievers in this chapter seem repetitive, I have achieved one of my goals. On the subject of time, high achievers do sound very much alike. They all value it.

Benjamin Franklin, no low achiever himself, summed up his feelings about time with the rhetorical question: "Dost thou love life? Then do not squander time, for that's the stuff life is made of."

# 4

# Persistence

*I was not an overnight success, even after I sold the strip. "Peanuts" did not take the world by storm immediately. It was a long grind. It took "Peanuts" about four years to attract nationwide attention, but it took ten years to become really entrenched.*

—Charles Schulz

*There is no success without failure.*

—Malcolm Forbes

*I happen to feel that failure sometimes prepares someone to maybe be stronger and better in the future. You learn from failure.*

—Harry Hoffman

*I was always willing to undergo hardship or whatever it took to be able to stay with my work. I could have quit many times—given up, because it is no great art in life to be poor and hungry, and that's what I was.*

—Erskine Caldwell

## Stubborn Dedication

Erskine Caldwell's novels are known around the world. In fact, for a few years *Tobacco Road* and *God's Little Acre* were selling at a brisker rate than the Bible. Translated into scores of languages, adapted into Broadway plays and films, they have established Caldwell as one of the important literary figures of our time.

In the mid-1920s, Caldwell was an unknown reporter, turning out unremembered stories for skimpy pay. However, in 1926, Caldwell quit his job and set out for Maine, where, he promised himself, he would learn how to write fiction. His program was to take five years. And there was a proviso that he would take an additional five years if necessary. Caldwell chopped firewood, raised potatoes and rutabagas for food, and wrote and wrote and wrote. In fact, he mailed so many manuscripts to publishers that finding enough money for postage became a problem.

Finally, after many, many mailings, Caldwell received a letter from the editor of an English-language literary magazine published in France stating that he was planning to publish one of Caldwell's stories. No pay was involved, but Caldwell would have the satisfaction of seeing his work in print. Caldwell was so delighted that he and his wife celebrated the event with a bonfire—which he started with several shoe boxes full of rejection slips that he had received through the years. Slowly but steadily other small magazines began to accept his stories.

In 1930, Caldwell received word that the renowned editor Maxwell Perkins—editor to Wolfe and Fitzgerald and Hemingway—had seen one of his stories and would like to see some more of his work. Caldwell responded by mailing Perkins a story a day for a week; but, alas, at first each story was promptly returned. Then, after Caldwell had almost abandoned hope, Perkins finally sent word that he liked two of Caldwell's stories and offered to pay "two fifty" for both of them. Caldwell declined. Perkins raised the offer to "three fifty." Caldwell finally agreed, protesting tactfully: "I guess that'll be all right. But I thought I'd get a little more than three dollars and fifty cents for both of them." Perkins, of course, meant $350, not $3.50. (Lamb 1982:F1,2)

Caldwell found, as all high achievers do, that *competence* cannot be attained overnight. A considerable amount of research evidence, as we have already seen, indicates that ten years is a minimum to be world class in most demanding fields. In Caldwell's case, he felt that his experience as a journalist did not qualify him to write fiction. He needed more experience, more practice.

Helen Gurley Brown, who gives herself high marks on persistence, says that one of the most common mistakes people make in their careers is that they "check out too soon." They don't want to do the grubby stuff. They want to get to the top too quickly.

Brown's approach, based on her own experience of progressively working upward to her present post as editor of *Cosmopolitan*, involves starting out at virtually any job and moving up gradually. She calls the strategy "mouseburgering," because in the beginning, the novice may feel as insignificant as a tiny mouse.

Brown says you can start at virtually any job, but stay at each job only as long as you are improving your skills. With each move, try to keep going "ever so gradually *up*." If you stay with that plan, she promises, the gradual moving will take you to the top. What matters, Brown says, is starting and not giving up.

Rarely does one man or one woman become an institution. But Jacques Cousteau has. My interview with the explorer, inventor, and environmentalist took place aboard a chartered jet, headed toward Atlanta, where he was scheduled to speak to a nationally televised convocation at Georgia Tech. During the trip, we talked about his television series on the Amazon, his experiences in Haiti, and another project he was heavily involved in— an experimental wind ship, the *Alcyone*.

"How have you managed to do all this?" I asked.

He paused for a few moments, then replied: "I am obstinate—when I have something in mind . . . I make a list of things I like to play with: the Amazon, Haiti, the windship. I try, and I don't get the money. I try again, and I don't get the money, and after ten years I get it."

Thoughtfully, purposefully, always pushing in the direction he wanted to go, sometimes quickly, sometimes slowly, he has chalked up his victories. In 1943, it was the Aqua Lung that he and Emile Gagnan developed, which subsequently opened up the underwater world to millions of scuba divers. Then he developed skill as an underwater photographer, and in 1956 won an Oscar for *The Silent World*. Nine years later he won another

Oscar for *World Without Sun*. Now well into his seventh decade, Cousteau is still going strong, still checking items off his list.

## Goals, Objectives, and Priorities

Caldwell and Cousteau share not only their dogged refusal to give up, but also their striving toward specific ends. Indeed, there is a close and important connection between persistence and setting out an agenda. The word *achievement* implies goals—purposefulness. So does the word *success*.

When we say that high achievers have priorities, we mean that they have rank-ordered their goals—they have decided to give more emphasis to some goals, less emphasis to others. By means of persistence they translate goals, arranged by priorities, into action.

That sounds very simple—almost machinelike in its logic. Too simple, actually. In real life no one behaves quite this way. Even the most disciplined individuals deviate from their goals and priorities, sometimes behaving emotionally, sometimes intuitively or even illogically. Who has not made a false start, then stopped and said: "Hey, wait a minute. Why am I doing this? This isn't getting me anywhere."

There is no consensus among high achievers about the actual way they implement their goals and objectives. Some have very explicit goals and objectives, and carefully plan each day's activities, often the night before. They jot down what they hope to accomplish, and alongside each activity they will pencil in an A for the most important, a B for the next most important, and a C for activities that can be postponed.

Others perform this task only mentally. They have goals that are less explicit but still very real. But all the high achievers I interviewed had a general sense of direction and a sense of what needed to be emphasized in order to get where they wanted to go.

What kept Erskine Caldwell going through the early years of adversity? "Just a starry-eyed objective I had to get my work into print," he says. "Being famous was something that was far beyond my perception, because to be able to write and to get something into print was satisfaction enough. All I wanted to do was to be able to write a story and to get that story into print—cold print, black and white print."

Caldwell says that this goal, and not ambition to be acclaimed, sustained him: "I was always willing to undergo hardship or whatever it took to be willing to stay with my work.... I can eliminate anything in life that's going to interfere with what I'm trying to do," Caldwell told me. "I'm rather hard-headed and cold-blooded, in a sense, because I do alienate many people by being able to turn down the easy things in life, like going to this party or doing something else instead of doing my work."

We also see in Caldwell's career how persistence has been interwoven with other achievement factors: *competency, focus,* and *commitment.*

When you look at the early days of many of these now-famous individuals' careers, you often find that they were simultaneously working at two or more jobs. One of the jobs they really cared about, and the others they took just to pay the bills. That is what Tennessee Williams did, working by day at a Memphis shoe company and writing by night. That is what Erskine Caldwell did. He agreed to review hundreds of books, wrote the reviews, then sold the books he had received to used-book dealers. That is what Emmylou Harris did. She waited tables and worked at a real estate firm, showing model homes. Those were her "day jobs," she says. But at night, Emmylou was singing. Kristofferson took a job in Nashville as a janitor. He could have done better, he told me, but he wanted a job that would not tire him out mentally. His priorities told him that mental energy should be saved for music.

Tennessee Williams and Erskine Caldwell and Emmylou Harris and Kris Kristofferson persisted at what they considered most important, and, as we all know, one fine day they were able to say good-bye forever to their day jobs. Emmylou Harris, incidentally, advises that young people just starting out in the entertainment field should learn some practical skill in order to survive the lean years that most performers go through.

Not many people know that Robert C. Byrd did not possess a college degree when he first came to Congress. For years he had wanted one. During his steady progress toward Capitol Hill, he had been a welder, a fiddler, a grocery-store clerk, then a butcher, and finally a store owner. But he had never completed his college work, though he had taken college courses part-time while serving in the West Virginia legislature.

On the campaign trail, Byrd's opponents had sneered at his humble beginnings. They referred to him as a "butcher" and a "fiddler." Byrd tried not to show it, but their sneers hurt. "That sort of cuts a little bit, and it leaves its mark, and one really feels he is inferior," Byrd told me.

In Washington, those feelings grew more intense. It was quickly apparent to this self-taught orphan from the coal regions that virtually everyone around him was college-educated, and many of them had law degrees. "I felt inferior," Byrd told me, recalling those awkward early days. "I didn't only feel inferior, I *was* inferior in some respects."

Instead of resigning himself to inferiority for the rest of his life, Byrd decided upon a way of resolving the problem. He approached the dean of the law school at

American University and worked out a program to attain a law degree. Because Byrd lacked an undergraduate degree, the dean insisted that he maintain a higher grade-point average than was required for other students. Byrd accepted the challenge. For ten years he attended classes at night after the punishing daily schedule in Congress was complete.

Finally, in 1963, at the age of forty-five, Byrd graduated from American University's College of Law. "It was as hard a task as I have ever had. There was no time for leisure—no time for anything but work, work, work." The senator paused with his narrative, surveyed the trappings of power and tradition that surrounded him in the office suite of the majority leader, held up both of his hands—spreading wide the fingers—and said softly, poignantly: "Ten years. Ten long years."

On the front page of the résumé that the senator mails to those who request it, there is a listing under the heading "Academic Degree," which reads: L.L.B., J.D. *cum laude*, American University.

## Tenacity

Edith W. Martin uses the word "tenacious" to describe her personal approach to problem-solving. "During my career, there have been times when I committed myself twenty-four hours a day, seven days a week—just kept my nose to the grindstone and never saw the light of day."

Asked how this tenacity manifests itself, Martin replied: "If a solution exists, I will find it. That's my tenacity. If a perfect solution does not exist, I will give you the best possible alternative."

Senator William Proxmire, originator of the "Golden Fleece Award," has been a U.S. senator since he was elected to fill the seat left vacant by the death of Senator

Malcolm S. Forbes

Isaac Asimov

*(Handmade Films)*

Bob Hoskins

Kris Kristofferson

Francis Crick

Aaron Copland

Ray Charles

Daniel Barry

Helen Gurley Brown

Emmylou Harris

John Huston

*Right:* The author,
B. Eugene Griessman,
interviewing
*(by Schulz)*

Charles Schulz

John C. Portman

David Rockefeller

Stanley Marcus

Julie Andrews

Ted Turner
(Turner Broadcasting Corporation)

Andy Rooney

(photo by B. Eugene Griessman)

Richard Petty

Jack Nicklaus

Steve Allen

Mary Kay Ash

(Turner Broadcasting Corporation)

Griessman (left) and Chet Atkins onstage at the
Grand Ole Opry during TV taping

Xavier Roberts

Hank Aaron

Joseph McCarthy in 1957. Something of the senator's personality can be gleaned from a record that he holds—the longest unbroken record in the history of the U.S. Senate in answering roll-call votes. For over two decades, he has not missed a single one. That's almost 9,400 at this writing.

When I asked the senator what qualities had worked for him, Proxmire replied: "Persistence. Sticking with an objective, accepting defeat, coming back and hammering away at it until you've succeeded." (His class at the prep school he attended in Pottstown, Pennsylvania, named Proxmire the class "grind" because of this quality.)

Proxmire has learned how to face defeat without being defeated. The Democratic senator began his political career by winning a seat in the Wisconsin legislature in 1950. Two years later he ran for governor against the Republican incumbent and lost by a whopping four hundred thousand votes. In a state that has a long tradition of rejecting Democratic candidates for governor, Proxmire helped to keep the tradition alive by losing again in 1954, and in 1956 losing yet again. At this point, his friends had begun to suggest that Proxmire think about a more promising line of work. Then in 1957, Proxmire was elected to the U.S. Senate. "I lost three straight elections," he said, looking at me steadily, "but I haven't lost since then."

Anyone who has done direct selling knows that nobody closes every sale. Even the supersalesmen hear the word no. But really good salespeople can predict the percentage of noes and yeses they will hear with a given product. They may hit a streak of rejections, but they know that if they persevere—doing the very best they can, without panicking—that the numbers will eventually turn in their favor.

Not surprisingly, high achievers in many fields think in terms of ratios and percentages. Charles Schulz is one.

He, like Hemingway, says there are some days when he will sit for hours before thinking of something he can use. Sometimes, an entire day will pass and nothing will be accomplished. How does Schulz handle that kind of frustration? "I just realize that it's a day wasted, which is kind of disappointing and a little bit depressing," he says, "but maybe tomorrow I'll come up with some of the funniest things I've ever thought of. I think it's like a ballplayer who may go zero for five today, but tomorrow he may hit three home runs in a row."

Actor Bob Hoskins says, "If I want to do something, I won't accept failure, because until I do something, I haven't failed. I've always done what I thought I should do. Some have turned out to be incredible disappointments. I can live with that. What I can't live with is remorse."

And what is the distinction Hoskins sees between disappointment and remorse? "Disappointment is doing something and finding it's not quite as good as you thought," Hoskins replies. "Remorse is not doing it, and realizing 'I wish I had.' "

Loretta Lynn, the country singer whose life was portrayed in the movie *Coal Miner's Daughter*, says that at one time in her career people called her "Colonel Parker" because she promoted herself as assiduously as the legendary Colonel Parker promoted Elvis Presley. On her first promotional trip, Lynn stopped at every country-music station between Washington state and Nashville. Once in Nashville, it was the same story. In her autobiography, she writes: "I'd be on people's doorsteps at eight in the morning, holding copies of my first record and of new songs I'd written.... I went over to the Opry and pestered the manager until he let me on the show." (1976: 111, 129)

"When I get determined to do something, I don't give up," multimillionaire J. B. Fuqua told me. "I've made some significant acquisitions and done some personal deals that other people would have given up." Fuqua then described one of those acquisitions: "About fifteen years ago, there was a company listed on the New York Stock Exchange that appeared to be a very attractive vehicle that someone could take and do something with. It was controlled by two families, but the families didn't trust each other.... I went to New York time and time again, and sat down with each family separately. Eventually I convinced them that I was dealing on the same basis with each family. I got control of the company and made many millions of dollars off the transaction."

Fuqua says there were many other people who saw the same opportunity and tried one or two times and then walked away. "They were not persistent. I won the prize in a big way."

General Albert C. Wedemeyer summed up his long and distinguished career in the army thus: "I have not given up easily." Wedemeyer, a recipient of the Distinguished Service Medal, served as American commander in China during World War II. In his eighty-ninth year, the old warrior told me: "I've kept on striving to accomplish my objectives. I've met with disillusionments; I met with disappointments. Sometimes I was confronted with deceit, but I kept on anyway along the avenue that I'd selected, and tried to reach the goals."

Why? I asked.

"I have tried to live up to the motto of West Point: Duty, honor, country," Wedemeyer replied.

## Surviving Disappointment

The high achievers enjoy their careers, but they—like General Wedemeyer—will quickly add that there are unhappy experiences associated with their work. Home-run hitters strike out, politicians suffer defeats, playwrights receive punishing reviews, songwriters produce songs that no one will sing, writers have days when the words simply won't come, and generals order men into battle knowing many will not return. On those kinds of days, what do they do?

They fall back on character, on commitment, on their core values. In the case of General Wedemeyer—on duty, honor, country.

Ray Charles once told me, "When the crowd's with you, it does something for you."

"And what do you do," I asked, "when the crowd is small and isn't with you?"

He paused, grinned, and began to sway his body back and forth in that rhythmical way of speaking that has become his signature: "That's when you find out whether you're a pro or not." He was beginning to feel the subject. "That's like playing on the other guy's home court, when everybody boo everything you do. That's when you've got to say to yourself, 'That's fine, but I'm still me.' That's when you say, 'I'm gonna be good in spite of myself.' That's when you want those twenty-five people, or however many people's there, to be able to go away and say, 'There weren't many people there. And the place was a drag, and the sound system wasn't very good, but, look, I tell you something, honey, they put on a show. You missed it. . . .' You can't let yourself *get* down. If you're able to drag on stage, you've gotta be true to thyself. I must be true to Ray."

People seldom hear of the failures of high achievers, perhaps because they want to think of these people in terms of successes, not failures. And high achievers often avoid talking about or thinking about their setbacks. Sometimes the setbacks are too painful to reflect upon. But occasionally they will tell about their failures, which is fortunate for those of us who want to learn practical lessons from others' experiences. As it turns out, the honest story of many achievements, perhaps most achievements, involves setbacks and rejections.

Kris Kristofferson had an early and short-lived rock-and-roll career in England under the name Kris Carson. At about the same time his early efforts at novel writing came to naught. His manuscripts were promptly returned by publishers.

Mel Kranzberg was denied tenure at Amherst College, an experience that devastated the young scholar. He considered leaving teaching forever. Kranzberg then received an offer from Case Institute of Technology, now a part of Case Western Reserve University. At Case he began to develop a new field of study—the history of technology. "If I hadn't gone to Case, I would have become just a good journeyman French historian. . . . The move opened up a new opportunity."

One footnote should be added. In 1983, Amherst College conferred upon Kranzberg an honorary doctorate.

"I have a good reputation and considerable notice because of the success that I've had," says Harry Hoffman, president and chief executive officer of Waldenbooks, "but there have been an awful lot of failures along the way." Hoffman believes one of his greatest strengths is his ability to shrug off failures and to say, "Well, at least we tried." Hoffman says he has had some ideas that he thought were terrific—and still thinks they are—but they didn't succeed. "We had to spend quite a bit of money to find out they wouldn't work." But the resilience Hoffman speaks of is not passive. It involves trying to learn from failures so that the next idea will have a better chance of succeeding.

Architect John Portman experienced a major setback early in his career, an episode that changed his career. At issue was the construction of a medical building that Portman had designed during the 1950s. "I won a national award in *Progressive Architecture* for the design of the building," Portman recalls, "but I was associated with an individual in real estate who was supposed to develop the project. The two things didn't come together—the design and the construction—and the project failed." Portman lost $7,500 on the project.

It was a traumatic experience for Portman. "I couldn't afford a financial failure . . . I lost all the money I had in the world at the time . . . It had quite an effect. The building was never built."

However, Portman profited from the failure. "It was from that experience that I decided to learn all I could about real estate and finance and development so that I could be my own developer. I resolved never again to get into a position where someone else could cause something that I was very, very much interested in—to cause it to fail."

The longtime producer of "Flash Gordon" states that in the very demanding work of cartooning, it's easy to slump off into despair. It's just hard work sometimes, Dan Barry says. Barry admits that, when the work doesn't flow, when it doesn't come easily, he finds himself hating his work. Those are the days when the ink is spilling and the pencil is breaking and the juices aren't flowing. "I find myself having to survey what I'm doing and consciously remind myself that I really love what I'm doing, and turn on the creative juices that way. It's very important to be aware that what you are doing is something that you have *chosen* to do."

Barry believes that once you have made a commitment, you can—through an act of the will—immerse yourself to a point of thorough enjoyment. "The greatest joy is known when we overcome pain," Barry says. "We don't know real joy except by comparison with agony. And so, this work is so painful sometimes. Sometimes you can't make it happen." But, he says, all those difficulties add to the real pleasure of coming through, of turning in the job.

Being able to produce in spite of difficulties builds character and is habit forming. It reinforces itself—Barry says. "I've had to produce work that had to be in Monday morning, every week, fifty-two weeks a year, with no vacations for 35 years. You have a deadline. You do the work. If it's not flowing, you stay at it longer."

## Executing Ideas

Any successful strategic plan, building, painting, automobile, or advertising campaign always has two essential elements—conception and execution. Without a successful linkage of the two, the plan fails. "There's many a slip 'twixt the cup and the lip," is the way Shakespeare described the uncertainty and difficulty of making such a linkage.

"People are always calling me with ideas, but I don't need ideas," says Cabbage Patch creator Xavier Roberts. "I've already got ten thousand ideas right now, and all of them could succeed. A few would make millions; some would make only a few thousand. I need people to *execute* ideas."

The Cabbage Patch phenomenon began with Xavier Roberts's idea that dolls could be marketed as babies. The idea was tested first in flea markets and art shows, then with merchants. As the idea caught on, Roberts employed family members and friends to make the "Little People." There were early setbacks, though. Roberts financed the operation initially with a credit card—which was withdrawn when he extended the business too far, purchasing material to make the dolls. But he weathered the storm, and within months, his company, Original Appalachian Artworks, Inc., was employing several hundred employees. In 1982, Roberts signed a licensing agreement with Coleco, and the following Christmas—after a very clever marketing campaign—the Cabbage Patch Kids became a worldwide phenomenon. More about that later.

What advice does Roberts give to entrepreneurs yearning to breathe free? "You've got to be willing to work hard enough to prove your idea will work. People like Coleco will be interested *after* you've proved your idea. Not before."

Implementing an idea usually involves a lot of hard work, but it is an old, proven way to attain one's goals. Benjamin Franklin called it *industry*, and described its results in his autobiography: "My Father having among his Instructions to me when a Boy, frequently repeated a Proverb of Solomon, 'Seest thou a Man diligent in his Calling, he shall stand before Kings, he shall not stand before mean Men.' I from thence consider'd Industry as a Means of obtaining Wealth and Distinction, which encourag'd me, tho' I did not think that I should ever literally stand before Kings, which however has since happened—for I have stood before five, and even had the honour of sitting down with one, the King of Denmark, to Dinner." (Labaree 1964:144)

## The Art of Compromise

Persistent people are not always pleasant to be around. In fact, even the word *persistent* has a disagreeable connotation. It suggests stubbornness and obstinacy, and often implies opposition to advice. Those qualities are, in fact, common among high achievers. They often refuse advice. They can be stubborn and obstinate.

However, as we have seen, some of them, like Jacques Cousteau, wait until the time is right before launching a project. Still others, with equal effectiveness, use compromise as a strategy in order to attain their goals. They persevere toward their goals, but they adapt their means to match the situation.

Many people are uncomfortable with the word *compromise*. For them, it smacks of unprincipled deals cut in dimly lit back rooms. They regard any deviation from one's position as morally weak. However, life in any complex society would be impossible without bargaining, without give-and-take, without concessions and middle grounds. Happily, some of our ablest leaders have known the value of compromise.

"I am persistent, but not to the point of being dogmatic about it," says Sandra Day O'Connor. O'Connor, who served in the Arizona State Senate from 1969 to 1975 and was elected state senate majority leader in 1972, stated that her experience as a legislator taught her the importance of flexibility in negotiations. You gain what you want through "the art of compromise," she says, "not dogged persistence to the bitter end at whatever cost."

Norman Vincent Peale says he never lets go of something that he desperately wants to do or that he believes ought to be done. "I've preached this and practiced this for a long time." Asked if he is obnoxiously persistent, Peale replied: "If I can't do it head-on, I will look for a circuitous way to do it. The idea is to do it no matter what method you use."

Is Peale comfortable with the idea of compromise? "Yes," the renowned clergyman replies. "I will compromise, but always within ethical boundaries."

There are two kinds of compromise, Stanley Marcus says. One is a compromise on principle, which he doesn't believe in at all. And there's a compromise on strategy, which he does approve of. Marcus recalls that his friend Lyndon Johnson used to refer to "areas of attainability," a concept that implies that it is better to attain part of a goal rather than to lose the whole thing because one is unwilling to make some compromises. That kind of compromise—one of strategy—Marcus believes is always worth considering.

## Self-Assurance and Its Corollaries

Isaac Asimov received numerous rejections before the first acceptance of one of his science-fiction stories. But even though Asimov says those rejections bruised his ego, he had enough confidence in his ability to keep trying. "I was always pretty sure that eventually I would sell. It was just a matter of how long I would have to wait."

Aaron Copland says it never really bothered him when his work wasn't well received. When asked to explain why, the composer whose work is now performed around the world replied: "You have a feeling always in the back of your mind that whatever happens now, they'll see. The future will prove that you were right and they were dumb not to be able to appreciate it now." Copland believes you're bound to get discouraged unless you have that feeling.

Bob Hoskins, who gives himself a score of nine on self-confidence, says: "My mum said to me very early— and it's stuck in my head—'Son, if they don't like you, they've got bad taste.'"

"And you believe that?"

"Yeah, I really believe that," the celebrated actor replied.

As a youngster, Hank Aaron realized that he had more ability than the average ballplayer. His task was to keep trying until someone noticed. "I was not going to let failure stand in the way of doing what I wanted to do.... I've seen a lot of athletes that were as gifted as I was, but yet could not concentrate and would accept failure a lot quicker. I concentrated on what I had to do and I was not going to accept failure."

These individuals tend not to sway from one opinion to another. In fact, several of the high achievers stated that they are not particularly teachable. Admiral Moorer referred to himself as "pretty bullheaded." That is probably a predictable corollary of self-assurance. Malcolm Forbes chose the word "persuadable" instead of teachable, and gave himself a score of eight. Hank Aaron stated: "I'm a little bit stubborn, and I think one reason for that is that I learned how to play ball very easily without having other people tell me anything about it. I felt like I knew as much about many of the little things as somebody else did. I would have to give myself a seven rating on that, but I wish it were a ten."

Charles Schulz stated that he doesn't test his ideas with anyone.

"You're that confident that you know?" I asked.

"Well, it's a combination of that and the fact that you really can't trust anybody. I don't want anybody else's opinion, anyway."

"Have you always been that way?"

"Yes."

"You don't want anybody else's opinion?"

"What good does it do? If somebody on my staff says that's not funny, or somebody says it is—just because they don't think it's funny doesn't mean I'm going to throw it away. I can't waste my time on that."

Erskine Caldwell told me essentially the same thing: "I'm really not interested in what someone else would advise me to do. I like to take my own advice. I'm sort of independent; I don't belong to a league." The famous author then observed: "An older person thinks he already knows it all. Right now, I would have to say, No, I'm not teachable."

Stanley Marcus has known and personally dealt with

a large number of high achievers from many different fields. Marcus says it is difficult to generalize about this attribute, but he says that many of the successful people he has dealt with—because they are successful—tend to depend upon their own judgment and resist others' opinions. He adds, however: "Some of them have been smart enough to listen to other opinions and enlarge their own perspectives.

Mail-order magnate Lillian Vernon Katz says nobody can move her if she feels strongly about something. She sees steadfastness as a part of having *character*. "However, if somebody says, 'I don't think you should do this kind of catalog,' I'll think about it, and if I feel they're right, I will change my mind and go in another direction. But they've got to convince me."

## *Reinforcement*

I first encountered the work of psychologist B. F. Skinner when I was in graduate school, back in the 1960s. At that time Skinner was regarded as something of a maverick, challenging many of the hallowed ideas of psychology.

Gradually, Skinner's ideas about conditioning, learning theory, and verbal behavior began to take hold, and, even though some scholars still regard him as a bit of a crank, his ideas have moved to center stage in the social sciences.

In 1985, I asked Skinner why his controversial ideas managed to gain such a wide following. The famous psychologist laughed: "Because I was right and the others were wrong."

But what convinced Skinner that he was right? Reinforcement, Skinner says. Reinforcement, he argues, explains why anyone continues at a task or stays with an idea. "I certainly have kept on going," Skinner says. "But

I don't call it persistence. I think it's due to the reinforcing consequences as I followed my work. I don't put
these things in people at all. I don't think people act as
they do because of their qualities. They act because of
what happens to them."

Reinforcement can come in many shapes and
sizes—as gifts, prizes, bonuses, good feelings, applause.
Skinner, it is clear, did not get much applause during
the early going, but some of his experiments with pigeons and mice turned out to be quite successful. He
found that he could modify animal behavior by giving
or withholding rewards. His pigeons, for example, mod-
ified their eating habits, and even learned to play a form
of Ping-Pong. During World War II, Skinner sought a grant
to train pigeons to guide bombs to their targets in air
raids. To Skinner's dismay, the plan was never imple-
mented, but the nose of an experimental pigeon-guided
missile is now in the Smithsonian Institution.

While Skinner was reinforcing his pigeons, he was
reinforcing himself. "I went on for about fifteen years
without making very much of a dent in the field. I think
my pigeons were the things that reinforced me, not people's reactions."

Jack Lemmon's experience supports Skinner's view.
At age eighteen, Lemmon was a summer-stock apprentice, building sets, pulling curtains, and auditioning for
small parts. It was a tough go. "I was ready to chuck it
and think that, well, maybe I should start out at the
bottom in my old man's business. Here I had dreamed
I was going to be a terrific actor, and I couldn't even
keep five- and six-line parts. . . . I got small parts and was
fired three times."

Lemmon says that young, blind hope kept him going.
That, and feedback from his friends and his peers who
told him he was talented.

"I don't believe in the old saw that talent will out

—like suddenly, if you have a painting talent, you will find yourself one day with a brush in your hand," Lemmon says. "I think it can happen. But I think what is more true is that you may stumble onto something that you have a talent for, and that if you are accepted doing it, you will continue it, because you want the acceptance."

# Enjoyment

As we have already seen, persistence is a matter of discipline and commitment for some high achievers—a matter of tenaciously hanging on. For others, it is not that grim. They seem to have found something they enjoyed doing so much that they just kept doing it. In effect, they got hooked on their work—which is one effect of positive reinforcement. Because they liked what they were doing, they spent a lot of time doing it. The result is that they became *skillful*, *proficient*.

That process describes what has happened in the career of writer Isaac Asimov. "I write all the time because I like to, and not because I'm disciplining myself," said he.

Charles Schulz regards drawing cartoons as a wonderful way to make a living. And, as we have seen, Schulz knows he is good at what he does. But he doesn't like to use the word *success* to describe himself. Asked how he accounts for the acceptance his work has received, Schulz replied, "I simply went ahead from day to day just drawing pictures."

For high achievers like Asimov and Schulz, the recognition, the fame, the money—though admittedly pleasant—seem almost incidental, almost like a side show to the main act. They are doing what they like to do. That is why they persist at it.

# Abundant Energy

The energy and stamina of many high achievers is downright astonishing—and that energy is often the driving force behind their dedication to goals and career. The day I talked with Jacques Cousteau, he had flown from Paris to New York early in the morning on the Concorde, caught a jet to Atlanta, where he delivered his speech and held a press conference. Then, the next day, he was off for the West Coast. A week earlier the seventy-five-year-old scuba diver had taken part in a two-hundred-foot dive off the coast of Haiti. Such stories seem to be typical of high achievers.

"One of the things people haven't stressed perhaps enough is, you need a lot of mental energy, or energy of some sort to do all this," says Nobel Laureate Francis Crick. "It's quite clear that the people who are good are not only sort of exuberant—but are also indefatigable. They have really got an enormous capacity to go on doing things for a long time. If you read accounts of [Sir Isaac] Newton, for example, it is clear that he just kept at it and at it and at it."

Renowned architect Hugh Stubbins, when asked what has contributed most to his career, replied: "Energy."

No one would accuse Steve Allen of being lazy. During an incredibly active career, he has hosted *The Tonight Show*, *The Steve Allen Show* (in Sunday-night competition with *The Ed Sullivan Show*), and *Meeting of Minds* for PBS, has written several books and several thousand songs, played the role of Benny Goodman in the movie *The Benny Goodman Story*, and still finds time to perform on stage.

Yet Allen told me, "I'm physically lazy.... I have to get ten or eleven hours of sleep each day." But laziness does not describe Allen's mental life: "I don't like to paint the fence or any of that stuff, but there is something up here that is just running all by itself. My will has, so far as I'm aware, very little to do with it."

Robert Shaw, the Grammy Award–winning conductor who has recorded scores of albums in his lifetime, names "above-average energy" as one of the qualities that has helped him most.

Norman Vincent Peale says he is endowed with "restless" energy. The eighty-eight-year-old clergyman says he still goes constantly all day long and all evening long, until he finally goes to bed. "That's foolish," he says. "Nobody should do that, but I do it."

## Persistence to a Fault

A word of warning about persistence. All of us know people who have worked persistently yet died poor, obscure and unhappy. Obviously, staying at a job brings no guarantee of success. Not by itself. There is an old saying to the effect that hard work brings only calluses.

Persisting at a career for which one has no talent leads inevitably to failure and frustration. What is more, the time spent unwisely in one occupation might well result in success in another. A maladroit, slow youngster will never win the Heisman Memorial Trophy, no matter how persistent he may be. An investor who holds on to worthless property is not going to become rich. And a scientist who becomes obsessed with a wrongheaded idea is not going to win the Nobel Prize. Linus Pauling believes that the most important characteristic of good, original researchers is the ability to recognize and throw away bad ideas. Otherwise, they will waste a tremendous amount of time following up one of the bad ideas.

Unfortunately, there are no hard-and-fast fules for telling the difference between good and bad ideas, or for knowing whether a setback is a signal to give up and try something else or to keep trying until the goal is reached. High achievers rely on facts when they can get them— they tend to be a hard-nosed about evidence—on their past experience, sometimes on the counsel of people hey really trust, and on what they will call their "instincts" or "gut reactions." But it is a critical issue. Being able to decide whether to try harder and longer or to try something else is one of the most important aspects of the achievement process.

\*     \*     \*

Clearly, high achievers possess the ability to keep at the tasks and careers they choose. They finish the jobs that they consider important and they stick by their guns when attacked.

They think about the future, but not too much. Mainly they are intent on doing well what comes to them each day.

They sometimes alter the direction of their careers, depending upon the times and the opportunities, but the changes are more evolutionary than revolutionary. Sandra Day O'Connor served in the legislature as a lawmaker and later in the courts as a judge interpreting the law. But both activities are in the public sector, and both have to do with the law. Jacques Cousteau has steadily enlarged the scope of his involvement with the sea— inventing equipment for underwater breathing, diving himself, becoming proficient at underwater photography, and creating a windship. John Portman began as an architect, beginning his career in a conventional way, but as a result of a setback decided to become a developer as well—thus breaking ranks with his peers.

Their styles differ markedly: frontal assaults, dogged persistence, gentle persuasion, deft compromise. Clearly, they receive reinforcement from what they do—many kinds of reinforcement. That helps keep them going. They remember their commitment—that they chose the field. They rely upon an inner sense of confidence that those who criticize or ignore them will one day be proved wrong.

Some seem to chug along, without worrying about why they do what they do. They have found something that they like, and they fell into the habit of doing it. Now they find the habit difficult to break. Indeed, most of them like what they do so much that they wouldn't want to break the habit even if they could. They are hooked.

We have thus far explored several of the achievement factors and some of their interconnections—*vocation, competence, time consciousness, time management,* and *persistence.* Next, we explore the question: Is the individual well enough motivated to be willing to make the long-term effort required to succeed?

# 5

# Wanting, Wishing, Needing

*For me, life is an incomplete experience without its expression in art. It simply is incomplete.*

*—Tennessee Williams*

*I've never called myself a genius. If other people want to call me that, that's their problem. I myself shoot for other more meaningful and more significant goals—like being the best science-fiction writer/ science writer/public speaker in the world. That's good enough for me.*

*—Isaac Asimov (1980:225)*

If you want something badly enough, long enough, consistently enough, don't be surprised if you get it. That is true of individuals and societies. Almost three decades ago, psychologist David C. McClelland examined the role of achievement motivation in several great historical societies. McClelland concluded: What each generation wanted above all else, it got. He wrote: "In the end, it is men, and in particular their deepest concerns, that shape history." (1961:437)

At the personal level, powerful motivation by itself does not always lead to high achievement. But, when combined with even modest ability, the results are often astonishing.

Paul "Bear" Bryant once told me, "I'm a poor coach of great players. I'm a good coach, I think, of that ordinary guy.... People that win the most are the people who can recognize those players who are not winners but don't know it. The walls of my office are loaded down with championship pictures of people who didn't have the ability to win, but didn't know it."

In all the social sciences, no field is more complex than the study of human motivation. Many scholars have grappled with the fundamental questions: What motivates us? Why? Are there universal nonbiological needs? Why are some individuals more highly motivated than others?

Those who have tried to answer these questions have made widely different assumptions about what we as humans are really like. Some have viewed us as living calculators who rationally weigh the costs and benefits of our actions. Others have argued that much of human behavior is not rational. Sigmund Freud, for instance, demonstrated repeatedly that human behavior is often irrational or nonrational. We tend to hide the real reasons for our behavior even from ourselves, he argued. B. F. Skinner has consistently maintained that motivation can be explained by reinforcement models. People—or for that matter, pigeons or mice—behave as they do because of the reinforcement they receive. (Skinner would not talk about internal psychological states, traits, or characteristics of individuals to explain achievement. He does not think this way.)

The sociologist W. I. Thomas believed that we all have four basic desires or "wishes"—the desire for new experience, the desire for security, the desire for response, and the desire for recognition. (Theodorson 1969:466.) Abraham Maslow arranged human needs into a hierarchy of lower and higher ones. He wrote, "We share the need for food with all living things, the need for love with (perhaps) the higher apes, the need for self-actualization (at least through creativeness) with nobody." (1954:147)

These theories are attempts to help us understand and interpret the raw data of human activity, and this chapter relies upon several of them. Whenever possible, however, the high achievers explain and interpret themselves in their own words. As you will see, many of the responses are profoundly perceptive and candid. This is particularly significant when you remember that the interviewees knew their responses would be published or telecast, not tucked away in thick folders marked "confidential." These are glimpses into the inner world of individuals whose accomplishments are remarkable.

## Economic Needs

An assumption often made in our society is that economic incentives are absolutely reliable, a surefire way of arousing individuals from lethargy into productive activity. Pay enough and you can get people to do anything.

My interviews with high achievers do not provide validation for this widely held view. Many high achievers admitted that economic considerations often mattered a great deal during their early years, but that after they crossed the subsistence threshold, money mattered less and less. There were also a few individuals at the ends of the continuum—those who said that money never mattered very much and those who said it still is a major consideration.

Asked to rate economic incentives, Kris Kristofferson replied: "Zero. When I went into this business, I was committing my life to be a songwriter, and all I wanted to do was earn a living as a songwriter. Tom T. Hall told me he had made ten thousand dollars the year before, and I said, 'I can live on that.'" Kristofferson told me in late 1986, "My decisions today are still not money decisions."

Multimillionaire J.B. Fuqua, who grew up poor as Job's turkey, says: "Making money is a measure we use in this country—sort of like a totem pole. But I don't think my major motivation has been making money."

"Was it at the beginning of your career?"

"I wouldn't say that it's ever been my major thrust." (Fuqua rated himself four on economic incentives.)

Sandra Day O'Connor says economic incentives are "not important" to her.

When Hank Aaron set out for the big-leagues training camp, he had one suit of clothes, two dollars in his pocket, and a cardboard suitcase. Aaron's parents had no money to give him. "Money was a ten then, because I didn't have any," the slugger recalls. "I still don't have a *lot* of money.... Today, it's about a seven."

Jack Nicklaus was in the insurance business, and doing very well at it, when he turned professional. "It was about a toss-up whether I could make more money playing golf or selling insurance. I was making thirty-thousand dollars a year when I was twenty-one—in 1961 that was a lot of money.... The only reason I turned pro was because I couldn't be the best at what I really enjoyed doing without playing against the best. And that's why I turned pro. It wasn't an economic measure at all." Nicklaus rates economic motive a one or a two.

Nicklaus says he has seen golfers make the mistake of being too concerned about economics. "They were out of the game in three or four years, 'cause they just couldn't stand the pressure of looking at the checkbook all the time.... I've always felt that golf is a game. If you play the game well, and pay attention to what you're doing, the financial part will follow."

Novelist Erskine Caldwell stated: "I have never written for money, but I expect to be paid for my work." He said that he never let economic considerations become primary because that would have turned him into a different kind of writer than he became. He would have had to write what he thought people wanted to read. "I do not do that," he told me. "I only write what I want to read, so for that reason I'm not a money chaser. I have no ambition to be rich as a writer." Caldwell summed up his attitude thus: "If money comes to me, fine. I'm very pleased to have it, but it's something that has to result from writing and not be the object of writing."

His is a typical response among high achievers. Economic considerations are somewhat important, they say, and they admit enjoying the good things that money will buy—BUT.

Mary Kay admits that at one time, economic incentives were "very important," but those incentives have slipped dramatically during recent years. "I once wanted to have a lot of money, but now that doesn't seem *that* important anymore. I think it would be if I lost it, probably. When you have two houses and a couple of cars, there's not much of a desire anymore, so I would say that's not very high on my list at this point."

Asked what number she would have assigned it at the beginning of her career, Mary Kay replied: "Early, it probably was, oh, at least an eight, and now it's more down to maybe four or five."

Ray Charles says that he's "just like everybody else" in wanting to live well, but he adds, "Money's not the key to me."

Lillian Vernon Katz is at the other end of the spectrum. She says money has always been important to her—at the beginning of her career, and today: "It's very, very important. There's no point in doing it unless you're going to be paid for it, and do well. I mean, business has a report card. It is money."

"Are you a ten?"

"No. I think probably a nine. It is not the only important thing. . . . But I went into this business to earn money—to be independent—and therefore I think money is very important."

Malcolm Forbes believes economic incentives are

important too, but as a by-product. "I don't think Roger Smith became president of General Motors spurred by an economic incentive," says Forbes. "The money is simply a measure of success." The publisher of the magazine that calls itself the "capitalist tool" feels that people like GM's Roger Smith are motivated by the power of power, by being able to implement agendas, by a sense of fulfillment, and by the authority and responsibility that high status brings. Wealth is an accompaniment to the main event. "The psychic income—once you're beyond a certain threshold—is infinitely more of the spur than the monetary."

Isaac Asimov told me there had been a shift during his career. "If I'm really aching for rent money, it would be near the top, naturally." But after Asimov no longer needed rent money, he kept on working just as hard as before, and with a lot more pleasure. "Economic motivation—provided you've got a certain minimum security—is quite low on the list," Asimov stated. "I would think almost anything else would be higher."

## The Esteem of Others

If economic incentives are not the explanation of Isaac Asimov's prodigious output, what is? It is desire for recognition, Asimov says. That, and his enjoyment of writing. "When I began writing as a student, I was content to have a little money to pay my tuition, but I was much more driven by wanting to see my name in print, by wanting to be known in the science-fiction world. I guess you would say that ego meant more to me than money at the time."

Everybody has to be somebody to somebody. All individuals, except for a few pathological exceptions, have a need for stable, firmly based high evaluations of themselves, for self-respect or self-esteem, and for the esteem of others. We need self-respect and we want respect from others.

Mario Andretti did not reply at once when I asked him if he would race if there were no crowd, no audience. He paused for a long time, trying to find an honest answer, trying to explain, perhaps to himself, just why he pursued such a risky occupation.

"That's a good question.... Probably not," the renowned racer replied finally. "It's show business. You want to show what you can do.... To show yourself— yes, that's satisfaction. You have to satisfy yourself first. You're going to be a tough critic on yourself. Then nobody *has* to come over and pat you on the back. But it's good when you know people are talking about it. It's good."

Hank Aaron answered the same question without hesitation. "I don't think I'd play without a crowd," said the slugger. "Everybody wants to be recognized, especially if you do something well. Give me a ten on that ... I got a kick out of the crowd; I got a kick out of the fans; I got a kick out of the sportswriters. I enjoyed that."

Then the quiet-spoken champion surprised me. Asked to state which attitudes and habits he had had to work at the hardest, Aaron answered: "Not being envious of the attention other ballplayers received.... I played in Milwaukee for ten years and then I moved to Atlanta and played ten more years. When you compete with the New York press, it's tough. You're hitting .350, and somebody else in New York is hitting .350, but when the newspaper comes out, they mention his name first and your name second. That was the toughest thing for me to overcome—to make sure that I played on the same level as I always did, and not let people know that that was bothering me."

For years that frustration had gnawed at the quiet,

modest man sportswriters called "The Hammer." In Aaron's case, W. I. Thomas was correct. The desire for recognition is a powerful wish.

"I think recognition is probably the least acknowledged and one of the more powerful propulsions for those who succeed," Malcolm Forbes stated "If you're a writer, how do you get any satisfaction if your work never sees the light of day?"

Chet Atkins says that his goal—ever since he was a little boy—was to be a famous guitar player. "I didn't want to be a movie star. I didn't want to host a game show. I didn't want to act. I just wanted to be a famous guitar player. And I did that."

J. B. Fuqua, who rated himself a four on economic incentives, chose a ten on desire for recognition. "That's the way you motivate people," says the man who believes one of his strongest business tools is his ability to motivate his employees. Fuqua, in fact, has become something of a legend doing just that. His forte is transforming small, undernourished or lethargic companies into highly profitable operations. For example, one of his companies, Snapper Power Equipment, the profit-leader in the lawn and garden equipment industry, has moved in annual sales from $10 million in 1967 to $266.7 million 1986 *with the same management that started the company.* When a business reporter asked him to explain the growth, Fuqua replied: "Motivate the management and provide funds for growth."

Mark H. McCormack says it is very important for him to be perceived as someone who has integrity and a degree of genius within a certain field—that, he says, is much more important than economics. McCormack gives himself an eight or nine on desire for recognition.

For artists, the desire for recognition is fundamental, absolutely basic, Dan Barry says. Art is a language, one that requires both speaker and listener. To make his point, Barry refers to Beethoven, who was deaf during his last years. "He couldn't have written that music if he knew no one was going to listen to it. This was his language. He was a man with enormous, noble, emotional messages—and they were messages that he had to write, that he had to say. Nobody talks to a wall. The need for recognition is absolutely primal. Even in a period when I'm painting without any intention of selling, there is an audience."

"How important is desire for recognition for *you*?" I asked.

"Oh, it's a ten. No, it's a twelve on a ten-point scale."

Barry's remarks reminded me of a comment Chet Atkins made: "I think most musicians want to be noticed and loved and accepted by their fellow man, but some of us are too shy to do it with conversation. I know that's true in my case. I was afraid to say hello to anybody, but I would play for them—I would play the guitar."

The same was true of Tennessee Williams. He told me that when he was in school, he was too shy to speak. His teacher had to judge him on his written work.

Some of us have been socialized to believe that only show-offs crave recognition. Nothing could be further from the truth. Not just artists but craftsmen and entrepreneurs and secretaries and ballplayers communicate through their work. They tell how much they care about what they do. They tell how competent they have become. Anyone who does outstanding work is saying something, and it is an absolutely basic need that someone listen, someone notice.

Mary Kay stated: "When you pour your whole heart into something, you really do need the recognition. You need to know that somebody sees that you're doing well." Mary Kay, incidentally, has made recognition of achievement—including her Awards Night spectacular—the centerpiece of her company's motivational program.

Nobel Laureate James D. Watson, in *The Double Helix*, frequently discussed his desire to become famous. "It was certainly better to imagine myself becoming famous than maturing into a stifled academic who never had risked a thought," Watson wrote.

His former colleague Francis Crick, who in 1962 was awarded the Nobel Prize with Watson, told me of his reaction to Watson's ambitions: "We had no idea that he was thinking of fame or prizes or anything when he was at Cambridge, and I say we—not only I, who saw him every day and talked to him for over an hour every day, but also other people. But when you read his book, you get the impression he was thinking about that all the time. But at the time he kept it to himself."

"Did the desire for fame or prizes ever cross *your* mind?" I asked Crick.

"No. People find this terribly difficult to believe, but it didn't cross my mind after we got the structure of DNA. Not till two years later, when somebody mentioned it, I suddenly thought, good gracious, that's the sort of discovery they give prizes for."

People who want to be famous often have a large and unfocused audience in mind. However, a number of the high achievers who said they had no desire for fame per se indicated that they did very much want the approval of a specific audience.

Admiral Thomas Moorer stated: "I think the greatest satisfaction one gets is derived from the opinion that people have about you—people who have been around you your whole life—as to your character and your compassion and your fairness, and the way you deal with people, and the way you do your job and whether you have tried to sacrifice other people for your personal benefit. . . . In the Navy, we call it *service reputation*, and I think that's the most important thing."

Edith W. Martin says: "It is extremely important to

me that the people I lead and champion and guide feel proud. It causes me to work very hard at what I do to be sure that I deserve their pride."

Ray Charles stated: "To be famous is a great thing. But I have never wanted to be famous. I have always wanted to be great. What I mean is that I've always wanted to be so good that the people who knew what I was doing would understand it."

Chet Atkins told me that he wanted to be a famous guitarist, but he also made it clear that one of his most deeply felt needs was to be well regarded by other musicians. "What is so important to me as a musician is the respect from other musicians. I've always longed and yearned and strived for the admiration of my peers."

Basketball coach Bobby Cremins says desire for recognition is important for him, but a special kind of recognition—a need that is rooted in the immigrant background of his family. "It's not important for me to get newspaper articles, pictures in the papers. I've had that. I just want to *be somebody*. I don't know how you define that . . . I think that comes from my family. They were born in Ireland, and they came over to America on the boat, and they just wanted to be somebody. They wanted to be American citizens. It was important for them to be recognized by their peers and family."

Nobel Laureate Paul A. Samuelson puts it bluntly: scholars seek fame. "The fame they seek, as I noted in my 1961 American Economic Association presidential address, is fame with their peers. I am no exception. . . . No celebrity as a *Newsweek* columnist, no millions of clever-begotten speculative gains, no power as the Svengali or Rasputin to the prince and President could count as a pennyweight in my balance of worth against the prospect of recognition for having contributed to the empire of science." (1986:2)

# Self-Esteem

Of all the questions I asked the high achievers, the one that produced the widest range of responses was about self-esteem. Those responses were also among the most poignant of the study.

Perhaps the wide variety of replies is due to the potential power of the need. Obviously, it can be an mighty force. In his study of political leadership, James MacGregor Burns states: "The most potent sources of political motivation—the key elements of political ambition—are unfulfilled esteem needs, both self-esteem and esteem by others." (1978:115,116)

Jack Nicklaus, unlike Mario Andretti and Richard Petty, says he *would* play golf even if there were no crowd, no one to watch. "I think I play for myself more than I play for people. I play for the enjoyment of being able to be self-satisfied and being able to accomplish something and be proud of what I do. If I'm proud of what I'm doing, the people who watch me are going to enjoy it, too." Obviously, the two kinds of esteem are related. Nicklaus's very notion of what constitutes an accomplishment is a social phenomenon, derived from interacting with other people.

Without such interaction there is no human personality, no self. A Zen proverb states: The self is the sound of one hand clapping.

Ed Turner pushed his son Ted relentlessly throughout his childhood and youth. He shipped him off to military school, and by the time Ted was twelve years old, during the summers, had him working forty hours per week at the billboard company cutting weeds and creosoting poles. Later, when Ted declared his intention of majoring in classics at Brown University, his father wrote a long, emotional letter demanding that he major in something more practical: "I am appalled, even horrified, that you have adopted classics as a major. As a matter of fact, I almost puked on the way home today," he wrote. "I just wish I could feel that the influence of those oddball professors and the ivory towers were developing you into the kind of a man we can both be proud of. . . ."

Turner gave his father's letter to the student newspaper to publish—and changed his major to economics.

Many years later, in a speech at Georgetown University, Turner told the audience what he did when he made the cover of *Success* magazine: he held the cover up toward heaven and said, "Well, Dad, is that enough?" (Vaughn 1978:153, 163–165; Cauthon 1986:A10)

Turner's story bears a striking resemblance to a childhood experience of Sigmund Freud's. When Freud was seven or eight years old, he "disregarded the rules which modesty lays down and obeyed the calls of nature in my parents' bedroom while they were present. In the course of the reprimand my father let fall the words: 'The boy will come to nothing.' This must have been a frightful blow to my ambition, for references to this scene are still constantly recurring in my dreams and are always linked with an enumeration of my achievements and successes, as though I wanted to say: 'You see, I have come to something.'" (Burns 1978:105)

## Defying a Sense of Inferiority

Several of the high achievers admit to having had inferiority feelings, although they say they have for the most part outgrown them. Arthur Murray told me, "I always had an inferiority complex and never expected to become even moderately successful."

"How did you overcome that?"

"I'm not sure," the celebrated dance master replied.

"But I think that when you know your subject, you have confidence in what you're doing. I think the answer is to study and analyze whatever you're doing so that you can do it as well as possible."

Norman Vincent Peale, one of the most influential clergymen this nation has ever seen, says at one time he had the "biggest inferiority complex ever developed in the state of Ohio, where I was born." Peale says he finally discovered not how to eliminate it, but how to deal with it—during his sophomore year in college.

Peale remembers an economics professor who one day asked him to remain after class. When everyone had gone, he began: "Norman, you are an A student, but when I call upon you to say something in class, you get red in the face, you're horribly embarrassed, and you don't show up at your best. What in the world's wrong with you?"

Peale replied: "I'm shy and I'm self-conscious and I have an inferiority complex." The professor knew that Peale's father was a minister, and that the young student was himself religious, so he challenged him to pray about the problem. Leaving the classroom, Norman walked outside and, standing on the steps of the main college building, did just that: "Dear Lord, can't you take a mixed-up young fellow like myself and make me normal?"

Peale told me that he expected a miracle to happen at that moment, but it didn't. Instead, a strange feeling of peace came over him, he remembers. A few days later, another professor gave him a book to read. It was *The Sayings of Ralph Waldo Emerson.* (The architect John Portman also discovered Emerson—at the urging of Frank Lloyd Wright.) Then another professor, a few days following, gave him *The Meditations of Marcus Aurelius.*

What was the result? Peale says: "Marcus Aurelius believed that the power resident in the human mind could handle the problems of life. Emerson taught the same thing. . . . And I began then to develop a philosophy which I later wrote down in a book. That book, as you probably have surmised, is entitled *The Power of Positive Thinking*." It has sold over 15 million copies and has been translated into thirty-eight languages.

Norman Vincent Peale, who says his greatest strength is public speaking, told me he still has an inferiority complex: "But I can master it now rather than it mastering me, I think."

Harry Hoffman, head of Waldenbooks, says the turning point in his life occurred when he was thirty-three years old, working as a sales representative for Bell .and Howell: "I was down in the sales territory of North Carolina, and something happened to me. All of a sudden, I realized that I was at least as smart and as good as the people I was working for. That was the major difference in my career. . . . From then on, I just started to grow."

Chet Atkins readily admits that he has had to wrestle with inferiority feelings throughout his career. "I went to Knoxville and got a job on a radio station, and I had an inferiority complex, because I don't have a ring on my finger that says Vanderbilt or something. I think I missed a lot, even though I don't think I would have ever developed the style on the guitar and everything if I had gone to college. . . . I've had to work very hard to get over my inferiority feelings."

Labor leader Joyce Dannon Miller says: "I'm sort of schizophrenic to the outside world. The whole world looks at me as being a very confident person, and my confidence has grown over the years. So, if I talk about today, yes, I would call myself a very confident person. Yet, underneath, at times I'm very insecure."

B. F. Skinner, in his autobiography, writes that his father was successful, but not successful enough. He constantly needed praise. Like father, like son. The noted psychologist admits that he too has had to cope with rather profound inferiority feelings. Skinner remembers that his classmates in college all seemed to come from better schools than he, that he spoke with a pronounced regional accent, that his fraternity was the least prestigious on campus. "Like my father, I needed reassurance, and when necessary, I reassured myself. I did so less often when I began to have something I could be proud of." However, as late as 1966, Skinner wrote: "I do not admire myself as a person. My successes do not override my shortcomings." (1983:409, 410)

Remember Robert Byrd's ten-year struggle to earn a law degree? Byrd says he still feels inferior about subjects outside his area of competence. But when it comes to politics, he claims a victory over those old nagging feelings. "I feel that if I had to assume the responsibilities of the presidency of the United States, I could do the job. I don't have any doubt about it. I can do this job in here—never had any doubt about it. When I became the majority leader, I knew I could do the job. . . . No, I have no feeling of inferiority any longer." And no wonder. Insiders say that few if any senators have a better grasp of the thousands of rules and conventions that regulate life in that venerable institution. *Competence* is good medicine for inferiority feelings.

Supreme Court Justice O'Connor states that she did not have self-confidence as a young woman: "I think most young people don't, and one of the blessings of getting older is that you get more self-confidence. My self-confidence has increased with my birthdays."

Thornton Bradshaw, former chairman of RCA Corporation, in an interview with Harold Stieglitz, stated that there is a considerable lack of self-confidence in the executive suites of the nation's largest companies—despite appearances to the contrary. "There is a considerable amount of insecurity. It is often masked—I don't think anybody wants to admit to being insecure in a job.

Remember, we have pretty bully kinds of guys at the top. They are quite sure of themselves, except perhaps in the dead of night."

Bradshaw says this insecurity stems from several sources. One is the need in a large corporation to select and supervise people for very different parts of the organization. "Since you, yourself, cannot possibly be an expert in—or cannot possibly have grown up with—all those businesses, there is a certain amount of self-questioning." (Stieglitz 1985:35)

John Huston has discussed the way he chooses a story for a film in his autobiography. Success stories per se, Huston says, do not really interest him, because he is convinced that there are more failures than men of achievement among us. The celebrated director writes: "The best men tend to think of themselves as failures." (1980:336)

I asked Huston if *he* ever thought of himself as a failure, to which he replied. "I question whether I've fulfilled all the potential that was there. It depends on my disposition at the moment, I guess. Sometimes I think, 'My God, I've gone three times as far as I should have gone with my endowments.' And at other times, I think, 'Christ, what I've done isn't worth shit.'"

Several high achievers said that inferiority feelings —especially if they take the form of fear of failure—can be used positively. Helen Gurley Brown stated: "I personally feel that inferiority is what fuels you and drives you; so instead of being a negative force, I think it's a very positive force." Brown calls it a fear, a kind of anxiousness, a kind of restlessness. "The successful women that I know, the successful men, all have this feeling that if they don't do it, something terrible is going to happen to them. So, it's hard work. It's drive predicated on being a little fearful that you must get on with it, or you're going to be in trouble."

Even though inferiority can be a positive force, it can be destructive in large doses, Brown believes. "You just wouldn't show up for work in the morning. You'd hide under the covers all day long."

Robert Shaw rated himself only a two on self-confidence. "I've been playing catch-up all of my career," Shaw told me. "There are days when I get so frightened that I get physically ill."

"Frightened of what?"

"Frightened of falling on my face ... of not being able to give the orchestra the direction they need.... It scares," replied the recipient of seven Grammys and over twenty honorary degrees.

Harry Hoffman says: "Inferiority was a factor, I'm sure, in motivating me ... I was fearful of people with reputations, and it probably affected my career negatively initially, and then as I found out that a lot of the reputations were unfounded—that's kind of cynical—that affected my career positively."

Lillian Vernon Katz, whose success in the mail-order business is a legend in her industry, is certain that her lack of self-confidence has been a positive force in her career: "I was awful, terrible," she told me. "I think one of the things that probably drove me to success was the lack of self-confidence—just wanting to pull myself together and do it for myself.... I think women generally have not had a really great self-image, and maybe just doing what we did improved our own self-image."

At the beginning of her career, Katz said her rating on self-confidence would be a one. Today, it is a six or seven. "Success brings its own self-confidence. But I don't think anybody is really totally self-confident. I have never met anybody who was."

However, some of the high achievers disagree. People like architect John Portman and businessman J.B. Fuqua and Hank Aaron all say they are totally self-confident about what they do—so there certainly is no reason to conclude that inferiority feelings are a prerequisite to success.

Fred Waring was supremely confident when he was doing what he was good at—popular music. Robert Shaw recalls hearing Waring say, "I just can't make a mistake with a popular song. I can do it naturally, and nobody in the world is as good."

John Portman doesn't think inferiority or superiority feelings are relevant concepts when he is involved in something he truly believes in. "I've always been so motivated and intent on accomplishing whatever it is I was trying to accomplish—and having a mind that truly focuses in singleness of purpose—that hasn't left much time to feel superior or inferior. If you're really into something, and you've got great conviction about it, I don't think these sort of feeling have a role to play." As a postscript, Portman adds: "The conviction is really the driving force, no matter what it is you try to do. If you don't feel extremely strong in your position—in the rightness of it—then all kind of feelings will start happening."

Isaac Asimov recalls old inferiority feelings from school. He remembers that he was an absolute failure in gym class. "I knew damn well I was worst in the class." But when it comes to writing ability, Asimov is the soul of self-confidence: "As far as my writing is concerned, I've never done things to try to prove that I'm not inferior. Never. I mean, I took it for granted I wasn't."

## Neurotic Needs

Some of the world's most talented and brilliant individuals have not been emotionally healthy—Wagner, for example, and Van Gogh and Byron. Dozens of names could be added to the list.

"I write to avoid madness," Tennessee Williams told me. He said he had never felt really comfortable loving anything very much—even writing—because when one loves, one is vulnerable. "Oh, it's haunted me all my life," said the gifted, troubled writer. "There've been times when I've trembled before I sit down at the typewriter, because writing is my great love. I really tremble."

Williams said that *Clothes for a Summer Hotel*—the story of the sad, tortured last days of F. Scott Fitzgerald and Zelda—was his way of describing the tortured minds he had known. "I've had a great deal of experience with madness." I've been locked up. My sister was institutionalized for most of her adult life. . . . Both my sister and I need a lot of taking care of . . . I'm a lonely person. I'm lonelier than most people. I have a touch of schizophrenia in me, and in order to avoid madness, I have to work."

The psychological problems of Tennessee Williams were severe, dramatic, and highly publicized. Other high achievers have struggled quietly through bouts of depression, loneliness, and frustration. Bob Hoskins and Art Buchwald spoke openly and freely about difficult periods in their careers, when they required professional help. Chet Atkins speculated that his periods of depression and his incessant striving for perfection might be linked to his poverty-stricken childhood: "If I'm not learning something, if I'm not educating myself all the time in some manner—musically, or if I'm not learning something on the guitar—I get very depressed, and I think it's because I'm afeared that I might be hungry like I was years ago. I'd be a good study for a psychiatrist."

It is extremely difficult to identify the many strands of needs and wishes that motivate us, even when we are trying to be completely honest. As perceptive individuals have always recognized, even our most sacrificial acts are mingled with selfish desires, our most healthy behavior motivated partly by neurotic needs.

## Self-Development/Self-Actualization

High achievers realize that they have attained success by honing their skills and specialties. They study and practice and listen to critiques by mentors and coaches and do the hundred and one tasks that are necessary to get up to speed. Like millions of Americans, a goodly number of them diet and jog and work out and read books on self-improvement. They hope to gain tangible rewards, to feel good, to be better persons—to feel fulfilled.

Senator Proxmire, you recall, stated that his success is due largely to persistence, to tenacity, to not giving up. But the senator cited another characteristic, perhaps equally important to his success—the desire to improve his talents as much as possible. People around the senator say that desire is almost an obsession with him. He jogs, works out regularly, diets. He published a book in 1973 about his exercise-diet regimen entitled, appropriately, *You Can Do It*. Proxmire works regularly on his vocabulary, constantly trying to improve his writing ability: "I write six hundred words every day—Saturdays, Sundays, whether I'm in the state, regardless of the pressures," he told me.

The senator related how he thinks he conquered a childhood habit of stuttering. One night his father took him to see a boxing match, where young Proxmire watched a light-heavyweight champion in action. "He had the most sensational left jab I had ever seen in action. That night when I went home, I threw three hundred left jabs, and I've been throwing them almost ever since. And the amazing thing is that when I started using my left hand a great deal in boxing, I stopped stuttering. . . . People have a theory that stutterers are people who are forced or intimidated into writing with their right hand when they are natural left-handers. Maybe it was because I developed confidence. Boys lack confidence when they are not very good in sports, and maybe I simply gained confidence. But I still maintain a regimen for self-improvement. Every morning, I do pushups, stomach exercises, back exercises, I run to work every day."

Ted Turner believes that the people who win in business are people who think harder, longer, and better than their competitors do. And how does one do this? By practice: "Your mind, as I understand it, is similar to the muscles of your body. You can take just a skinny little guy, and he can run thirty miles if he builds himself up to it. The same way with your mind. The way to strengthen your mind is thinking. The more you think, the more you use your mind to handle problems—just like a runner stretching himself by the distance he runs each day—you keep building yourself up, and you can do the exact same thing with your mind."

Turner doubtless remembers an experience he had at McCallie School, a military prep school he attended in Chattanooga. Disappointed with the score he had made on his college board verbal exam during his junior year, he set a goal of reading a large number of books and learning a several new words per day during the summer—strengthening his mental abilities and improving his vocabulary while he was working at his father's billboard company. His senior year, when he took the test again, his test scores were considerably improved.

Turner told me that he still likes to set challenges for himself in order to stretch his mind. "I like to sit down and outline problems and see if I can come up with solutions. . . . In school, while I was blessed with perhaps above-average ability, I wasn't a brilliant person. But as I've grown older, I've tried to keep working on improving my mind and my general attitude, and I've reached levels I didn't think I could ever have reached if I hadn't gone out and tried to improve myself."

Hank Aaron stated that he has always felt the need for improvement. "No matter whether I hit .300, I always felt like I should have hit .320; if I hit forty home runs, I should have hit forty-four."

To hear Chet Atkins describe his accomplishments, one would think he had never won an award or produced a successful recording. But the winner of eight Grammys and ten of the Country Music Association's "Best Instrumentalist" awards says he never listens to his recordings. "I make records because I realize there are people out there who like what I do, but I can't stand them. I detest what I do and I always will. I listen, and I think, 'Why did I play it that way. It's terrible.' I'm not one of my greatest fans. . . . I am still trying to get it to sound right.'

Dan Barry explained why artists experience the feeling Chet Atkins described: The discontent derives from striving for perfection. "Artists are never content with the work they do; they are never completely satisfied." Then he added a comment similar to John Huston's: "I sometimes think I'm magnificent while I'm doing something. As I see something realizing before my eyes, I think, 'God, I'm really good!' And then a week later, I've reproduced it or I get proofs back from the syndicate and I see it in print and I say, 'God, that's awful! I can do so much better.' I think that's built into the artist, that he never really is content with what he's done. There's always a step ahead. . . . I still, to this day—after all the years of acceptance and relative success—feel pretty much the way I did when I came out of art school: 'My God, this stuff is so hard, and I have so much to learn. I've got to try harder.' "

Self-improvement for some high achievers is not a conscious goal, but rather a kind of by-product that accompanies doing what they enjoy doing. Asked if he is working hard at becoming a better actor, Bob Hoskins replies: "No. It's not a conscious effort. It's a natural process, like making bread. The yeast in it grows."

Malcolm Forbes says: "I don't set out each day and say 'How can I be better today than I was yesterday?' " He believes that anybody who's active is self-improving all the time, but that isn't why you're doing it. Forbes maintains that self-improvement is a by-product of doing work that is satisfying and fulfilling.

That idea—fulfillment—is central to the psychology of Abraham Maslow. Maslow is well known for his pioneering work on self-actualization. Maslow used the term *self-actualization* to refer to a special form of self-improvement. He described self-actualization as "the desire to become more and more what one is, to become everything that one is capable of becoming." (1954:92)

Edith W. Martin speaks for many high achievers when she says, "Money's not a consideration. Reward is not a consideration. It's that you feel there's a void and you feel a responsibility to fill it."

Mario Andretti describes the racetrack this way: "This is the only place I find fulfillment. I know that sounds corny, but it's true."

The same Tennessee Williams who told me he wrote in order to avoid madness also spoke eloquently of his need for fulfillment. It came in response to a question I had asked about fame—that his reputation was assured with only one or two of his plays, and I named several.

Why continue to write? I asked. His eyes flashed as he answered: "That's not what I'm after. That's not what it's about," he exclaimed with raised voice.

"What is it about?" I asked quietly.

"That's not where it is. . . . For me, life is an incomplete experience without its expression in art. It simply is incomplete."

# The Need to Create Something That Will Endure

Art Buchwald's office is located on Pennsylvania Avenue, a short distance from the White House, which through the years has provided him with such abundant data for his newspaper column and books. On his wall are letters from readers, some of them famous, some unknown. He is particularly fond of one from a woman who calls Buchwald a smart alec, a sadist, and stupid. Another is from a minister, taking him to task for using the word *damn* in a column.

While I wait for the appointed time of my interview, America's best-known satirist is taking a phone call from someone who wants to know if he will do an advertisement for cat food. Buchwald tells the individual on the other end that he doesn't do advertisements for cat food or anything else, thank you very much.

Buchwald hangs up the phone, walks into the reception area where I have been waiting, invites me into his office, and asks his assistant to bring us lunch—sandwiches and soft drinks from the deli downstairs. He offers me a cigar, leans back in his chair, and motions for me to me to push my Sony's record button.

A few minutes into the interview, I ask if he plans eventually to fade away. "No," he replies, "I want to do something big."

"What's your big thing?"

"A novel. I think these colums of mine are really based on topical events, and therefore they're not going to survive."

"They're throwaways?"

"Yeah. So, I'd like *one* thing to be remembered by."

Playwright Tom Stoppard understands that kind of wish. In his award-winning play *The Real Thing*, Stoppard gives Harold, who's an author, the following lines —which explain what good writers sometimes think about when they put words on paper: "If you get the right ones [words] in the right order, you can nudge the world a little or make a poem which children will speak for you when you're dead."

Isaac Asimov told me that his fondest hope is that some of his books will survive: "I suppose it wouldn't matter if I die, if at least some of my books live. I would like to have my books remain alive and remembered. At least some of them. If that's the case, then I've achieved a fair chance of immortality. . . . I don't know how much longer I have to go. It's not important, but my books are."

Asimov told about a conversation he had years ago with his daughter Robyn. "One time she got onto my lap and looked up lovingly, and said, 'Daddy, do you love me?' And I said, 'Certainly, Robyn, I love you.' And she said, 'Do you love me a lot?' And I said, 'Oh, I love you a great big lot.' She is a very shrewd little girl. She knows exactly my feelings toward her, and she has no scruples whatever. Perhaps no little girls do. She says, 'Do you love me as much . . .' and I figured she was going to say 'as a million dollars' and I'd say 'More,' and she'd say 'billion, trillion, zillion'—and it's going to be easy. But she didn't. She said, 'Do you love me more than *writing*?' And I said 'Yes, love.' And I do, but there had been a long hesitation before my reply. And she noticed it, because she said, 'You hesitated, Daddy.'"

"Did you lie to her?" I asked.

"No, I guess I didn't lie. If they pointed a gun at Robyn and said, 'If you don't promise never to write again, we're going to kill Robyn,' I'd have to promise never to write again—but I might as well die."

"You might as well die!"

"I think so. . . . Yes, because that's worse than dying."

Asked what gave him the most satisfaction, Kris Kristofferson replied, "My kids and my work."

"In what order?"

"The kids first, definitely."

"And if you had to make a choice?"

"I don't think it's necessary to, but if it were, the kids are definitely more important to me. . . . It's easy to say that when you can't envision having to give it up. I feel very dedicated, as dedicated as William Blake to his art, but the thing is, that's an old song, and that's a little girl, and I'll take the little girl over those old songs any time—any time. But I hope my work's going to continue to be important to me until they throw dirt on me. . . . I hope I keep getting better. I feel like I can get smarter. I feel—I feel like the best is yet to come."

B. F. Skinner answered a similar question in a different way than Kristofferson. Skinner writes that, given a choice between burying his children or burying his books, he would bury his children. But he says he would give the same answer if he were asked to choose between his own death or the death of his books. "If some Mephistopheles offered me a wholly new life on condition that all records and effects of my present life be destroyed, I should refuse." (1983:411,412)

## Pleasure/Having Fun

This particular achievement factor did not get my full attention until fairly late in the interviewing process.

In fact, it was an interview with Nobel Laureate Francis Crick that convinced me of its true importance.

We were talking about what motivates great break-throughs in science, when Crick responded that desire for recognition had not been a major force in his own work. "I like to *enjoy* science," he said. "I have gotten much more recognition than I feel I deserve."

"So, for you, it's been fun?" I asked.

"That seems to me the *proper* motivation, person-ally," replied Crick. "Of course, there have been ups and downs, but by and large, yes—enormously. Especially *that* one [the discovery of the structure of DNA]. There is a wonderful remark by Leo Szilard, the physicist who patented the atomic pile. He said when he went to visit the Rockefeller Institute [now University], he could see written on all the walls, in invisible writing: 'Science is serious.' He wanted to cross it out and say, 'Science is fun.'"

I asked Crick who makes the best contribution, the serious scientist or the one who is having fun?

"Both," he replied. "If you want solid work, in which you plod away, then the serious-minded person is likely to do that. If you want to have the things you're talking about—making major discoveries and having insights— I think it's much better to think of science as fun. It's that exuberant overflow of energy which is what you need for this."

After the Crick interview, I looked back through my earlier interviews and discovered several direct or oblique references to playfulness, to having fun.

Linus Pauling had said he won the Nobel Prize in Chemistry by "simply having fun." In a later interview with Norman M. Lobsenz, Pauling said: "I enjoy thinking about problems and making discoveries about the world. Pursuing the questions is part of the pleasure of finding the answers."

Jacques Cousteau had told me: "My life has been spent playing with nuts and bolts. . . . I am passionate to play. . . . I do not live anywhere. I have a hand in the Concorde, a toe in the 747, my lungs in the *Calypso*, and my heart in the water."

Xavier Roberts stated that his Cabbage Patch Kids are little jokes. "I tried to go for a comic view of a child."

Dan Barry explained that playfulness often releases his ability. He calls playfulness the "floodgate for all of the intensity that can build up and engulf the creative powers."

Other researchers have found playfulness to be an important dimension of high achievers. Michael Maccoby, who interviewed Pehr Gyllenhammar, chief executive officer of Volvo, Sweden's largest corporation with seventy thousand workers, described Gyllenhammar's psyche as "subtle and playful, with kinds of contradictions that characterize many creative people." (1981:157)

Paul "Bear" Bryant stated: "Coaching for me is fun. Coaching is my hobby. You can laugh at this, but I honestly get a thrill out of going out to practice. The only working about coaching is the things you have to do that's not coaching."

"Like what?" I asked.

"Like doing this interview," said the crusty old coach, and then roared with laughter.

Playfulness, sometimes call *ludic* behavior, occurs in many species of animals. For example, birds have a "sub-song" that is unlike their species-specific full song. The "sub-song" is often amorphous and rambling, sometimes imitative of the song of another species of bird— a kind of vocal play. It is possible that art, science, and technology derive as much from playful activities as from necessity.

The literature of science and technology is full of references to the play element in discovery: "I was playing around in the laboratory one day," a scientist says, or "I was fooling around with this device...."

Playfulness typically involves activity that has as its main aim the pleasure which the activity brings. It exists for its own sake. It sometimes seems detached from serious ends and means. However, as the financial success of "Peanuts" and the Cabbage Patch Kids makes clear, playfulness can be transformed by shrewd marketing techniques into very serious, very profitable activity.

There is no consensus on this point, however, among the high achievers that I interviewed. J. B. Fuqua ranked himself at zero on playfulness/having fun. Sandra Day O'Connor does not consider this factor relevant to high achievement in her profession. When I asked Erskine Caldwell to rank himself on playfulness/having fun, he asked me how that applied. "Some people say that they have fun doing what they do," I replied.

"No, no, no. I would not say that," Caldwell exclaimed. "I would not use that term as applied to me, because to me writing is a very serious occupation. It's not having fun; it's doing something that you want to do. You're very serious about it. There's nothing funny or humorous about what you're doing. To me, it's a very serious occupation."

\*    \*    \*

Maslow was right. We can think of our needs as a hierarchy, ranging from biological drives to emotional and spiritual cravings. Typically, our needs and wants evolve, corresponding roughly to changes in our careers and to stages in our life.

The observations of high achievers bear this out. Most admit to a concern for finances, especially when just starting out, but that concern diminishes as success brings economic rewards. Then other needs and desires loom larger.

However, Maslow's self-actualization seems not to be an inevitable occurrence that automatically comes with acceptance and economic success. In fact, self-actualization—as a motivating force—seems to be present in many high achievers' lives long before they achieve wealth and acclaim.

One mild surprise of the interviews is the role that desire for recognition plays in high achievement—not its presence but its overpowering importance. As we have seen, Hank Aaron and Mario Andretti and Richard Petty admit that they probably wouldn't bother to play or race if there were no audience. Fuqua and Forbes observe that wealth is a symbol—a way of letting others know. Barry states that he is thinking about others' seeing what he has done even when he is working in solitude.

Every seasoned coach, teacher, and manager knows of people who shouldn't have succeeded but did. They all can tell of individuals with modest abilities and inferior training who outdistanced more gifted, better-trained competitors—because they were more powerfully motivated. That is one reason why good schools and companies require recommendations as well as records, transcripts, and résumés. They want to look beyond the records to see how motivated the individuals are, how much they *want* to succeed.

The personal message seems clear. If you want to attain significant goals, obviously you must want them very much. The high achievers I interviewed do. There is a hot fire burning within.

Their motives vary—from a deep commitment to high standards of excellence to the craving for applause. But they want to attain their goals. Very much.

I recall the way my interview ended with Paul "Bear" Bryant. I had asked the man who eventually won six national championships and thirteen Southeastern Conference titles if there were any goals he had not yet attained. He replied: "I haven't beaten Mississippi in two years. I haven't won a conference championship in two years. I haven't won a national championship in a long time. I haven't had an undefeated season [at the time of the interview]. I haven't heard much singing in the dressing room lately."

"And if you got those," I asked, "would you be satisfied?"

"No . . . I'd want another."

And so it goes. The high achiever begins with *competence, learns to value and manage time well, is persistent, wants—indeed, has a powerful need—to achieve.* The next chapter explores how high achievers channel those wishes and needs in order to get maximum results.

# 6

# Focus

*I think what separates the superstar from the average ballplayer is the fact that he concentrates just a little bit more.*

—Hank Aaron

*Q. What human quality is most important for you?*
*A. Passion—to do whatever you do in a passionate way.*
*Then you do it well.*

—Oscar de la Renta

*I have not wavered, really, in whatever my goals were, from the time before I could even get a job to today. The basic goal, without really changing, has been to be as good an actor as I can be.*

—Jack Lemmon

# Concentration

It is six-thirty on a slate-gray evening at Indy. The outside gates of the famed Speedway have been closed for a half hour. The qualifying runs for the thirty-three starting positions begin tomorrow.

Earlier in the afternoon, three racers managed to hit two hundred. Mario Andretti didn't. Not even close.

Now the lights are on in Andretti's garage on Gasoline Alley. His mechanics are back at work again—tightening, adjusting, listening, frowning a lot. The car just won't play in tune.

Andretti is huddled in a corner with his manager, Don Henderson. After a few minutes, Henderson edges his way through the mechanics and comes outside to tell me what everyone already knows. Things are not going well. "I just called Newman about it," he says. Paul Newman and Budweiser are partners in this venture. "Mario's canceling everything this evening. He just wants to think; but he'll still do your interview. Just keep it short. If he gives me a dirty look, we'll have to stop. He's a real pro, and you probably won't be able to tell that he's upset, but he is."

About five minutes later, the premier chauffeur of fast cars saunters out, smiles at the cluster of fans who have been hanging around a long time to catch a close-up glimpse of the lithe little performer.

He is a handsome man. In his tight-fitting, flame-proof racing suit, the 145-pound, five-foot-seven, Italian-born racer looks like a helmeted Nureyev in running shoes. His complexion is tan and so unflawed that he disdains makeup for the television cameras. His hazel eyes flash, sending little quivers through more than one pretty fan.

And he is a genuinely nice man. He smiles when he signs autographs. The fans pick up on it. They adore him. All kinds of fans. Little kids with their Instamatics and shirtless good ol' boys with beer cans held heavenward, pit kittens and grandmothers.

A grandmother pushes through the crowd, and before the interview can start, announces: "I'm Italian. Can I have my picture taken with you, please?" Then, with one deft move, she slips an arm around his waist, presses her cheek against his, and with the free hand shoves a camera into the waiting hand of her sister.

"That's my husband over there," she whispers to Mario. Then she calls out, "Try not to be jealous, darling." The crowd laughs appreciatively as she snuggles closer to Andretti. Andretti grins. Her husband manages an embarrassed little smile.

"It goes with the turf," Andretti explains after she has made a triumphant departure.

He tells me his ambition is to be known as the most versatile race car driver of all time. That goal probably will be achieved, even if he quits racing this year. He has already won every championship possible in his dangerous trade—on the dirt tracks, at Daytona (which he won as a rookie), Indy, and the jet-set circuit with the formula-one racers.

Mario Andretti's racing career in the U.S. began in 1958, when he and his twin brother, Aldo, rebuilt a 1948 Hudson and began racing on a track near their home in Nazareth, Pennsylvania. Since then, Andretti has seen it all. He won at Indy in 1969, and he still believes he won the hotly disputed 1981 race as well.

"Racing is all I want to do," says Mario Andretti. *"I don't have a plan A and a plan B.* This is the only place I find fulfillment. I know that sounds corny, but it's true. I'm one of the lucky people who gets paid very well to do what I love doing." (Italics mine)

"Being exposed to danger is what makes this sport so unique," he says. Then he describes the discipline that is required. "When you're sitting out there and the crew's trying to get the machine to work properly, the stomach is churning inside—it's Rolaids time—but what can you do? Jump up and down. . . . One of the most difficult parts of racing is being able to control your emotions properly."

And during the race itself, it's concentration time. "If you lose your concentration in an office, you can lay your head on the desk, or maybe take a nap. If your boss finds you, maybe you'll get fired. If you lose your concentration out here, they scrape you off the wall."

The scene changes, and I am in the office of Hank Aaron, with its view of the field where he broke Babe Ruth's home-run record. Aaron is talking about what is different about superstars: "I think what separates the superstar from the average ballplayer is the fact that he concentrates just a little bit more . . . I knew the pitchers like the back of my hand. If I saw them once, I could tell you about how they were going to throw in what situation, because I studied them. And I think every superstar player does the same thing. He can almost tell you in any situation what a pitcher's going to throw you. . . . He has the ability to think a little bit more than the other players."

Concentrating was a habit for Hank Aaron. It even took over his dreams before a game. "If it was going to be a night game, I would take a nap about one o'clock, and for some reason, I would always remember if I had to face a particular pitcher, and I could see him in my sleep pitching to me. When I woke up, I was ready to go to the ballpark."

When Hank Aaron arrived at the ballpark, he continued that same level of concentration. In the dugout, Aaron would use a "keyhole" in his baseball cap as a kind of lens. It helped him block out distractions and see only the pitcher he was about to face. "If a pitcher got me out with a fastball, I would focus in on that one pitch the next time up and make sure that he didn't get me out the same way. If it was a pitcher that gave me trouble, I would take my baseball cap, pull it down over my face, and look through a little hole in my cap, and focus on nothing but him. . . . I'm not bragging, but I think I focus on things very well."

U.S. Supreme Court Justice Sandra Day O'Connor has developed a similar skill. O'Connor, who spent her early childhood on an isolated ranch, was subsequently sent off to live with her grandmother in El Paso so that she could attend a good school. Her grandmother, whom Justice O'Connor remembers as a delightful, outgoing person, had one very distracting habit. She talked incessantly. The fact that her granddaughter might be reading assigned homework did not dampen her enthusiasm for nonstop chatter. "I learned to let her talk, but to go right ahead and concentrate on what I had to do," the Supreme Court justice told me. "I learned to just automatically respond to what she might be saying at appropriate intervals, but never let it deter me from concentrating on what I was doing."

Learning how to concentrate in spite of distractions has become habitual for O'Connor. She can still do it, at work and on the golf course. "My husband and I play golf sometimes. . . . It is very distracting to him if someone is talking when he's trying to make a shot. I'm exactly the opposite. Anyone can move, talk, do whatever they want, and it doesn't affect my shot, because I tune extraneous things out and focus on the task at hand."

Norman Vincent Peale is another high achiever with the same ability: "I can write on planes, in airports, with thousands of people around—I can focus on what I'm doing at the moment."

O'Connor and Peale have discovered and developed a very useful skill, the same one that Hank Aaron utilized effectively throughout his major-league career. These three high achievers, who have attained the top rank in disparate fields, can concentrate intensely—in spite of distractions.

Concentration—the ability to devote full attention to the task at hand, and, long-term, to concentrate on a career—that is one aspect of focus. But focus has another aspect—intensity. Intensity involves the ability to channel large amounts of energy into the task at hand, and by doing this habitually, to further one's career, as well. By analogy, focus has the same effect on one's work as a magnifying glass does when it is held over a piece of paper on a sunny day. If you hold the glass just right, so that the rays concentrate on one spot, you can set the paper on fire.

## Intensity

Oscar de la Renta is sitting behind his desk in the corner of a room where assistants are scurrying back and forth with samples and drawings and messages for the Prince of Ruffles. We have begun to talk about the widely reported dinner parties he and his late wife Françoise gave. "Your dinners are legends in New York society," I comment. "What has been your secret?"

"Françoise never thought, 'Let's have a wonderful dinner,'" this vibrant, courteous, elegant man replies. "What we always wanted to achieve was for people we cared about to have a good time. I have great curiosity, and I have a very wide range of friends. We tried to put people together who would have a good time together, even if they came from different ways of life."

"Was there a common denominator in your choice of guests?"

"Yes. People who have a commitment to what they do and who have something to say. There is always a link among people who have a commitment and who care."

"What human quality is most important for *you*?"

"Passion—to do whatever you do in a passionate way. Then you do it well. I am also impatient."

"Impatient?"

"Ah, yes. Very much so. It is a part of being passionate."

I left Oscar de la Renta's workplace thinking about how few individuals I have met who could say, "I am passionate about what I do." But many of the high achievers have said it, in their own way.

Agnes De Mille, who choreographed *Oklahoma* and is considered by many to be *the* choreographer of the Broadway musical, has said: "It takes great passion and great energy to do anything creative, especially in the theater. You have to care so much that you can't sleep, you can't eat, you can't talk to people. It's just got to be right. You can't do it without that passion." (Beilenson and Tenenbaum 1986:13)

When people really care about their work—when they do it with passion, as Agnes De Mille says—they are less likely to skimp on quality or attempt shortcuts. Chet Atkins states: "Maybe there are a few shortcuts for a rock star who becomes an overnight sensation and is forgotten about tomorrow. But you take a guy like Glen Campbell, who's a very good guitarist, or Roy Clark, a great entertainer, or Jerry Reed. They spent twelve hours a day for many years playing the guitar. They may tell you different, but they did. Everybody does. I took the guitar with me to the bathroom, everywhere I went, I played it—because I loved it. Jerry Reed says, 'You gotta be eat up with it.' You've got to love it with a passion that will follow you to the grave.... If you don't have that, you might as well forget it, I think."

Paul "Bear" Bryant summed up his approach to winning football games thus: "It's a life-and-death affair with me. It's whether you want to live a good life or a sorry life. There's a whole lot of difference between winning and losing; there's a whole lot of difference between going to heaven and going to hell."

This is not to say that you must live your life in a constant state of high-voltage energy to be a success. As Arthur Ashe told me, "You've got to be intense when it counts." "If you try to be intense twenty-four hours a day, you're not going to last very long."

Ashe spoke of trying to be relaxed, so that he could play loose, and being focused, so that his performance was not careless and error-prone. "People perform best when they're relaxed—athletes, at least. I mean, you're focused and you're concentrating, but you've got to feel tension-free."

Given a choice between being intense and being relaxed, Ashe said he would choose the latter. "I know what you mean by intensity," he said. "It's just I wouldn't rank myself very high there, because I always thought that when you got too intense, you got overanxious and didn't do well."

Hank Aaron told me that he was "consumed" by baseball, but he—like tennis champion Arthur Ashe— found that intensity could be counterproductive. "I'm a pretty relaxed fellow," Aaron says. "I don't get too intense, because I've always felt like I had to work within my own means. Some people can get intense and be better. If I get intense, I get nervous. I'm not able to concentrate on what I have to do. I always tried to keep myself as loose as I could."

High achievers from many fields say that passion sustained for too long results in diminished energy and power. "It can drain you—not just of your energy, but of your creative power," says cartoonist Dan Barry.

Many high achievers are able to control and harness their passion, thereby using it effectively. They learn to be focused and loose at the same time, or they segregate their roles so that they are intense about their work, but are relaxed in other settings.

Oscar de la Renta turns to gardening, a hobby that forces him to be patient. "The reason I love to garden is because it is a challenge to my patience. You might plant a seed that will become a tree, but you know in your lifetime that you are not going to see the tree at its best. But still you do it. Gardening teaches you patience." Here is an instance of segregating roles. He is intense and impatient in one, relaxed and patient in the other.

Striking a balance between intensity and relaxation is wise. Intensity, if sustained for too long, is emotionally damaging. Coach Bobby Cremins says, "During basketball season, I always have a book in my hand. Always. Biographies, autobiographies, rarely books about basketball." Reading is his outlet, because Cremins believes intensity has a danger level: "Intensity can destroy you."

In July of 1890, Vincent Van Gogh wrote to his beloved brother Theo. "I apply myself to my canvases with *all my mind*. I am trying to do as well as certain painters whom I have greatly loved and admired." (Italics mine.) Van Gogh describes himself as someone with a "mind diligently fixed on trying to do as well as possible." Of his work, he writes, "I am risking my life for it, and my reason has half-foundered because of it—that's all right."

There is a note written on this letter, in Theo's handwriting: "Letter found on him on July 29."

July 29, 1890, was the day when Vincent Van Gogh fatally wounded himself. (Bernard 1985:214, 215)

## Surge Modes and Flow States

High achievers in many fields speak of being able to regulate their intensity—of being able to phase in and out of an intense state. Edith W. Martin calls this intense state the "surge mode." She explains: "I feel that I can do most of what I want to do in my stride. By and large, tremendous intensity becomes counterproductive. Once you know how to do things, intensity should be the *surge mode* you turn on when you have to, and the rest of the time you should be able to glide through decision-making, and the like. When I'm in the surge mode, look out."

Asked about focus, architect Hugh Stubbins rated himself only a five. Stubbins explained that an architect is trained to focus on many different things at one time. "One has to have an eight-track mind to be a designer. You've got to think of so many things simultaneously. If you thought of them, each one at a time, you'd never get anywhere. It's like driving a car. It becomes second nature to think of all these things. It's like shifting gears and pushing the clutch and putting your foot on the accelerator. Once you get used to that, you don't have to think of those things. They just come automatically."

This balance between the automatic flow of the work

Stubbins speaks of and the "surge mode" described by Martin sounds very much like a phenomenon being studied by University of Chicago psychologist Mihaly Csikszentmihalyi (pronounced "chik-zent-me-high-yee"). He calls the phenomenon "flow state." Csikszentmihalyi has developed the idea over a twelve-year period—studying athletes, artists, mountain-climbers, surgeons and others whose work requires intense concentration.

According to Csikszentmihalyi, a flow state is most likely when an individual's ability is about equal to the difficulty of the task. If the difficulty is too great, anxiety results. If the difficulty of the task is not great enough, the individual gets bored.

The flow experience requires deep concentration, usually on a few stimuli. People in the flow state do not think about or even notice activities that are irrelevant to the task. They may not even realize that they are hungry or tired. They do not hear distracting noises. Many of these individuals report a euphoric feeling when their thoughts were exceptionally clear. People report a loss of awareness of time passing, a loss of self-consciousness, or self-doubt, or the concerns of everyday life, where goals, feedback, and concentration are not well structured. Little or no attention is left over for the person to think about himself as separate from the interaction. (Gross 1982:167–187)

Many of the comments of the high achievers I have interviewed fit Csikszentmihalyi's flow-state model very nicely:

Jack Nicklaus: "I don't know how you can describe it. I think it's what I experienced last year [1986] at the Masters. All of a sudden I was fifteen years younger, and I could do things the last round that I haven't been able to do for, you know, five or six years. And the distance I hit the golf ball, the shots I was going to make, the feeling that I knew I was going to do it—it just happens every once in a while."

Emmylou Harris: "There is no term to explain the exhilaration and the sense of accomplishment.... It is not just a matter of singing well, which you try to do every night on every song—at least I do—but there are moments on stage when you click with the right song at the right time for the right people, and you're giving everything and you're getting everything back."

Mario Andretti: "Anybody could take it [the racing machine] out there and do two hundred miles an hour on the straightaway, and one hundred fifty miles an hour on the corners. Anybody. The trick is to be able to take that machine down the straightaway at two hundred miles an hour, enter the corner at two hundred miles an hour, and come off the corner at about one hundred ninety-two. That's the trick. That's where the excitement is. That's the thrill that we really get—measuring yourself against time and that machine."

Dan Barry: "I'm not at all aware of time going by when I'm working. I've discovered that after about four intense hours of painting, the quality and the concentration start to drop. And yet I've had people come into my studio and say, 'Hey, you're still working? Do you know it's midnight?' I hadn't noticed that it had gotten dark. So when I'm completely involved in concentration, I have no concept of how much time something has taken."

Robert Shaw: "I guess I'm so good at concentrating that I don't hear anything that's going on. I'm sort of monomanic."

Mary Kay: "Whatever it is that I'm doing, I'm very much into and have to get it done. If I start doing something at one in the morning, until I finish it, I can't quit."

Csikszentmihalyi found that the individuals in his

research created their own self-contained little worlds. Hank Aaron told me about a similar kind of experience: "The greatest thing about sports, I guess, is the challenge. A lot of people say the reward is money, *but to stand out there and have nobody but you, the pitcher and the catcher*—to stand up there and try to hit the baseball, trying to hit a baseball that's being thrown ninety miles an hour—that's the challenge of it." (Italics mine)

Csikszentmihalyi respondents described the flow experience as exciting, fulfilling, enjoyable—as an experience that is rewarding in itself, rather than a means to some external reward. So do many of the high achievers I interviewed.

Dan Barry: "Sometimes it's not whether the work is good or bad; it's the act that's so exciting. The art transcends everything—the purpose, the product. It is the doing that is so exciting."

Hank Aaron: "It feels good . . . it just feels like nobody can get you out—no matter what they throw you, it's right down the center of the plate. It's right there for you to hit. And it's almost as big as a watermelon."

Jack Nicklaus: "It's hard to describe, 'cause when you go through it, it's something you know is happening to you. . . . All of a sudden, why do you hit the ball fifty yards farther? The adrenaline is flowing, you're excited, you're in total control of yourself, your concentration level is such that you know—it looks like everything else could be in slow motion—you have enough time to do everything you wanted to."

I tell Julie Andrews about flow-state research, and what Hank Aaron and Jack Nicklaus have said about the experience. "Has anything like that ever happened to you?" I ask.

"Oh, yes," she replies. "It doesn't happen very often. . . . Let's say I'm singing with a grand orchestra, and it is heavenly. It's one of the most exciting things anybody could do, I think, and the excitement, or the 'flow state,' as you say, rises up and almost threatens to choke one off. It almost drowns one, it's such a splendid feeling."

She pauses, says she isn't sure what she has experienced is the same thing that I have described, and continues: "For me, it's almost dangerous, because one can enjoy it so much that one forgets to send it out and project it. One wallows in one's delight but forgets to remember what it is one's doing. It's very easy to drown in it sometimes, it's such a pleasure. . . . It actually does physically threaten. I mean, when I'm singing and the joy rises up, it almost cuts the power of my voice out. . . .

"There are days when a kind of pure joy happens, and you know you're in very good health and you are doing something fairly well. Those are rather rare times, when everything comes together. But I'm talking about that sheer thing you're talking about, which is just a state of ecstasy that's just wonderful. For me, it can be quite dangerous, because the ecstasy can actually threaten to cut out the very thing that I'm enjoying so terribly."

Abraham Maslow, whose research influenced Csikszentmihalyi's, discovered that many of his respondents had had what he called "peak experiences." During these transcendent episodes, they experienced delight and heightened clarity. Then, things seemed to flow in harmony.

When I asked Nicklaus if he had learned how to consciously induce the flow state, he said no: "It happens occasionally when you really all of a sudden get excited and charged up and emotionally involved, and all of a sudden you just focus and channel in on it. Fortunately, it's happened to me on a variety of occasions, but mostly when it's important."

Presently, research is underway to see if people can

be taught to induce the flow state. "I am trying to learn how the flow state can take place in everyday life, and not just for exceptional people," says Csikszentmihalyi. He believes that we all have the ability to transform any situation into a flow activity. That is accomplished by mentally transforming our environment into gamelike situations—by pitting our skill against some task that we select, letting some challenging but do-able goal emerge in the situation. We focus intently on that task and goal, then strive to attain it.

## Holding a Point

Two years ago, I attended a conference where I heard Clifford W. Rackley, former president of Tenneco Oil Company, discuss how difficult it is to find people who can eventually move to the top of a corporation. "We begin to look at new employees almost immediately to see if they have management potential. If they do," Rackley said, "we put them on a fast track. One of our problems is that many of the people we would like to promote can't hold a point."

*Hold a point.* I wasn't sure I understood that expression. Did it refer to a pencil point, and therefore imply that some people didn't stay sharp and alert? Or, did it have some other meaning? When the meeting adjourned, I asked Rackley what he meant.

"Have you ever been hunting?" he asked.

I knew immediately. Holding a point is what a good hunting dog does. It points until the bird flies. Later, a hunter-friend amplified on that idea. A good bird dog, he told me, will hold its point "till hell freezes over" or the dog's owner releases the dog from the point, usually with a whistle or some other signal.

That down-home metaphor was Rackley's way of describing constancy of purpose. The kind of people

Rackley's company seeks for its top positions are individuals whose goals are not continually changing.

When I interviewed Xavier Roberts for the first time in 1985, his company had just begun to ship his Furskins to dealers. Roberts told me the initial response to the new product was excellent, but added, almost wistfully, "It'll be hard to come up with a second Cabbage Patch.... I've made only one investment, really, and that's Cabbage Patch. I've spent seven years working on Cabbage Patch, and that investment's paid off. If I had started out and spent a little bit of time on several products, I probably wouldn't be where I am today. One good investment is sometimes worth twenty different investments."

Roberts's philosophy has been confirmed at the cash register. In 1986, sales of the Cabbage Patch line totaled $250 million—down $350 million from the previous year. But the Cabbage Patch line was still the largest-selling toy line in North America—for the third straight year.

Jack Lemmon told me that he had never deviated from his original goal of trying to be the best actor he could possibly be. But Lemmon acknowledged that he has had great difficulty overcoming his impetuosity. "I would keep jumping and flying off in eighteen thousand different directions, of trying to play a part fifty-two different ways, instead of slowly stripping down and methodically peeling the layers off—of getting down to the simplicity of one way and one thing at a time in a scene."

The philosophy of focusing is the discipline of the gardener's shears—which prune the plant so that the main stems will grow fuller and more luxurious. Focus often means less but better.

Arthur Ashe feels that the time-consuming responsibilities he experienced as the nation's first black tennis star cost him in terms of his own career. "Had I felt comfortable enough to be more selfish about the use of my time, I might have been able to win more titles. But when you're part of the first wave, you can't afford to be single-minded."

Ashe recalled that there was tremendous pressure on him to do things other than training and competing. "Bjorn Borg or Jimmy Connors or McEnroe or Chris Evert Lloyd or Martina Navratilova have all been able to be completely single-minded. They don't have to go off and do any clinics. They don't have to worry about discrimination. They don't have to worry about whether they're going to be refused service in some restaurants. They don't carry that mental baggage around—of having to worry about things like that. I'm not saying that they don't have some baggage of their own, but they certainly don't have that type."

These are the words of a man, in midlife, looking back on his early years as an athlete—knowing that he did well, extremely well. But he knows that he could have done better, perhaps much better, had he been more single-minded.

## Keeping Your Priorities Straight

Priorities are implicit in the idea of focus. "If something unexpected comes up, I don't hesitate to change it and put the most important thing first, but by and large I operate on a basis of priorities," says the former chairman of the joint chiefs of staff, Admiral Thomas Moorer.

A sense of priorities is vital in any intensive undertaking. For example, watch a bond trader or a stock trader in action. He will take a position in the market by sifting through all the data, and then—in terms of priorities—look for the germ of truth that will tell him whether to bid high or low, or pass. Then, in the minute-by-minute flow of activity—with a phone pressed against each ear, his eyes glued to a monitor, with people excitedly shouting all around him, he sorts out all the messages aimed at him. He ranks them in order of importance, simultaneously tuning in some messages, tuning out others, and listening intently to the critical ones. A momentary lapse of attention can result in losses of hundreds of thousands of dollars.

In her book *Having It All*, *Cosmopolitan* editor Helen Gurley Brown discusses what she calls the "number-one secret of success." Do you know what that number-one secret is? *Priorities*. Brown says you can determine what the top priority at work is by thinking carefully about what the company hired you for, which activity of your activities will most favorably affect the company's profit and loss statement and therefore means most to *you*, in terms of your rise in the world.

Brown says a lot of people make the mistake of working hard at every task that confronts them, with little or no regard for the relative importance of those tasks. "At day's end, exhausted, they may even be self-congratulatory about all the work they've done, while the important work goes further in arrears." She approves of an idea developed by time-management consultant Alan Lakein—of putting letters and memos and reminders of all the other tasks that beckon into folders marked A, B, and C priorities.

In order to be reminded that her first priority at *Cosmopolitan* is producing a product—the magazine itself—and not decorating the reception area or working at some other lower-priority task, Brown always keeps a copy of the magazine on her desk. (1982:60)

\*　　\*　　\*

In their career choices, high achievers tend to be narrow, rather than broad. They certainly do not resort to the shotgun approach. And even when they branch out into related fields, they have the ability to focus in on the task at hand. Jack Nicklaus, who has become almost as well known for his golf-course designs as he is for his game, states: "If playing golf was the only thing I do, life would become very boring. But I have been able to channel my mind in many different directions. I am able to focus on one thing, concentrate on it, and keep channeled on it until I get finished with the problem and then move on to the next thing."

This kind of concentration—a focus linked to the performance of some task—is called *instrumental concentration* by some psychologists. Psychologist Auke Telegen, who has studied the phenomenon, says that people who rank high on instrumental concentration are those who have the ability to keep their focus in spite of other tempting distractions. They are more able than others to put constraints on what they do, better able to learn in depth, less likely to make mistakes.

Dr. Daniel Goleman, author of *Vital Lies, Simple Truths*, believes we develop our mental muscles of concentration by concentrating. He recommends meditating every day, not for mystical purposes, but for the purpose of learning how to rule out every other thought except one.

Goleman feels that our culture weakens our ability to concentrate through its many distractions. "So much richness finally dilutes each of the individual experiences." The result, he writes, is too often "a mindlessness, a state where each thing distracts us from the other, so that we focus on none of it with full awareness."

We have been socialized to think of temptation as a choice between good and evil. That is a mistake. Often, we are tempted between two or more goods, not between good and evil. Only a few decades ago, most Americans had far fewer choices than they do today. Now, on a given evening, many of us can choose between going to a concert or a play, between reading a book or magazine or watching television, going to a movie or renting one, going to a party or dinner, doing aerobics, or taking a night class. And any one of those choices might enrich us mentally, physically, or emotionally.

But these choices can become distractions if they divert us from our priorities or cause us to lose focus. Goleman makes a valid point when he observes that our culture—with its many opportunities for entertainment or careers—can dilute our focus.

Distractions can be overcome, as Hank Aaron has demonstrated. The last place on earth to concentrate, it would seem, is a ballpark, with fans cheering and booing, vendors clamoring for customers, players yelling, and umpires shouting. However, Aaron learned how to concentrate on one object only—the pitcher.

# 7

# The Right Place at the Right Time

*Had they tested me six months later, I may not have gotten a contract, because the system was beginning to change and they weren't doing that as much. Also, the picture I was so right for might have been made and done and another picture might not have loomed at the time. So, I might never have gotten that kind of start. I might have been at MGM three months and gone. . . . Timing and luck had a great deal to do with the start of my career.*

—Janet Leigh

*Nobody ever makes it the same way. I made it by being a fiddle player. They needed a fiddle player and I got the job—for three dollars a night. Then they heard me playing the guitar a few nights later and gave me a job as a guitar player. You gotta be in the right place at the right time.*

—Chet Atkins

$I$t is tempting for high achievers and their admirers to emphasize the internal factors—characteristics of the individual, such as competence, focus or single-mindedness. Understandably. High achievers like to believe that they had something to do with their successes. It is, after all, heartwarming to accept praise for being persistent, hardworking, and talented. Moreover, when we give out awards for achievement, we seldom get around to mentioning that the great scientist made his discovery because he had available a new but unheralded technology or that the great political leader achieved his goals primarily because the people were ready for them. When is the last time you heard of a testimonial dinner for, say, the electron microscope?

Yet many of the factors involved in high achievement are external to the individual—factors like having good equipment or being exposed to a good teacher, like being born into the right family or having a passport from the United States.

In reality, the achievement factors are never exclusively external or internal. There is always an interplay between the individual and the environment. It cannot be emphasized too strongly that high achievement consists of making successful connections between internal factors and external ones, between one's self and the physical, social, and cultural environment—between competence and opportunity.

High achievers frequently mention external factors, sometimes gratefully, sometimes grudgingly, but always with respect. External factors are the elements of context, the situational elements that, though they may not make or break a career, certainly shape it profoundly.

## The Right Place

Many a career has been advanced when an individual left an out-of-the way town or a stifling environment, made a break with the past, and moved to a new place. Kris Kristofferson did that. For several years, he tried mailing his material to publishers and producers and performers, hoping someone would notice. But they didn't. Gradually, the message seeped in. He would have to go to the place where things were happening. In the 1960s and 1970s that meant Nashville for the kind of music Kristofferson wanted to write.

Kristofferson recognized that if he stayed in the Army, he would have to abandon all hope of ever becoming a songwriter. "I saw that if I was going to be sending stuff in from West Point, nobody was going to listen to it or do anything with it. You have to be there." He made an irrevocable decision, as we have seen, that involved considerable hardship.

Interestingly, Kristofferson says that putting yourself where the action is makes a difference even after you achieve recognition. In 1986, Kristofferson stated: "Even after I left Nashville—after I had made it—if I wasn't actually back there pitching the songs myself, the songs weren't going to get recorded. And they haven't been."

Things might have been different, Isaac Asimov says, if he hadn't lived within subway-commuting distance of a science-fiction editor by the name of John Campbell, whose office was in Manhattan. "John Campbell is the guy who made me what I am today," Asimov says. Campbell worked with Asimov, showed him how to revise his manuscript and encouraged him to resubmit. The point is that a talented editor was readily accessible to a persistent youngster with raw talent.

Cartoonist Dan Barry tells a similar story. "I lived in New York. . . . In those days, there weren't any outsiders in the business. The first outsider I ever met was a guy from Georgia, Jack Davis, but he had to come to New York to show his stuff. Today, the business has dispersed itself somewhat, but still people have to be where it's happening."

Robert Shaw was a junior at Pomona College in Claremont, California, when Fred Waring brought his orchestra and chorus to the campus to film some scenes for the movie *Varsity Show*. That year, the director of the highly regarded college glee club was ill, and Shaw was filling in temporarily during his absence. Waring heard the glee club and was impressed by the young Shaw. He asked if he had ever considered music as a career. Shaw said no. He was thinking about becoming a college profesor in comparative religion or English literature.

A few months later, Shaw reconsidered and wrote to Waring, saying he would like to discuss "the professional music business" with him. Back came a telegram from Waring asking Shaw to come to New York City and form a new choral organization for a radio show. Shaw accepted the invitation, and his professional career in music began.

"It wasn't the fact that the discoverer [Waring] promoted anything," Shaw told me. "It was the fact that he lifted me up out of Red Bluff, California [Shaw's hometown] and put me in New York City, where I met Julius Herford, and where I met Toscanini, and where I met Koussevitsky."

Finding the right place involves more than discovering an appropriate physical location. It often involves making a move in social space. Qualities that are essential at the bottom of the corporation pyramid—which, for the most part, consist of doing what you are told—are not the same ones that are important at the top. Thus, what may be sound advice for people at one end of the pecking order may spell disaster for people at the other end. The qualities that bring generals fame—like audacity and stubbornness and haughtiness—lead to courts-martial for privates.

Sometimes, high achievers don't *find* the right place. They just happen to be there when an opportunity presents itself. Such an experience occurred early in the career of Hank Aaron. When Aaron left his hometown of Mobile, Alabama, he had big-league hopes, one suit, and two dollars in his pocket. Arriving at training camp in North Carolina, Aaron received an unenthusiastic reception. "The older players greeted me like I was a disease," Aaron recalls. And the coaches were paying most of their attention to the other players, not Aaron.

"It was two weeks before I even got on the practice field," Aaron recalls. "They weren't looking at me." Aaron realized he was about to be cut, which would mean a long bus trip back to Mobile, where he would have to face his friends and explain his failure. "Unfortunately," Aaron recalls, "one of the players got hurt, and the manager said, 'You go out there, kid, and play shortstop.' And I went out there, and I got three hits that day, and the next day I got three hits, and they said, 'We'd better take

a serious look at this kid; he might have something. . . .'
After that, I kept right on going."

Paul "Bear" Bryant did not grow up in a sports-
minded household, and had it not been for an unplanned episode, the legendary coach might never have
called a play. His parents were strictly religious, and
regarded football as a "worldly" sport. They were also
poor, and football was played when all available hands
were needed in the fields picking cotton and getting the
corn in.

One afternoon, when Paul was in the eighth grade,
he lingered for a few moments behind the school building to watch the football team practice. He was a big
youngster, a physical characteristic not lost on the coach.

"Would you like to play?" the coach asked.

"I don't know, sir. . . . You want me to?"

"Yeah. I'd like to play you."

"What do you want me to do?"

"Well, you run down there, and when that guy catches
the ball, you try to kill him."

Bryant lined up, and the punter kicked a good high
ball. Racing down the field and following the coach's
instructions to the letter, Bryant demolished the receiver,
almost killing himself as well.

He started the game that week. Thanks to a coach
who knew raw talent when he saw it, and Bryant's mother,
who appealed to his father on the boy's behalf, Bryant
began a career that led to his posthumous induction
into the Football Hall of Fame in 1986. Neither of his
parents, incidentally, ever attended a game Bryant played
in or coached, something he always regretted. But he
liked to tell the story about a prayer his mother prayed:
"Dear God, keep him from playing, but if he does, please
let him win."

High achievers frequently mention unplanned meetings, accidents, and serendipitous discoveries when they tell their stories. Even the most sophisticated and scholarly will use the word *luck*. But they do not mean Lady Luck, magic potions, or horseshoes nailed over barn doors. What they mean is that there sometimes seems to be an element of sheer chance in being chosen or rejected, being in the right place instead of the wrong one, choosing one line of experimentation and not another.

Novelist Erskine Caldwell says luck in the beginning is a "very small, almost invisible object." Caldwell explains, "You may not recognize it immediately. It is something that grows upon you. My good luck, so to speak, came in bits and pieces—nothing in one fell swoop."

Some believe that chance explains fads like the Cabbage Patch Kids and Pet Rocks and hoola hoops. Lightning has to strike somewhere, so the argument goes. If it doesn't strike the Cabbage Patch, it will hit somewhere else. The public always needs some new diversion to satisfy its whims. Xavier Roberts, as a matter of fact, recognizes that element in marketing and has taken steps to capitalize on the public's shifting moods by creating his line of toy bears, named "Furskins," and developing a resort in the Appalachians.

Psychologist B. F. Skinner uses the word *luck* to describe his career. But Skinner is careful not to describe *himself* as lucky. "I don't think people are lucky. Lucky things do happen to them, but not because *they're* lucky. . . . I did some experiments that paid off. And it was lucky. It wasn't my doing; it's just that what I happened to do happened to be the thing that worked."

Eric Hoffer, the self-taught folk philosopher who wrote the best-selling *The True Believer*, believed that the element of chance is very important in human affairs. "I don't believe in purpose," he told me. "There is no purpose in life, only chance."

Norman Vincent Peale doesn't believe in luck or chance, but he does believe "fortuitous things" happen —which he attributes to divine guidance. Peale cites one such episode: In the winter of 1932, a church in New York City which was without a pastor had engaged a famous clergyman to preach on the following Sunday. However, that weekend there was a major snowstorm, and the clergyman, who lived out of state, notified the church leaders that he could not get to the city. On Saturday, when the leaders were desperately trying to find a replacement for Sunday, a man walked into the meeting and suggested that they try Peale, who was then pastor of a church in Syracuse. "They telephoned me," Peale remembers, "and I said to Mrs. Peale, 'Can we go to New York this Sunday?' She was not about to pass up a weekend in New York City, and she said we could. I went; I received a call to the church; and was there fifty-two years."

# Timing

Opportunity always involves timing. The same society that will reject an idea or politician or music or an art style at one time may receive them gladly only a short time later.

Such a development accounts for the success Arthur Murray has enjoyed. Until the turn of the century, not many Americans danced—contrary to the image created by romantic movies and novels. Dancing was frowned upon by many religious groups and often strictly forbidden. Those Americans who did dance usually followed the traditional steps of European dances: waltzes, quadrilles, and polkas.

Then, between 1910 and 1920, Americans went dance crazy. New dances appeared: the Bunny Hop, the Turkey Trot, the Grizzly Bear, the Crab Step, the Chicken Scratch, and the Kangaroo Dip. Marathons and dance contests drew huge throngs to ballrooms, auditoriums, and improvised dance halls. The nation had never seen anything like it.

With exquisite timing, Arthur Murray launched his business at a time when millions of Americans wanted to learn these new dances. He geared his business to the opportunities around him. Sears and Roebuck and Montgomery Ward were making fortunes selling Americans merchandise by mail, so Arthur Murray decided to sell dance lessons by mail, too (a preposterous idea, if you think about it). Millions of Americans were reading magazines, so that is where he advertised. And he was the first to recognize that radio could be used for dancing. When television came along, he and his wife Kathryn were pioneers in using that medium, too.

Janet Leigh has played important roles in many of the major films of our time, including *Touch of Evil*, and *The Manchurian Candidate*, and Alfred Hitchcock's *Psycho*. Her career in movies began when Norma Shearer happened to see Leigh's photograph at a ski resort in northern California. Here is how she tells the Cinderella story: "My daddy and my mom were working at a ski lodge, and I went to visit them over Christmas break. Daddy took a picture of me in the snow and put it on his little desk. Norma Shearer visited the ski resort, saw the photograph, and took it back with her to Hollywood."

The people at MGM were impressed by the photograph of the fresh-faced, eighteen-year-old girl in the snow with her hair blowing and no makeup on and invited her to come down for an interview. After meeting with the drama coach and reading for her, the director and producer decided to test her for a role in *The Romance of Rosie Ridge*. She got the lead. Her name was changed from Jeanette Helen Morrison to Janet Leigh, and she starred opposite Van Johnson in her first film.

As for timing, Leigh says: "Had they tested me six months later, I may not have gotten a contract, because the system was beginning to change and they weren't doing that as much. Also, the picture I was so right for might have been made and done, and another picture might not have loomed at the time. So, I might never have gotten that kind of start. I might have been at MGM three months and gone.... Timing and luck had a great deal to do with the start of my career."

Coca-Cola chief Roberto Goizueta is a strong believer in timing, in taking advantage of the ebb and flow of business—a belief that was inculcated in him by his grandfather. His grandfather understood that fortunes are made, not just lost during depressions. "My grandfather bought a sugar mill [in Cuba] for practically nothing, because when the depression hit, he had such a strong cash position. You could pick up a lot of bargains [then]. He always said: 'Spend much less than you need to live, and always have a very strong cash position in the bank. That way, you can take advantage of opportunities when they arise.'"

Great political leaders have always recognized the importance of timing. Franklin Delano Roosevelt was a master at it. He would try to outmaneuver his opponents before they had a chance to organize, or failing that, would wait until the opposition crested before he acted. Then he would strike quickly, because he knew the public soon tired of reform. He once said, "I am like a cat; I make a quick stroke and then I relax." (Burns 1978:281)

Timing has been essential in the great revolutions that have shaped history. "All successful revolutions are the kicking in of a rotten door," writes Harvard economist John Kenneth Galbraith. (1977:96) That is what Lenin found when he arrived at the Finland Station in Petrograd April 3, 1917. The situation was ripe for a leader who was self-assured and who was ruthless enough to carry out a bloody agenda. The Russian army was starving and in retreat, the masses were demoralized, the serfs and workers were ready to rebel, and the aristocracy was weak. In October, a scant six months later, Lenin became Russia's absolute leader.

Sports consultant and entrepreneur Mark H. McCormack writes: "Many ideas fail not because they are bad ideas, not because they are poorly executed, but because the timing is not correct. A lot of salespeople are far too quick to write off a good idea simply because their timing was bad." Often a salesman is turned down because of economic reasons or internal reasons that the salesman doesn't know about.

McCormack recommends listening, really listening, to the potential buyer for what he calls "timing cues." These cues involve the rhythms of the organization, for there are times when the organization is receptive to buying, times when it is not. "There are any number of timing opportunities that drop in your lap," McCormack writes. "While you don't have to be a fortune-teller to spot them, you do have to be sensitively attuned to their significance to tailor events to your advantage." (1984:94, 100)

## Resources

A dedicated, resourceful, and competent—but not necessarily brilliant—individual often will gain recognition just by having early access to advanced research tools. In fact, discoveries are virtually inevitable whenever there is a major breakthrough in, say, telescopy. If an astronomer can see stars and galaxies that no one else has ever seen before—because he has a more powerful telescope—he gets credit for the sighting. (It goes without saying that if he knows where to look, his chances of success are improved considerably.)

Many an idea has been conceived before the resources were available to implement it. Leonardo da Vinci conceived of the airplane centuries before the concept became reality. The technology needed to transform his dreams into great aluminum birds had not yet been invented, so the ideas got no further than the pages of his sketchbook.

The availability of resources explains why so many of the great names in the world of science are to be found in only a very few universities and research centers. That is where the bright students, skilled assistants, world-class colleagues, money, and state-of-the-art equipment are.

That also explains why the United States is where things are happening today in most fields of science. Nobel Laureate Francis Crick says it would be difficult to name a single field of science today in which the United States is not the predominant power. There are some branches of mathematics that have advanced further in the Soviet Union, he observes, and there are other exceptions, but you have to search for them. That's quite an admission, coming from a Cambridge-educated Englishman.

The center of scientific gravity shifted to the United States during and after World War II, when scientists fled from Europe, finding refuge in American classrooms and laboratories. That gave a degree of sophistication to American science that had previously been lacking. Asked to explain the change, Crick replies: "Partly it's because the United States has a large population, partly because it's got a lot of money, and partly because it's now got a lot of sophisticated scientists who train good young people," he replied. "It still attracts lively young people."

The presence or absence of resources explains high achievement in a great many fields, not just science. Take stock-car racing as an example. Richard Petty, the winningest racer in the history of the sport, says there is probably no harder sport to become a winner in than stock-car racing, grand-national style. Only five or six people have the cars that can win major races, says Petty. The reason? Money. To win consistently, a racer needs expensive racing cars, garages, equipment, trucks, and competent crews. A newcomer has a lot going against him. "If you're not in one of those cars, no matter how good you are, you're not going to win," Petty observes.

Petty says he's actually grateful for those drivers who don't stand a chance, the weekend racers who drive second-rate cars with catch-as-catch-can crews. "They help the fans realize how good we are, when we're passing 'em."

High achievers are not passive when it comes to finding resources. Typically, they start out trying to exploit the resources of their native environment, even if those resources are limited. Some succeed, like Xavier Roberts, who was able to use the assets of his mountain home to good advantage in producing the Cabbage Patch toy line. Others are not so fortunate, but they keep trying, sometimes longer than they should, because they are a persistent lot and hate to give up. Kris Kristofferson, as mentioned elsewhere, organized a band when he was stationed overseas and wrote songs for several years, dutifully mailing them off to the States, but met with only limited success. Eventually, high achievers do move on if they can't find what they need in their own environment.

That is what Aaron Copland did when he realized that he had progressed as far as he could with his music in the United States. He left for Paris and there encountered Nadia Boulanger, a consummate musician and teacher, who helped Copland get his first major break.

# Significant Others

"It's who you know that counts," like most clichés, contains an element of truth. Virtually all the high achievers mention a *who*—a mother or a father, a teacher, a colleague, a coach, a boss, a mentor, an editor—who found them, supported them, criticized them, inspired them, became a role model for them. But even though there seems always to be a significant other, just who that person is varies enormously. Parents of high achievers figure prominently in some accounts but not in others. Some high achievers have discoverers but not mentors, teachers but not discoverers.

## Parents

We have already seen that architect John Portman knew he would become an architect at an early age. Portman's mother, whom he describes as a Grandma Moses type, would draw for him by the hour. Those early experiences deeply impressed him. "It fascinated me to watch her do this," he recalls. "I think I came to a love of drawing and art at a very, very young age."

Hugh Stubbins says his mother helped him choose architecture for a career: "My mother told me I was going to be an architect when I was about fifteen or sixteen years old," Stubbins recalls. "I wanted to be an artist and she didn't think an artist was anything to be, so she said, 'Why don't you be an architect?' "

It was Herbert Marcus, a successful merchant in Dallas, who taught his son Stanley merchandising skills and principles for dealing with customers. Stanley Marcus says that one of the first declarations of business philosophy he ever heard came from the lips of his father: "There is never a good sale for Neiman-Marcus unless it's a good buy for the customer." He truly believed that,

Stanley Marcus told me. "He also taught me that the public was always willing to pay the price for quality."

Richard Petty attributes many of his attitudes about racing to his father, Lee Petty, who he says was the best driver he ever saw. Petty remembers that the other racers "would blow his father's doors off" for about half the race, but then they would begin to head toward the pits with worn-out tires and blown engines. "He'd just putter along, and when the race was over, he'd be getting the flag. I figured he was a little smarter than most of those kids. And when he quit racing, he had won more races and more money than anybody had won up to that time." From his father, Richard Petty learned not to take foolish chances, not to try to win at any price. There would be other races where with better luck and with a better-running car he could win without risking his equipment or his life.

The forty-one-year-old chief of the Waffle House chain, Joseph W. Rogers, Jr., credits his father with grounding him in the principles of good business practice. "I was fortunate in having a father who talked a lot about management and self-discipline, and was able to see himself honestly and share that perception with me at an early age. Because I took an interest in the business back in my teens, I was able to soak up a lot of that."

Parents' styles vary widely. Some are patient and teach quietly, often by example. Others are demanding, sometimes neurotic. Historians say that John D. Rockefeller's father's treatment of his son probably toughened him up, even though the son never fully appreciated the lessons. "I cheat my boys every chance I get," the father would brag. "I skin 'em every time I can. I want to make 'em sharp." William Rockefeller would lend his son money for investments, but at a high interest rate, and he would call the loans due unexpectedly, just to see if his son could come up with the money. The son always paid his father promptly. (Collier and Horowitz 1976:13)

John D. Rockefeller was not as capricious with his children as his father had been, but he taught them to be disciplined toward money and generous toward philanthropic and religious causes. That tradition continued into the next generation. Rockefeller biographers Peter Collier and David Horowitz describe the upbringing of the Rockefeller brothers: "Like their father [John D. Rockefeller, Jr.], they earned their spending money— by killing flies for pennies, shining shoes, hoeing the garden." The brothers were required to keep a record of income and disbursements. Grandfather's Ledger A, with its yellowing, brittle pages, was the model. "Any child with an unaccounted-for item in his ledger at the end of the week was fined five cents. . . . " (1976:180, 181) Like father and grandfather, the grandchildren were required to give at least a tithe—ten percent—of their income for religious and philanthropic causes.

When I asked David Rockefeller about those lessons, he replied: "One that I think has been important to me and probably to all of my brothers and sister was the notion that with opportunity goes responsibility." Rockefeller said his parents made much of the fact that their wealth gave them opportunities and responsibilities other people did not have. "We were taught that we should use the wealth to do things in a way that would be constructive and helpful to mankind."

Mary Kay grew up poor—at the other end of the economic spectrum from the Rockefellers. When her father contracted tuberculosis early in her childhood, her mother had to go to work in order to support the family. "I seldom saw her, because she left at five in the morning and she came home at nine at night. For many of my early years, I was in bed when she left and when she came home. But I could call her on the phone when I was taking care of my father at the age of seven, and she would always tell me in great detail how to do what I needed to do. Then she would invariably finish up every direction she gave me with: 'Now, honey, Mother knows you can do it. You can do it, darling. You can do it.'"

Mary Kay says that her mother's "You can do it" became a kind of watchword of her life.

## Teachers

For some high achievers, it was a teacher who got them started, or brought out some latent ability. Businessman J. B. Fuqua attended a high school that had only three teachers, one of whom was the principal. One of those teachers taught Fuqua speed-reading, which he says has been invaluable in his career. One of the teachers taught him how to debate. "Today," Fuqua says, "I can get up and talk before ten people or ten thousand people." The third told Fuqua he could borrow books by mail from the Duke University Library. "I lived out on a farm and didn't have access to a library. The Duke University Library gave me a basic education."

Tennessee Williams told me about a school teacher who, without knowing it, helped him decide upon writing as a career. Williams was about ten years old at the time. "I remember the English instructor, and the walls of the schoolroom. They were covered with color lithographs, you know, romantic pictures. I chose the most romantic, of course, which was the Lady of Shalott, floating down a river on a flowery barge, and I wrote a theme about it, and she read it to the class. She said, 'This is very beautiful writing.' And from then on, I thought writing was my profession, and I just took to it."

Former secretary of state Dean Rusk remembers a high school Greek teacher, Preston Epps, who taught a group of about twenty teenage boys: "He just brought us to life with the great questions and the great ideas that the Greeks had raised and discussed. And that, I think, was the principal thing that started me on the line of curiosity and inquiry and speculation and a hunger for more education, more learning."

Kris Kristofferson, like Dean Rusk, was a Rhodes scholar. Kristofferson says a philosophy teacher nudged him toward the world of ideas. "I'd never have been a Rhodes scholar if it weren't for a philosophy professor who pushed me into doing it," Kristofferson admits. "I was very lazy. Football was the most important thing in my life."

U.S. Supreme Court Justice Sandra Day O'Connor credits a Stanford University professor, Harry Rathbun, for influencing her to turn to the field of law as a profession. "I had a hard time deciding what I should major in in college, because I liked geology and history and political science and economics and languages." Rathbun's course in business law and informal meetings with students tipped her scales toward law. In 1952, O'Connor graduated from Stanford University *magna cum laude*— with a law degree.

Labor leader Joyce Dannon Miller says she became vitally interested in her present work because of the influence of the late Kermit Eby, a professor of social sciences at the University of Chicago. "I don't know if he picked me out or I picked him out, but there was a small group of people at the university he was like a guru to, and he made it possible for me to come into the trade-union movement." Today Miller is one of the most prominent women in the trade-union movement.

Aaron Copland had a number of excellent teachers, but *the* teacher in his life was Nadia Boulanger. Through Boulanger's efforts, Copland met Serge Koussevitsky and thus began a career-long partnership. "Nadia Boulanger read in the Paris papers that Serge Koussevitsky had just been appointed the new conductor of the Boston Symphony. She said to me, 'We must go and visit *him*.' So we went and visited him, and by the time the visit was over, as we were about to leave, he said to me, '*You* will write an organ symphony, Mlle. Boulanger [who was an organist] will come to America and play the solo part, and *I*, Serge Koussevitsky, will conduct it.'"

The twenty-three-year-old Copland—who until that time had not written many long pieces—was unnerved. As soon as they were out of earshot, Copland asked his teacher, "Do you *really* think I can do it?"

"*You* can do it," Boulanger replied.

Copland returned to The United States, where he commenced work on the symphony, completing it within the deadline. Nadia Boulanger played it with the New York Philharmonic Orchestra and the Boston Symphony Orchestra. "That was really my debut as a composer of serious music in my own country," Copland recalls.

A high school art teacher took a special interest in Cabbage Patch producer Xavier Roberts. "I never could take but one year of art in high school, but I had a teacher that really liked me, and she let me kinda independently do art in study hall. If I saw something I wanted to pursue, she would give me instructions."

Teachers do not figure prominently in all the high-achiever accounts, however. Architect Hugh Stubbins, who taught architecture at Harvard University for thirteen years and headed its architecture program for a year, believes that it is impossible to teach a person to be an artist or a designer. "You either have the ability inherent in you, or you don't. The only thing a teacher can do is to create a climate in which you can develop and grow."

Erskine Caldwell, who, like Stubbins, attributes to teachers only a modest role in his career, does mention fondly a professor at the University of Virginia: "This teacher inspired me to be myself," Caldwell recalls. "That's what I was looking for. I cannot describe his influence other than the fact that it made me be myself."

## Discoverers

"Talent is common. It's everywhere, but it usually gets wasted," the celebrated writer and folk philosopher Eric Hoffer told me. One reason talent gets wasted is that it often is not discovered. That has always been true, although some societies are better than others about screening for talent and providing resources for the nurturing of talented individuals.

One reason people get discovered in our society is that there are people who, for a living, *look*. We call them agents, casting directors, editors, coaches. Like so many other jobs that need to get done, we as Americans let the profit motive help us deal with this one.

"I used to think editors and readers were out to *reject* manuscripts," says Jesse Hill Ford, author of *The Liberation of Lord Byron Jones*. "But they have to *find* manuscripts. They literally have to publish or perish. One way for a reader at a publishing house to make it to editor is to find an author." They live in hope that they will find another Hemingway or Wolfe or Krantz in the next batch of manuscripts.

Every agent hopes that a Clark Gable or a Marilyn Monroe will show up at an audition. Every coach hopes that another Joe Namath or Don Meredith or Herschel Walker will try out for the team.

Being discovered has been the theme of romantic stories, from Joseph in Pharaoh's court and Cinderella at the ball to today's stories about an obscure individual being discovered at a large casting session (known affectionately in the trade as a "cattle call"). Our biography shelves are filled with accounts of people being "accidentally" discovered.

The motivation for discovering talent often is not limited to the desire for economic gain. Chet Atkins, who was an RCA division vice president during Nashville's most prosperous years, discovered and produced some of the nation's best-known artists. Admittedly, those discoveries helped make Atkins successful at his job, but they also have brought him immense personal satisfaction: "I want to be remembered for helping a lot of artists become stars," Chet Atkins says. "People like Jerry Reed, Jim Reeves, Dolly Parton, Charlie Pride—that I signed up for RCA records."

The individuals who discovered tennis champion Arthur Ashe were not agents; nor were they motivated by financial gain. One was a student by the name of Ron Charity, who had seen Ashe play at a local public park. Charity introduced Ashe to R. W. Johnson, a local physician who had long been a patron of promising black tennis players.

"I have had several lucky breaks," Arthur Ashe recalls. "One was being discovered by Dr. R. W. Johnson at age ten. He thought he saw some talent, and also, when I was eighteen, the tennis coach at UCLA [J. D. Morgan]—sight unseen—thought my record was good enough to warrant a phone call to ask if I would like to attend UCLA."

Ashe more than justified Charity's evaluation, Johnson's support, and Morgan's phone call. While at UCLA, Ashe was named to the Davis Cup team, won the NCAA singles and doubles titles in 1965, was an All-American from 1963 to 1965, and paced UCLA to the national championship before going on to a brilliant career as a professional.

A businessman in Vancouver by the name of Norm Burley discovered Loretta Lynn and became her first promoter. In 1960, Burley happened to see the then unknown singer win an amateur contest on *The Buck Owens*

*Show* on a Tacoma, Washington, television station. Convinced Loretta Lynn had talent, Burley formed a recording company to help her get started. He signed her to a contract, but promised that he would never stand in her way—if she ever had an opportunity for a better one. Later, Burley did just that, releasing Lynn from her contract.

Sometimes the discoverer remains in the background. Thirty-year-old Billy Graham had a very narrow constituency when he pitched his "canvas cathedral" in Los Angeles for a city-wide campaign in 1949. It was his first campaign in a major city. Graham was a gifted orator, but he was not a national figure, not by any stretch of the imagination.

Somehow Graham attracted the attention of the publishing magnate William Randolph Hearst, who dispatched a two-sentence telegram to his lieutenant telling him to "Puff Graham." The motivation for Hearst's decision may never be fully known. Perhaps Hearst saw a feature story that would sell newspapers. Or he may have done it to please his middle-aged maid. According to one account, the maid who worked for the bed-ridden Hearst in his California mansion had heard Graham in Chicago and told her wealthy and powerful boss about the young preacher.

Whatever the reason, the results were instantaneous and gratifying to Graham. The evening after the telegram arrived, Graham found his tent swarming with reporters and photographers. The next day, Graham's meeting was proclaimed by headlines in the Los Angeles *Examiner* and *Herald Express*. The story was carried in the other Hearst newspapers around the nation and by the Associated Press as well. The campaign was extended from three weeks to eight, and the tent was enlarged so that it could accommodate nine thousand nightly. When Graham folded his tent on November 20, he had spoken before audiences totaling more than three hundred fifty thousand, and the young evangelist had become a national celebrity. (Pollock 1985:45, 48)

One of Jack Lemmon's early discoverers remained in the background. Literally.

Lemmon was on the verge of quitting show business when he had the opportunity to try out for a major part in a play with the British actor, Roddy McDowall. One of the main actors in the play became ill just two days before opening. The story was cast in an English boy's school, and the producer was flying boys in from New York and from Boston—anyone they could think of who could do an English accent. The mother of Roddy McDowall, who was fifteen or sixteen years old at the time, was helping screen the auditions from the front row of the balcony. Lemmon remembers waiting backstage while the boys in front of him were reading for the stage manager. No sooner would they begin to read than a voice would ring out from the balcony: "The boy is not British." And whack, off they went. One after another.

"Wouldn't you know, I'd be the last one," Lemmon recalls. "And not only that, as far as I could see, I was the only American." Lemmon had resigned himself to rejection, and looked on the audition as a way of gaining a bit more experience: "Out I go, and the sweat is flying, and the stage manager gives me the cue, and he looked at me and smiled. He knew I was scared to death and that I had no chance of getting this part. I said a line, and waited to hear 'The boy's not British.' But there was a silence, and I said some more lines, and waited. And I got through the entire speech. And then, so help me God, I hear: 'Thank God for a British boy.' Now, you want to tell me that luck is not involved or that there isn't a higher power somewhere? I never needed anything more in my life than that shot in the arm."

## Mentors

Many talented individuals do not have good contacts or they are not aggressive enough to push themselves into the spotlight. Hence the need for mentors who will make strategic introductions for them and give them gentle nudges and sometimes sharp kicks. Mentors usually have a long-term relationship with their protégés, seeing to it that they develop properly, meet significant people, avoid career hazards, obtain opportunities to display their talents, and not grow disheartened when setbacks come.

Nadia Boulanger introduced Aaron Copland to Serge Koussevitsky in Paris, thus performing the role of mentor as well as teacher. That single contact paid off handsomely for Copland. The performance of Copland's symphony in Boston was the beginning of a long and productive connection with Koussevitsky. "I knew in advance that whatever I would write for orchestra, he would play with his Boston Symphony Orchestra. And you can't imagine what a stimulus that is. Most composers—poor devils—write their music and *hope* somebody will play it."

Roberto Goizueta readily credits two men for his ascent to the top of the Coca-Cola hierarchy. One was Paul Austin, Goizueta's predecessor, who brought Goizueta to the corporate headquarters from the Caribbean and subsequently asked Goizueta to put the corporate engineering program together. Goizueta also caught the attention of Robert Woodruff, the legendary patriarch of the company. In 1974, Goizueta's office was moved to the same floor as Woodruff's. Goizueta began to be among the four or five guests who would lunch with Woodruff. A close friendship developed. Toward the end of Woodruff's life, Goizueta would go by his mentor's house once or twice a week and talk about business.

On one of those visits, Woodruff told Goizueta, "I'm pleased with what is happening at the company, now that you're the boss."

"I'm not the boss," Goizueta replied.

"You're the chairman, aren't you?"

"Yes."

"If the chairman isn't the boss, who is?"

"The man who chooses the chairman," Goizueta replied.

Arthur Ashe believes that having a mentor is critical for tennis players. "On a scale of one to ten, I'd give that an eleven," he says. "In my field, you start off very young, and the younger you are, the less likely you are to be able to fend for yourself. So you need a mentor when you're young."

Cartoonist Dan Barry believes having a mentor is important in the field of cartooning. "Coming out of art school, you are totally unprepared for professional work. All you've learned are the rudiments—all you've learned is the vocabulary. You have to learn how to speak and what to say with it. And then there is the hard, hard machinery of what the business is like and how work is produced, and how you go about not only doing it, but getting it and dealing with the people you work with." Barry says it was the same person who put him onto the idea of doing comic strips in the first place—George Mandel—who later would come up to Barry's studio and watch him work and offer advice and steer him with comments and criticisms of Barry's first efforts.

Hank Aaron feels the same way about mentors. "No matter who you are, everything is not going to be smooth, you know. You're going to have times when you're going to wish that you had somebody to talk to—somebody to get you through some of those trying times."

Norman Vincent Peale found such a person when Peale was a ministerial student at Boston University in the 1920s. He was foreman in an industrial plant in Providence, Rhode Island, and a member of a church Peale served on weekends. "I went to him one day in great discouragement," Peale recalls, "spending the time telling him what I couldn't do, what I couldn't handle. Finally he said, 'Listen, son, and never forget it. Never build a case against yourself.' That man's name was Robert Rowbottom; he helped me realize that I was building a case against myself. . . . People have asked me at times how I developed the idea of the power of positive thinking. Well, that was one building stone."

Rowbottom continued to serve as Peale's mentor and confidant for years—over fifty years, in fact. "I never let go of him," Peale told me in his eighty-eighth year. "I conducted his funeral. I went up to Rhode Island and saw his body to the cemetery."

However, not all high achievers have a mentor. *Cosmopolitan* editor Helen Gurley Brown says, "I just worked it out as I went along." But Brown says she's been helped by some people who gave her a break. "They let me write advertising copy when I was a secretary. That was a real breakthrough, because in those days, you didn't let your secretary do anything except be a secretary. There were no women copywriters." Her boss never told her to write copy or inspected it afterward. He simply permitted Brown to do it. "I haven't had much teaching," Brown says. "It's all been pretty much self-taught, but it took a long time. If you do it that way, it takes longer."

Justice Sandra Day O'Connor says there were few women she could emulate in the legal profession or the judiciary when she began her career. "In most instances, I was the first in a particular area," she says. However, in the early days of O'Connor's career there was an Arizona judge, named Lorna Lockwood, who proved helpful and encouraging to the young lawyer.

Admiral Thomas Moorer plays down the importance of the mentor in the military. In fact, Moorer says he didn't have a mentor or a discoverer. The critical factor in promotions in the military, Moorer says, are the performance reports that junior officers get every six months.

Asked if those who catch somebody's eye higher up are more likely to get promotions than those who don't, Moorer replied: "You may get assignments more rapidly that are prestigious, but I don't think that an individual can get you promoted in the service. An individual can get you assignments, and he can talk you up, but he really can't directly promote you."

Of course, not all mentor-protégé relationships turn out well. History is full of accounts of relationships that started out well but turned sour. Perhaps the best-known recent instance is the highly publicized hostility between Lee Iacocca and Henry Ford II. "Henry really thought of me as his protégé, and he treated me that way," is the way Iacocca describes his early days at Ford Motor Company. But the Ford-Iacocca friendship gradually withered, as millions of Americans now know, and the protégé was fired, after being with the company over three decades.

When Robert Shaw eventually struck out on his own with his own chorus, his mentor Fred Waring felt betrayed. "As he grew older, he had counted on my taking over his organization. . . . He felt I was stabbing him in the back. . . . The only thing I could tell him was 'I've been here for seven years, and I haven't done a piece of music on this show that caused me to cry.' What I missed was music that had an intellectual quality and an emotional and spiritual quality."

Until Robert Shaw's choruses came on the scene, Fred Waring's Pennsylvanians was the prime sophisticated instrument in the United States, even though it was in entertainment only. "Now there was one that was equally sophisticated in the field," recalls Shaw. "One that found itself on the proper page of the *New York Times*."

The relationship was never fully repaired. And many years passed before the two became friendly again; or, as Shaw says, "before it worked itself around."

Bitterness and pain are always the risks in any close, personal relationship—especially mentor-protégé relationships. Mentors often want to remain the mentor, even after their protégés have developed strengths and reputations of their own. They find it difficult to stand on the sidelines, watching someone younger break old records, and be gracious about it. And protégés develop needs to try out their wings and assert their independence. They get tired of calling somebody boss after they have become the chairman. Eventually most protégés want others to know that they did something on their own. The relationship of mentor and protégé, like that of parent and adolescent child, is often filled with frustrations and jealousy.

## Colleagues

The secret of success in science involves being able to distinguish between good and bad ideas. Francis Crick believes that having good colleagues makes it less likely that you'll pursue bad ideas. "The way to make a discovery is to get rid of false ideas or false assumptions," Crick says. "With two or more people, that's easier to do. If there's one of you, you take things for granted. If there are two of you, the chances are one will query the false idea. When a close collaborator produces an idea, you try to destroy it. If it's any good, it will survive."

To be effective, colleagues must not only be capable, they must be candid, as well. "You can't be too deferential to one another, or it won't work," Crick says. You can be polite, but not *too* polite. Crick believes that the need to save face has hindered the development of *basic* science in Japan: "It's very difficult for the Japanese to operate properly in science, because they're too polite to senior people. I heard a Japanese-American scientist make the astonishing remark that he revered his professor in Japan so much that he would not deliberately step on the man's shadow."

Crick admits that when he and Watson were working on DNA, they made "terrible" conceptual mistakes. Asked how that affects him, Crick replied: "It depends whether you've published it, which in our case we hadn't. I'm personally very resilient. You soon learn that nine out of ten of your ideas—although they seem terribly attractive—turn out to be wrong."

"That many?" I asked.

"Certainly," replied Crick. "That's the difference between the professional and the amateur. The amateur has one idea and gets so carried away, he thinks it must be right and sticks to it. But the professional has ideas all the time, so he knows he's going to have to abandon them—sometimes with reluctance. You shouldn't abandon them too early, though. It's a nice judgment as to when you should say, 'Too bad,' and throw it away."

Linus Pauling told me of an incident that occurred back in the 1930s. One of his doctoral students had asked him how he went about getting good ideas. And Pauling replied: "You have a lot of ideas and throw away the bad ones."

Later, when I told Francis Crick about Pauling's reply, Crick chuckled: "Pauling publishes *all* his ideas, and leaves it to us to spot the bad ones."

When Crick received the Nobel Prize for his work on DNA, he said: "The soul of collaboration is perfect candor, rudeness if need be. A good scientist values criticism almost higher than friendship: no, in science, criticism is the height and measure of friendship." (Judson 1979:146)

The wisdom of that observation is borne out by the experience of Rosalind Franklin, an excellent researcher who was working on the structure of DNA at the same time that Crick and Watson and Linus Pauling were struggling with the problem. Franklin was well ahead of Crick and Watson early in the race. But she was not the one who made the great discovery. Why? Because Rosalind Franklin did not have a good collaborator—not the kind Crick described. Horace Freeland Judson, in his splendid book *The Eighth Day of Creation*, writes: "It is evident from her notebooks that she needed one." (1979:147)

Not everyone can take criticism, even when it is constructive and sound. "I don't critique other people's novels anymore," Emily Ellison, a fine novelist, recently told me. Ellison admits that she feels unhappy about making this decision. "I haven't paid my debt yet to the people who read my early work." But her experience at offering suggestions and criticism to aspiring writers who have come to her for advice has not been pleasant. "People want to hear praise, but few can bear to hear criticism," Ellison has concluded.

**Competitors**

Whether one decides to write a book, open a business, draw a picture, do research, or compose a symphony, someone else is probably already doing it, and perhaps doing it very well. It would be difficult to think of a field where there are no competitors. Sometimes the competition is impersonal, sometimes face-to-face; sometimes friendly, sometimes ugly and ruthless.

Competition can be very intense in some fields. "I have been on several selection boards for admiral," former chairman of the joint chiefs of staff Thomas Moorer told me, "and we have examined as many as four thousand records for thirty-six vacancies—and many of those people, perhaps half of them, were very good indeed."

Demo tapes are produced every year by aspiring musicians, who press them into the hands of producers and stars at concerts, hoping for an audition or an encouraging phone call or letter. Emmylou Harris says she gets at least one tape that way at most concerts, and she says she listens to all of them, because there was a time when she was doing the same thing.

The struggle to be recognized, to outdistance rivals, to be accepted as one of the best can be tiring and traumatic. But the effect often is to raise standards and improve quality. "People are usually no better than they have to be," says Dan Barry. "Twenty, thirty years ago, whenever new illustrators came to the *Saturday Evening Post*, they showed them the work of Norman Rockwell, and asked them to learn to do as well."

Stanley Marcus is convinced that competition is a tremendous stimulant toward productivity and improved service in any customer-oriented business. He uses a horse-racing metaphor to describe a strong competitor's effect: "A course always needs a pacesetter to stretch out and do his best. If you don't have a pacesetter, you get fat and lazy."

\* \* \*

High achievers are people who learn to use the environment for their own purposes. They are not passive. They do not simply float on the social currents. When the competition is keen, they strive to enlarge their abilities and outdistance their rivals. If the resources are present, they utilize them. If not, they move on to a place where they can do what they want to do.

They "use" significant others—parents, teachers,

mentors, colleagues, competitors—not necessarily in exploitative ways, but certainly in ways that further their own goals. They hear the messages they need to hear. Erskine Caldwell hears a college professor say, "Be yourself," and he decides to do just that. Mary Kay hears her mother say, "You can do it," and makes that word of encouragement a guiding value in her life. John D. Rockefeller's father plays tough games, loaning his son money at high interest rates, calling in the loans capriciously, but the son plays along with the father, pays him what he asks, and thereby develops character and financial shrewdness.

In the next two chapters, I will discuss in greater detail what happens when alert, talented, and decisive individuals meet up with opportunity.

# 8

# Perceiving Opportunities

*Having eyes do you not see, and having ears do you not hear?*

—Jesus (Mark 8:18)

*The greatest thing a human soul*
*Ever does in this world*
*Is to see something*
*And tell what he saw*
*In a plain way.*

*Hundreds of people can talk*
*For one who can think,*
*But thousands can think*
*For one who can see*

*To see clearly*
*Is poetry,*
*Prophecy,*
*And religion*
*All in one.*

—John Ruskin

*I try to look for opportunities.*

—J.B. Fuqua

*Everybody gets a lucky break. It's recognizing it that's important.*

—Bob Hoskins

## Seeing Clearly

We all tend to see and hear only those messages that are congruent with our interests and attitudes. We avoid exposing ourselves to information with which we disagree—a process called *selective exposure*. If exposed to such information, we will either reinterpret it so that it fits nicely with our interests and attitudes—a process called *selective perception*—or we will forget it, a process called *selective retention*.

I encountered numerous instances of high achievers doing just that—hearing what they wanted to hear, seeing what they wanted to see, using their environment selectively. For instance, when I asked Erskine Caldwell if he was a good listener, he replied: "I wouldn't say I'm a great listener, no. I'm usually thinking something else when I hear somebody say something. " Mrs. Caldwell quickly added: "He listens to whatever he wants to listen to."

Other high achievers admit having the same attitude. Mark H. McCormack says he listens attentively only when he's interested in the talker or in the subject matter being talked about. Stanley Marcus puts it this way: "If it's interesting, I'm a good listener; and if it's mush, I'm a bad listener. I have no ability to listen to small talk." Rather than being a hindrance, however, this behavior often turns out to be a focusing technique often developed into an art by high achievers.

Many of these individuals seem to have the ability to pick up signals a lot of other people miss. The achiever sees a pattern that spells opportunity, or perhaps danger. This sensitivity to cues may come from reading, conversation, research, or long involvement in the field. This is not to say that the vision of high achievers is always 20/20. Far from it. But high achievers *want* to have clear vision in the areas that interest them.

Oscar de la Renta says that he keeps his creative forces at work "by keeping my eyes open."

Asked a similar question, Charles Schulz replies: "I've remained alive to everything that's going on about me. I don't think that I've settled into being a boring person who lives only in the past. I think that I'm aware of new things that are happening in the world—new twists to our language and new activities among young people."

Schulz says he's always thinking about funny things. "I'm always getting ideas by listening to talk shows on the radio, or by just driving around in the car, or if I'm at home conversing with people—little things are always coming to mind."

Scientists often find the germ of an innovation by searching through the research literature to see what others have discovered. Francis Crick told me that he "immersed" himself in the subject he was studying, sometimes for months.

"I have flashes of inspiration," says Nobel Laureate Linus Pauling. "*They often come after long periods of preparation. . . .* What happens is that I suddenly have an idea that I recognize as the solution to the problem or the answer to the question." (Italics mine)

Nikola Tesla claimed to have conceived of the AC induction motor in a flash of insight while reciting Goethe: "Oh, that spiritual wings soaring so easily/ Had companions to lift me bodily from earth."

Tesla later said: "In an instant, I saw it all." What Tesla saw was a motor without brushes and commutator, turned by a rotating magnetic field. (Florman 1986:24)

Jonas Salk, the famous scientist whose research helped conquer polio, has developed a mental game that helps him see and hear what he otherwise might miss. Salk imagines that he is the object that he is studying. If it is a virus, he tries to think how he would behave if he were a virus attacking an immune system. Then, mentally playing on the other side of the net, Salk tries to reconstruct what he would do if he were the immune system that was being attacked. In his book *Anatomy of Reality: Merging of Intuition and Reason*, Salk calls this mental exercise the "inverted perspective."

Salk says that he uses this exercise to design his laboratory experiments. In effect, Salk participates in a dialogue with nature, posing his questions in the form of experiments. (1985:7)

In 1839, during an experiment, Charles Goodyear accidentally dropped some rubber mixed with sulfur on a hot stove. The rubber did not melt as expected. Instead, the heat seemed to "cure" the rubber and produce a substance that remained tough and hard in heat and cold. Using this chance event as a lead, Goodyear did further experiments until he developed a process that is known today as vulcanization.

Goodyear was looking for something to happen. His was an informed mind. It is to people like this that happy accidents happen. (In the next chapter, we will see how high achievers court such accidents.) And when the accident occurred, Goodyear recognized its significance.

## Seeing In Nontraditional Ways

When B. F. Skinner was an eighth-grade student, researching material for a term paper on Francis Bacon, he discovered an idea that has stuck with him throughout his career: Study nature, not books. That accidental encounter with Bacon's idea has reinforced Skinner's determination to stick by his own insights and observations, and not to be unduly swayed by conventional ideas. "I am poorly read in psychology," Skinner writes. "That is one of the ways in which I neglect my contemporaries."(1983:406, 407)

While one must know enough to be able to know what to look for, Skinner is correct in believing that it is deadly to be bound by old ideas. Perhaps for this reason, high achievers are often newcomers to the field. But even when they are old hands, they do not feel duty-bound to follow old rules slavishly.

"The cat that comes up with something different is the cat that doesn't know any better," is the way Chet Atkins explains his distinctive guitar style. "I taught this country how to play finger-style guitar. A lot of people don't know it, especially the younger people, but I influenced an awful lot of people. When I came along, everybody made fun of me—the way I played."

Atkins grew up in poverty on a farm in eastern Tennessee, where there were no trained musicians for miles around. Atkins developed his style by listening to phonograph records: "I heard a record of some black guy—"Stump" was his name, I think—on a big Edison record. And then I heard Merle Travis, and I thought he was playing with three fingers and a thumb. I learned years later that he plays with one finger and a thumb. But I began playing with three fingers and a thumb, and it turned out to be classical style. That's the way classical guitar players play, but I had never heard classical guitar playing. It's things that I stumbled on over fifteen or twenty years—out of ignorance—that made me different."

## Seeing Uses for Old Ideas

Xavier Roberts has made untold millions of dollars with his Cabbage Patch Kids—when many toymakers with more experience, more money, and better traininig have not. Why? Clearly, Xavier Roberts has done something different from other toymakers. But what? And how?

The Cabbage Patch phenomenon, like any innovation, began with ideas that already existed. "It was in art class that I got introduced to soft sculpture," Roberts says. "I would like to think that nobody else was doing it. But the Germans were doing fabric sculpture in the seventeenth century. Maybe earlier. They would paint the fabric and make it hard. I learned about soft sculpture from books and from other artists around 1975."

However, it is what is done with the existing idea that separates the ordinary from the exceptional. And therein lies the difference between Xavier Roberts and the thousands and thousands of struggling artists and craftsmen who set up tiny booths and peddle their creations for a pittance. Xavier Roberts decided not to make a doll. He decided to create a person: "When I learned about the soft-sculpture technique, I set out to make a baby. A real baby. We scaled the arms to a real baby— the belly button, the birth certificate—the whole concept. I think we actually captured a baby."

At the time, Xavier Roberts did not consider himself a dollmaker. He was a maverick—someone who considered himself an artist in a field dominated by craftsmen. "I hadn't ever made a doll before, and neither had Debbie [Morehead, his girlfriend]," Xavier says. "We thought of ourselves as serious artists."

Until his idea caught on, Roberts lived in a trailer on a backroad in the mountains. He paid the bills by teaching crafts courses, managing a gift shop at a state park, and selling his productions at art shows and flea markets.

"At first I called my trailer the 'crackerbox palace,' but when the babies came along, it became 'Babyland General Hospital.' It was just a fictitious name at that time. Home delivery—that's the way the first babies got into the world." Xavier and Debbie began doing art shows, selling quilts and paintings and a few of the "babies." The babies attracted most of the attention, however, because everyone had already seen his other items many times before. "They had never seen me take up the babies and treat 'em real nice," he explains. "When I was making the babies back in the beginning, in 1977–1978, I kind of puppeted 'em . . . to make 'em do funny things, like fly. Sometimes when people were standing around, I made 'em exercise. They'd just bust out laughing."

He remembers that the look of his creations would take customers by surprise. "People would come up and say, 'That's the ugliest thing I ever saw.' In order to keep his babies from hearing such indelicate remarks, the next generation of babies was born without ears. (His own line of soft-sculpture babies still have no ears. The Coleco Cabbage Patch Kids do.)

Gradually he elaborated upon the basic concept, giving the dolls birth certificates. Unfortunately, Xavier didn't have the money to get the birth certificates printed. So, whenever he made a sale, he wrote down the customer's name and address. Within a year, he had enough money to print up a batch of certificates, and sent out the birth certificate, along with a second embellishment—a birthday card.

Roberts decided not to "sell" his original babies. "I was at this art show," he recalls, "and people kept coming up asking, 'How much are they? How much are they?' like a broken record. That's when I came up with the response, 'You can't buy em; they're not for sale. They're up for adoption.' "

He subsequently bought a building that had once housed a hospital in his hometown. That building—renamed Babyland General Hospital, after the name of his trailer—today produces several million dollars of revenues each year on its own.

Inside the hospital, his salespeople, who are dressed in nurses' uniforms, walk down the corridors cuddling the little creatures. There is a viewing window where the preemies are being fed. Down the hall from the nursing station is *Dr.* Roberts's office. As I stand outside the door, several nurses are talking in hushed tones to visitors who seem to have questions about child care.

One of the nurses, with a baby in each arm, approaches. "Surely there's one here you want to adopt," she says, and asks me to hold one. I indulge her. I look down into its flat, chubby, not-very-pretty face. I feel its soft body pressing close to mine. It's about the same size my own daughter once was. "I can tell you'd make a good father," she tells me. And I begin to understand the magic that prompts so many people to spend the dollars that have made Xavier Roberts very rich.

Many high achievers do not regard themselves as particularly creative, and do not seek innovation simply for the sake of innovation. They let other people do the innovating, and try to profit from their experiences. They look for ways to apply others' ideas, often old ones, to their own situation.

In the case of law, judges and lawyers have traditionally done that, seeking guidance from past decisions. Sandra Day O'Connor states: "I don't rank myself high on creativity. I wish I were higher, but I think my training and my nature has been to try to subjectively analyze something and apply precedents and construct a sound response and a solution." O'Connor sees a need for creativity—discovering an idea that bridges the gap between what's been decided before and what's needed in a new situation. But, she says, that's not one of her greatest strengths.

"I daresay I haven't had an original idea in fifteen years," says Waffle House President Joseph W. Rogers, Jr. "Every one of them has been stolen from something that I read." He says his company is on the *trailing* edge of technology.

Rogers gives himself a high score on curiosity, but a low score on originality. Because Rogers believes that very few concepts are truly original, he says he doesn't have to make any original decisions: "I've always thought that everything I needed to do to run this business appropriately, somebody else had already figured out sometime throughout history, and had applied that decision or that principle successfully. I felt that if I read everything I could get my hands on about business— biographies of corporate leaders, any sort of material even close to business history—I would find in them all the wisdom I needed to make appropriate decisions."

## Seeing Uses for New Ideas

Arthur Murray has been able to exploit several mass-media developments during his career. The start of that career can be traced to an episode that occurred in 1912, when the nation's dance craze was reaching full tide. Murray, a shy student intent on a career as an architect, attended a dance contest held in a huge exhibition hall in New York City. As he watched from the sidelines, a girl brashly grabbed him by the arm and escorted him to the dance floor. Murray knew enough about dancing to make a presentable partner, and the two of them proceeded to win a silver loving cup. Later, grasping the trophy in one hand, she gave Murray a hug. "Thanks, fella," she smiled. "I know a place on Sixth Avenue where I can hock this. So long!" And she was gone.

Murray had no trophy to show for his efforts, but he did feel emboldened to ask the manager if he could have a job as an instructor. The manager reluctantly agreed, and Arthur Murray's career as dance teacher began.

Murray steadily gained confidence and skill and began to teach wealthy pupils in New York, Asheville, North Carolina, and Atlanta. It gradually dawned on him, however, that he would never be rich simply teaching dance lessons. He would have to do something dramatic. As he cast about for an idea, he came up with the idea of organizing a radio dance. That was in 1920, before there were even commercial radio stations.

Arthur Murray says the idea occurred to him when a friend in Atlanta told him that he could talk to friends in Augusta, Georgia (about 170 miles away), without wires. "I didn't believe it," Murray recalled, "so I went to his room and he talked with his friends. And then it occurred to me that it would make a good publicity story if I could have a dance by wireless—send music from the Georgia Tech campus to the roof of the Capital City Club in downtown Atlanta, about a mile away."

Murray recruited several members from the military engineering department and the Army Signal Corps to assist in the technical aspects of the broadcast. The forty-member school band agreed to help with the experiment, and, the day of the dance, a group of his students and friends gathered on the roof of the Capital City Club, all wearing headsets. The idea worked. A crowd assembled in the street below and camera crews and reporters gathered to cover one of the important human interest stories of 1920.

The radio dance brought Arthur Murray momentary publicity, but not much money. Shortly afterward, however, he conceived of an idea that, after one false start, did bring him money. Murray learned of a primitive moving-picture machine, known as a Kinetescope, which he felt could be used to teach dancing. He bought a thousand of the little contraptions and placed ads in magazines and newspapers that read: "Learn to Dance at Home."

Orders began pouring in, and Murray began to expand the operation. Then, to Murray's dismay, customers began to return the Kinetescopes—almost all of them. The flimsy little machines had fallen apart in the mail. When Murray tried to get his money back, he discovered that the company had gone bankrupt.

Now Murray needed to pay the bills he had incurred during his first venture into the world of mass marketing. Returning from the bank, the despondent dancer fretted about what to do next. That evening, the thought occurred to him that he did not need motion pictures to teach dance steps. He could do it with diagrams. As a college student, he had learned mechanical drawing, so he sat up all night drawing pictures of dance steps.

The next morning, Arthur Murray showed the drawings to a friend, who was impressed enough to endorse a bank loan, and Arthur Murray was in business once again. His product—a dance-instruction book with diagrams—was a great success, and Arthur Murray was on his way. (Murray:1960:40,41,54–57)

The appearance of new technologies always spells opportunities for those who recognize their potential and prepare themselves to exploit them. J. B. Fuqua made his first fortune putting to use his hobby as a ham radio operator. As a teenager, Fuqua had read a twenty-five-cent book on radios. When he graduated from high school, he passed the test for a commercial radio operator's license and joined the merchant marine as a radio officer. Following his discharge, he took a job as chief engineer of radio station WCSC in Charleston, South Carolina. Not long afterward, he realized he could be running a station of his own, so he conducted a survey to determine which town could best support a second radio station. Augusta, Georgia, looked like a promising market. So, at age twenty-one, Fuqua and several investors launched WGAC, and Fuqua became the youngest station manager in the nation.

In 1953, Fuqua was able to implement a new technology he had first seen years earlier at the New York World's Fair—television. Fuqua launched Augusta's first television station at a time when owning a television station was like owning your own mint. Twenty-seven years later Fuqua sold the station for $25 million. It still bears his initials—WJBF. "I try to do the same kind of thinking in other businesses that I did with that television station," Fuqua says.

Today, if you own a home computer, you can communicate with other computers by means of a device called a modem. The modem enables computers to talk to one another over telephone lines. However, modems were not generally available for home computers until the late 1970s, when Dennis C. Hayes designed one on his dining-room table. At that time, the large mainframe computers had the capacity to communicate with each other, but small computers were still little isolated islands of information.

Hayes, who was an engineer for National Data Corporation, saw a mass-market opportunity. With one associate, he founded the company that today produces thousands of modems annually. When Hayes resigned from his job, his boss told him he would be lucky to sell a dozen units.

"I didn't invent the modem," Hayes once told me. "I simply was involved in packaging a technology so that the public could use it." Hayes says his perspective was developed while he was a physics major, working his way through college as a co-op student at AT & T Long Lines. "During my co-op job, I met several people who helped me get an insight into the impact technology can have on large populations of people and large geographic areas. These individuals were interested in more than demographics and geographical range and technical requirements. They influenced how I see things," Hayes's ability to see what could be done with what was then a technical device with a limited market has led to a major industry and to his own financial success.

Three important events occurred in the world of communications in the mid-1970s. A communications satellite—SATCOM I—was launched, Home Box Office began operation, and the FCC changed one of its regulations, thereby permitting any independent television station to be brought in by cable systems.

Ted Turner saw a big opportunity for his small, independent UHS television station in this combination of events. Why not use the communications satellite to create a new television network? Turner wondered. The cable network would bypass local stations and link up with countless viewers by means of cable systems, not just in the Southeast, but in the entire nation.

Turner ordered his people to get busy on the project. In December 1976, WTCG-TV went on satellite as "The SuperStation." Within days, cable systems all across the country were signing on for the station's package of Braves baseball, Hawks basketball, old movies, live wrestling, documentaries, and public-affairs specials. That makeshift arrangement has since grown into two networks —the "SuperStation" and Cable News Network— that reach 38.5 million and 33.1 million subscriber households, respectively.

## Seeing Opportunities in Unexpected Events

Bob Hoskins, a 1987 Oscar nominee for best actor, began his acting career through an unexpected invitation. Hoskins was having a drink at a pub in a small amateur theater at Kings Cross in London, waiting for a friend who had volunteered to paint scenery for the theater, when a man appeared and announced: "You're next."

"Next for what?" inquired Hoskins, who had had enough to drink by this time to try most anything, he now admits.

"Next to read for the part," replied the man, thinking Hoskins had come for an audition. Hoskins went upstairs into the theater, read the script that was handed to him, and was given the lead in the play.

"When I started showing up at rehearsals," Hoskins told me, "I was at home; I was at peace; I was content. I didn't know what I was doing, but I was really happy."

An agent attended the first night's performance, and afterward said to Hoskins: "You must take this up professionally."

"You get me a job, and I will," replied Hoskins. "She did, and I've never been out of work since." That first appearance on stage occurred in the winter of 1967. Hoskins became a professional in January of 1968.

That episode illustrates several of the factors involved in achievement that have been presented thus far. An event occurs, the individual sees it as an opportunity and makes a decision, something clicks, and the individual knows it is the right thing to do. And there is often someone to help, in this case an agent who recognized Hoskins's latent ability. Then follows steady growth—a series of steps, some small, some large. Hoskins describes the process thus: "Everybody gets a little chance here, a little chance there. They are part of the jigsaw. Something happens here and you use it; something happens there and you use it. Everybody gets a lucky break. It's recognizing them that's important. If you're going in the direction you want to be, you're in the right place already. The right place is you."

Practically everyone has heard of the Neiman-Marcus "his-and-her" gifts that are advertised each holiday season in the Christmas catalog. That tradition began with phone calls that Ed Murrow and Walter Cronkite made to Stanley Marcus, inquiring if any unusual purchases had been made by wealthy customers. It occurred to Marcus that if the store deliberately created some exotic gifts and put them in a catalogue, the store would receive an immense amount of free publicity.

Marcus and his colleagues came up with the idea: his-and-her airplanes. Photos of two Beechcraft planes were duly printed in the Christmas catalog as a double spread. That year, when the phone calls came, Marcus reported that the store had sold a "her" plane. The story was carried on television and in hundreds of newspapers.

The idea worked so well that the next year the store marketed his-and-her miniature submarines. "The ultimate in togetherness," the store hyped. Over the years, that marketing and public-relations coup netted the store millions of dollars in free advertising.

*   *   *

Horace Freeland Judson, who has interviewed virtually all the major figures in the history of molecular biology, including Linus Pauling and Francis Crick, writes: "In the process of discovery, there comes a unique moment: where great confusion reigned, the shape of the answer springs out—or at least the form of the question. The insight occurs *in the prepared mind* of some one person." (Italics mine, 1979:25,26)

That ability to perceive patterns in the real world and to be able to recognize their significance is valuable in many fields, not just in the world of science. Dennis Hayes has been successful with his modems because he introduced a well-engineered product at a time when hundreds of thousands of people were buying PCs—people who wanted to do more with their new purchases than just play games and prepare reports. Hayes knew this. He probably would never have quit his job, risked his savings, and gone into debt had he not realized what was happening in the world of computers.

Mary Kay's product is cosmetics—a commodity that has one of the highest profit margins in retailing. She markets that product in a society whose members are getting older—and are trying not to show it. She knows her market, understands the people in the niche she targets, and has shrewdly utilized the party-in-the-home concept to exploit it.

These kinds of risks are *calculated* risks—where the accuracy of the calculation rests upon knowledge, upon being able to see clearly. "What appears to be a reckless gamble may be just that," says Herbert A. Simon, "but it's more likely that it was much less of a gamble than it appears, just because the risk-taker understood the situation better than competitors did." (1987:17).

The ability to see can be developed and strengthened. Jonas Salk has carried on his dialogue with nature for so long that he calls it "second nature." Oscar de la Renta and Charles Schulz, as we have seen, keep their eyes and ears open, thereby encountering stimuli for creative contributions of their own.

This ability to see opportunities has connections to achievement factors considered earlier in the book:

*Competence*—High achievers "know" what to look for. They have patterns stored in memory that alert them to opportunities.

*Persistence*—High achievers transform an alert attitude into a habit. They keep on looking, listening.

*Wishes and needs*—High achievers want to see, want to hear. They thirst for knowledge.

*Focus*—High achievers know that not everything they observe is equally important. They focus in on situations and data that are relevant to their wishes, needs, and goals.

*Situational factors*—High achievers are alert to what is happening around them.

In the next chapter, we look at ways high achievers not only see but seize opportunities.

# 9

# *Seizing Opportunities*

*There is a tide in the affairs of men,*
*Which, taken at the flood, leads on to fortune;*
*Omitted, all the voyage of their life*
*Is bound in shallows and in miseries . . .*
*And we must take the current when it serves,*
*Or lose our ventures.*

—Shakespeare, *Julius Caesar*

*I seem to have been very blessed with an unusual number of very*
*fortunate incidents that have helped me along the way. And then the*
*rest had to be up to me.*

—Julie Andrews

*I've got to think that more important than the big break is the*
*readiness—being ready for the opportunity when it occurs. If it*
*occurs.*

—Kris Kristofferson

*. . .You have to be willing to move on opportunity. Courage is so*
*important.*

—J. B. Fuqua

S eeing well is essential to seizing well. As we will see, high achievers, to an extraordinary degree, do both. They see and seize. Of the several elements that go into such activity, one of the most important is decisiveness.

## Decisiveness

Our nation has never had a more decisive public figure than Harry Truman. In 1950, Truman authorized the Army to take over the nation's railroads in order to avert a general strike, returning them to their owners two years later. That same year, Truman ordered the nation's armed forces into Korea without a formal declaration of war. In 1951, he fired General Douglas MacArthur, one of the most popular and brilliant generals in American history. In 1952, he ordered a seizure of the nation's steel mills to avert a strike, an act that was ruled illegal by the U.S. Supreme Court two months later. And, in the most momentous decision of all, he authorized the raids on Hiroshima and Nagasaki, thereby ushering the world into the atomic age.

Each of these decisions involved a weighing of costs. In the case of the dropping of the atomic bomb, for instance, Truman engaged in the gruesome task of calculating how many lives would be lost if the United States invaded Japan. He already had some sense of the cost of invasion from the Normandy experience and the resistance of the Japanese on Iwo Jima and other Pacific islands. That cost would be too great, he concluded, and chose instead to unleash the terrifying power of a nuclear bomb, whose power and after effects could only be surmised.

Whether or not we agree with Truman's choices, there can be no denying his decisiveness. Once he had made a decision, he would not permit himself to look back. Truman regarded feelings of regret as the most enfeebling of all emotions.

I never met Harry Truman, but I have interviewed former secretary of state Dean Rusk, who worked closely with Truman during his career at the State Department. "We were very fortunate in Harry Truman," says Dean Rusk. "Harry Truman was a genius at making decisions. When he saw a complicated problem, with all the factors in it, it was as though he were looking at a heap of jumbled-up jackstraws. He would listen to all the briefing and think about it. Then he would decide which one of those jackstraws was the crucial one, from his point of view, and he would pull that one out of that complicated pile and make his decision, go home and go to sleep and never look back. He was a genius for that necessary oversimplification at the moment of decision. The alternative of that is paralysis."

The paralysis of which Dean Rusk spoke is a problem in many fields, not just government. Businesspeople encounter it regularly in various disguises. Sometimes, indecision comes under the cloak of fact-finding.

Thomas R. Williams, former chairman of First Wachovia Corporation, one of America's largest bank holding companies, recently told me about a failing of many of the young people he has seen in the banking and finance business: "A lot of young people with wonderful educations and wonderful minds come to us who have a terribly difficult time knowing when to stop researching and when to start building." Williams admonishes: "While fact-finding is important, you reach a point where you must stop fact-finding and start working toward a solution."

Coca-Cola chief Roberto Goizueta dislikes the term *management science*. It is not an exact science, he says. The tendency to quantify everything occurs primarily because it makes managers feel more comfortable when they make a tough decision. When he was chief technical officer of the company, Goizueta was fond of quoting Yukio Mashima: "To know and not to act is yet to know." He would explain, "All the research work in this world will produce only information. If we don't act on that information, we haven't done much."

In his essay "Self-Reliance," Ralph Waldo Emerson writes, "A man should learn to detect and watch that gleam of light which flashes across his mind from within." Emerson warned against rejecting our own ideas, refusing to act upon them simply because they are our own: "Tomorrow a stranger will say with masterly good sense precisely what we have thought and felt all the time, and we shall be forced to take with shame our own opinion from another." (1947:384)

Decisiveness involves working through all the perceived options and reaching a conclusion about the one to go with—often not waiting for a perfect solution or even a clear-cut choice between good and evil. A great many people are not able to do this. They see danger lurking behind every decision, a price to be paid for every choice, an unseemly mixture of good and evil. And, as Dean Rusk says, they are paralyzed, they do nothing.

Sandra Day O'Connor says she learned an important lesson when she first came on the bench as a trial judge, and, O'Connor says, she has never changed. What is that lesson? She does the very best she can when a case comes before her, weighing evidence and doing the necessary research. But when she has made her decision, she—like Harry Truman—does not look back: "I put all the time and effort at the front end in trying to decide it correctly in the first place and do the best I can. Then I don't look back and have regrets and agonize over it. I may have to live with the consequences, but I'm going to live with them without regrets, because I did the best I could with it at the time."

# Agility

Opportunities often have an evanescent quality about them. The stock market builds and builds, finally reaching a crest, and then hesitating for a moment plunges downward, triggering sell orders at each level in its descent. A coveted painting appears at auction, the bidding takes place, the gavel falls, and it disappears from sight perhaps for generations. Opportunities are usually for the moment, and as they pass by, there is often only a brief moment to grab them. The greater the opportunity, the less time we usually have. "We must take the current when it serves," Shakespeare admonished, "or lose our ventures."

Some of the individuals I interviewed are today recognized as high achievers because they seized opportunities, grasping them just as they appeared to be slipping away, seemingly out of reach. If you ask them, they can tell you when and how it happened.

In 1940, Ronald Reagan's film career was proceeding smoothly, although not spectacularly. He had already played the lead in *Love is on the Air*. That film had been made on the B lot of Warner Brothers in 1937. In those days, the major film studios made two kinds of pictures, the big A blockbuster pictures that would lure the people in, and the pictures from the B lot that ran for about an hour instead of the normal ninety minutes. Pictures from the B lot usually received second billing on double-feature programs.

Getting to play the lead in one's first film , even if it was on the B lot, was a tremendous break for any young actor. "I since have learned that I was very lucky," Reagan told me, "because many times people were put under contract, and then months would go by without their ever setting foot in front of a camera."

After making *Love is on the Air*," the studio continued to use Reagan on the B lot, and, from time to time, would send him over to the A lot to play parts in the major pictures. One of those pictures made on the A lot proved to be a major turning point in Reagan's life.

That idea for that picture seems to have originated with Reagan. Shortly after arriving at Warner Brothers, he had begun to talk about the need to make a major film about football. "Everybody that comes to Hollywood, I guess, begins to get ideas about what would make a good picture," Reagan told me. He knew whose lives should be portrayed in the film: Knute Rockne, the legendary Notre Dame coach, and his great ballplayer George Gipp.

"I'd been a sports announcer, and I'd told the story of George Gipp on the air on a sports program one day," Reagan explained. "I knew the lines without having to memorize them. I thought a story of Rockne would make a great picture. But being new, I talked all around the lot, asking people's advice on this Rockne thing."

One day, not long afterward, Reagan picked up a copy of *Variety* and came upon an announcement that Warner Brothers, his studio, was going to make a movie on Rockne. Reagan was thunderstruck. "I went to my mentor, who was head of the B unit, and said, 'Hey, they're going to make Rockne.' And he said, 'You talk too much. You've been talking all over the lot. It was a good idea, and they're going to make it.' I said, 'Look, I didn't want anything for it. I just wanted to play George Gipp.'

"'Well,' he said, 'You'd better get on the ball, because they've already tested about six guys already.' "

Reagan hurried over to the producer's office and requested a screen test. However, the producer was not overly impressed by the young, eager actor who stood before him—at least, not for this particular part.

It was excruciatingly painful for Reagan to see the role he had dreamed about slipping away from him. Then, in a flash, he realized what he had to do: "I suddenly remembered, standing there in clothes like this [business suit], that football players don't look like football players, usually, unless they're in uniform. And I also remembered that a cameraman told me that in Hollywood all they knew was what they saw on film.

"So I said, 'Excuse me.' I went home—drove home as fast as I could and dug down in the trunk. And I came up with my college football pictures—I had played on the line for eight years in high school and college."

Reagan rushed back to the studio, hurried into the office, and triumphantly placed the photographs on the desk in front of the producer. Looking at them intently, the producer finally asked: "Can I keep these for a little bit?" Reagan, of course, agreed.

Returning to his home, Reagan had only a few minutes to wait before the phone rang. "Be in the studio at eight o'clock in the morning," the voice on the other end said. "You're testing for Gipp."

The next morning, Pat O'Brien, who was already cast to play Rockne, played the test with Reagan. "I got the part," Reagan told me, "and *it was the one that opened the door*."

*Current Biography* agrees with Reagan's assessment: "Reagan's performance in the role [of Gipp], climaxed by a stirring deathbed scene, established his reputation as a serious actor." (1967:338)

The Reagan story illustrates several of the factors that are important in high achievement. The young actor had a *mentor*—the head of the B lot—who gave him timely advice and criticism [which Reagan took]. Reagan even used the word *mentor* to describe him. Reagan had conceived of a good idea, actually an innovative idea—a serious sports movie—that he believed in enough to try to promote it. And Reagan by this time was not a rookie anymore. He was well along the road toward *competence*. He had played important roles in several films, and—in the words of Herbert A. Simon—Reagan had stored in memory a number of "patterns," or "chunks of information." Finally, and perhaps most important, Reagan moved *decisively* and *quickly* on the *perceived opportunity*.

Frank Borman told me of an experience he had with a fellow astronaut, William A. Anders, as they were circling the moon: "Bill's responsibility was to take pictures for future landing sites. He was the scientific member of the crew, and he was a very confident, dedicated person who was doing just that. When we went around about the sixth or seventh time, I looked up and saw the earth in the background and I said, 'Bill, let me have the camera. I want to take a picture of that beautiful earthrise." And he said, 'I'm sorry. We don't have enough film.'

Patricia Roberts Harris

Art Buchwald

Robert Shaw

Janet Leigh

*(The Coca-Cola Company)*

Roberto C. Goizueta

*(photo by Gary Meek)*

Sandra Day O'Connor

Melvin Kranzberg

Arthur Ashe, Jr.

*(ProServ, Inc.)*

Mark H. McCormack

Gloria Steinem

Joyce Dannon Miller

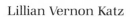

Lillian Vernon Katz

Linus Pauling

Harry T. Hoffman

Hugh A. Stubbins, Jr.

Erskine Caldwell

*Above:* Tennessee Williams during TV interview with Griessman

Jacques Cousteau

Robert C. Byrd

Norman Vincent Peale

B. F. Skinner

Paul "Bear" Bryant

Jack Lemmon

*(Salem Productions)*

Edith W. Martin

Ronald and Nancy Reagan

Loretta Lynn

*Left:* Frank Borman (right), Commander of Apollo 8, with Lunar Module Pilot William A. Anders (center), and Command Module Pilot James A. Lovell, Jr.

Frank Borman

*(NASA)*

Frank Borman's famous photograph of the Earth as seen from lunar orbit *(NASA)*

"We must have had eight thousand frames on board," Borman explained "So I asked Bill, 'Please let me have the camera, because you will have all the scientific shots, but I'll have the one that will make the cover of *Life*.'" (The photograph Borman took did make the cover of *Life*, and was used on a postage stamp, as well.)

"Was that an *order* you gave?" I asked Borman.

"That was finally an order. Bill surrendered the camera only reluctantly," Borman replied.

A forty-eight year-old gem broker by the name of Roy Whetstine saw an opportunity most people only dream of at a gem and mineral show in Tucson in 1986. He was looking for some pretty stones to take home to his two sons when, on the last day of the event, Whetstine discovered a stone he knew he had to buy for himself. It was lying in a Tupperware dish, along with the other minerals and gems the amateurs and dealers were selling. A hand lettered sign read: AGATES, YOUR CHOICE $15.

"How much do you want for this one?" Whetstine asked, pointing to an orange-size rock. "Fifteen dollars," came the reply. "You're kidding. You want fifteen dollars for this?" Whetstine asked. The owner replied, "O.K. Tell you what, I'll let you have it for ten dollars. It's not as pretty as the others."

Whetstine left the show with one of the world's largest star sapphires in his possession. L. A. Ward, who personally appraised the stone and verified the story for me, stated that the 1,905-carat sapphire Whetstine bought for ten dollars, when cut, will have a value of over $2 million. Ward stated that he has never known of such a discovery in all his experience as a gemologist. So the likelihood of finding another massive star sapphire in a Tupperware dish is remote. But it illustrates the principle that having a trained eye enables one to seize opportunities when they appear.

*A footnote to the story*: Whetstine and the man who

sold him the stone, whose name Whetstine will not disclose, are rumored to have become partners in a venture to locate more star sapphires where the big one came from.

## Courage, Chutzpah, Risks, and Gambles

"I've got more courage than most people," J. B. Fuqua said in answer to the question, "What separates you from your peers?"

Fuqua continued: "I had courage as a kid. I've always had more courage. I'll take risks, and have taken risks that other people are afraid of. When I was a kid, I'd pick up a snake—other kids wouldn't do that. I'd walk in the dark. And the same thing is true in my business experience. I'll just figure out what my risks are. I'll take a big risk. I try to look for opportunities. Let me add to that, you have to be willing to move on opportunity. Courage is so important."

Asked if he was brave, Kris Kristofferson asked rhetorically, "What's brave, you know? I think bravery is overcoming your fears, so I think I'm brave. . . . I went to jump school and ranger school and I was a boxer and did different things where you really put your life on the line. You risk it all. I played football for years after I was told that I could die from another blow on the head. . . . But I don't know whether that's bravery."

Later in the interview, when I asked Kristofferson to choose two or three qualities that helped put him where he is today, he replied: "A creative imagination and a compassion for my fellows and strength of spirit, which doesn't come from me but from God. I think I have a strong spirit. I allow my spirit to be strong."

Coach Bobby Cremins has a motto on a plaque on his desk: "Courage Is The Quality That Guarantees All the Rest." "I lose my confidence sometimes," Cremins admits, "and that's where the courage comes in."

Jack Lemmon told me that he was "scared to death" of some of the roles in which he triumphed. *Days of Wine and Roses* frightened him because, prior to that film, his successes in Hollywood had been comedies. "I knew it was a great part, but I was afraid I might not be able to play it well enough," he admitted. Lemmon says he's been aware of this aspect of his personality ever since. Now he tries to harness the fear and make it work for him. "I work on fear," he says. "I have not overcome a certain insecurity, and God help me, I hope I never lose it, or I'll be lousy."

We have already seen that Senate Majority Leader Robert C. Byrd is not easily deterred from his goals. Byrd's quest for a law degree is but one of many successful ventures in his remarkable career. In politics, not once but many times, better-financed, better-educated, better-known candidates took him on but lost.

Few would have predicted such accomplishments, looking only at his origins—for they are humble indeed. His name is actually Cornelius Calvin Sale, Jr. When his mother died soon after his birth, he was reared by his mother's sister and her husband, Titus Dalton Byrd, who gave him his present name. The Byrds took the young child with them to West Virginia, where Dalton Byrd worked in the coal mines, and where Robert subsequently began his education in a two-room schoolhouse. He was an excellent student, read avidly, and in high school learned to play the violin.

There was no money for college, so the young man worked at a number of jobs—as a gas station attendant in Helen, West Virginia, and as a produce salesman in the company store in Stotesbury. He studied a meat cutter's manual at night and after apprenticing in several small stores, became head butcher in a supermarket. He took a welding course, and worked as a welder in the shipyards of Baltimore and Tampa during World War II.

At war's end, he returned to his native state, where he ran for and won a seat in the state legislature. Byrd subsequently decided to run for the United States Congress, and it is during this race that the following episode—told in his own words—took place:

"There were three persons running for governor that year, and each had his own supporters. The supporters for one candidate would have their rallies in one community and the supporters for another candidate would have their rallies in another community.

"I was running for Congress and wanted to go to all the rallies so that I could have contacts and support in every group. However, I wasn't very welcome at the meetings of one of the supporting groups for a particular candidate, because they thought that I was supported by another voting bloc.

"I wanted to attend all the meetings, so I went over to this particular meeting. The person in charge was a lawyer. I said to him, 'I'm Robert Byrd, and I'd like to be introduced tonight. I'm a candidate for Congress.'

"Well, he merely introduced me at the end, thinking that I would get up and sit down. He introduced me as a candidate for Congress, who is a butcher and a fiddle player. Well, there's nothing really wrong with being a butcher or a fiddle player. But he didn't intend for those terms to be complimentary.

"I got up, and said, 'This gentleman here is a lawyer. He has introduced me as a butcher and a fiddle player. What's wrong with being a butcher? Shakespeare worked in his father's meat shop. What's wrong with being a fiddle player? Thomas Jefferson was the town fiddler. This gentlemen is a lawyer. I'm not. I grew up in a home of coal miners. If it's the last thing I ever do, I'm going to get a law degree, if for no other reason to show people like this that a coal miner's son can do it, too.'

"So, I won the crowd. They were coal miners, too, sitting there in the audience. The fellow had forgotten that. They weren't all lawyers.

"The next Saturday, there was another meeting, and the same person was the master of ceremonies. I was there with my violin, and I had with me an individual who played banjo and one who played guitar. When the main speaker finished his talk, the attorney said, 'Now, we're going to have the benediction.'

"Well, an old fellow in the back raised up and said, 'We want to hear Byrd.' The master of ceremonies said, 'You can hear Byrd some other time. We're going to have the benediction,' But he did say, 'After the benediction, you go over into the next room and get your refreshments.'

"After the benediction, they all went over to the other room, and while they did, I sent out for the violin, got my two musicians together, tuned up, started playing, and people began coming back with their refreshments.

"I said, 'Now, ladies and gentlemen, don't block the door, just come on in and sit down. So they all came back in . Well, that was *my* meeting now. So I said, 'Ladies and gentlemen, I've traveled seventy-five miles here to-night. I'm a candidate for Congress. It's important that you hear your candidates for Congress. I'm entitled to be heard.'

"If it hadn't been for that violin, I wouldn't have had an opportunity to speak to that group that night. When I finished, I daresay I had a hundred percent—really a hundred percent—of that group with me."

Byrd won that election and every one since then.

We do not have an English word that adequately describes the way Robert Byrd used his violin in the West

Virginia election, or the decision Ronald Reagan made to show his football photo when confronted by a skeptical producer. One word that comes close is a Yiddish one—*chutzpah*.

*Chutzpah*'s closest English equivalents are audacity, nerve, daring, guts, brazenness. The English talk about a person being *cheeky*, but that is not quite the same thing. And, people will sometimes say an individual who does something audacious "has a lot of brass."

Is chutzpah absolutely essential for success? Many high achievers say no. Helen Gurley Brown says she has *drive*, but not *chutzpah*. Don't depend on razzle-dazzle, she recommends, and don't push people to give you a break too soon. "Study. Inch along," Brown urges. "Pile up 'goodness' until you are *so* good everybody can see it and not ignore you. . . . if not in this present job, then in the next one."

"I'm not a pushy type," says Erskine Caldwell. "I'm determined—sure—and tenacious. But not pushy."

When I asked the tennis champion Arthur Ashe to rank himself on bravery and nerve, *chutzpah*, he replied: "I think bravery and nerve are almost part of the American fiber, as far as athletics are concerned. I think it's important. I'd give it a rank of nine, in my case. But you can take it too far. That's always a danger in athletics—especially in individual sports—to try something that you know is a high-risk venture, and sometimes it backfires."

Arthur Murray, who has tried a number of innovative projects during his career, told me: "I'm a logical person. I don't think I really take on things that are impossible." Stanley Marcus says he is a risk-taker but not a gambler. Asked to explain the difference, Marcus replies that ten to one is a gambler's odds. Six to five is a risk-taker's odds.

There are instances when high achievement requires gambles, not risks—sometimes great gambles,
where the odds against success are far greater than ten
to one: risks of fortune, risks of social displeasure, risks
of reputations, even risks of death. I am struck by how
often I have encountered instances of people who have
been willing to take them: people who have quit cushy
jobs, people who packed up their belongings and moved
out of their old offices, mortgaged their homes, borrowed
money from their friends and relatives, and sometimes
failed and began again.

Dennis C. Hayes left a good job and, with borrowed
money, built the modem that has become the standard
of the PC modem industry.

Mary Kay put "every penny from her retirement"
into her untried business plan, whose main product was
a cosmetics formula that had never made much money.

Lillian Vernon Katz borrowed two thousand dollars
from her father in 1951 (the equivalent of twenty thousand dollars today) and started a mail-order company
with a five-hundred-dollar advertisement in *Seventeen*
magazine.

Mario Andretti and Richard Petty literally risk their
lives every race.

Here is what they say:

Jacques Cousteau: "Everything I've earned has been
thrown into our organization."

Kris Kristofferson: "I've been a gambler. When I decided that I was going to be a songwriter at the age of
twenty-nine, I had a comfortable career ahead of me in
the Army. It's scary to leave something safe and secure."

Jack Lemmon: "I think we worry about failure too
much. I don't think that failure very often can hurt anybody. It's fear of failure that will absolutely destroy you.
Then you walk down the middle of the street. . . . You're

never going to go down the little side streets that you look down and say, 'Jeez, that looks interesting. But I don't know that. I know this street. I'll stay right here and just walk on this straight line.'

"You'll never take chances. If you did, you might find out that you can play the hell out of parts that nobody ever dreamed you could play."

# The Use of Luck

We have already seen that many high achievers see luck, or chance or fortuituous events, as playing a key role in any success that may occur. But they do not take a passive view of luck or chance, as the following comments make clear.

Harry Hoffman believes in looking for luck, asking for it: "When you want something, you've got to ask for it. A lot of people hear about a new job or a new opportunity, but very few people come in and say, 'I really want to do that.'" Hoffman says he did that with his former boss, and he likes it whenever someone does it to him: "I think most CEOs respond favorably to people who really want to take on additional challenges and responsibilities. It's so rare to find somebody who says. 'I'll pack up my family and go—wherever you want to send me, send, if it's additional responsibility and a chance to do something else.'"

Erskine Caldwell says that luck was one of the three main qualities that had served him well in his career (the others being talent and persistence). "But you have to create luck," Caldwell says. "It doesn't come to you." Caldwell links luck to the recognition of opportunity. "You have to recognize an opportunity, and when you see this opportunity, you foster it in some way. You use it as a springboard to something better or something higher."

Caldwell says luck is not inevitable and it is something very illusive. "When you get a glimmer of it, when you see a suggestion of good luck, then you have to enlarge upon it, you have to foster it, you have to encourage that good luck to bring the kind of result you anticipate."

Luck involves courting fortunate accidents, John Huston believes. "One must recognize a fortunate accident, and utilize it," the celebrated director told me. Asked to explain, Huston says that when he is directing he doesn't tell actors specifically what to do, but gives them scope, hoping that something unexpectedly satisfying will occur. He tells of the experience he had directing his father, Walter, who played the gold miner in *The Treasure of Sierra Madre*, a performance that won an Academy Award. The script called for the old miner to do an impromptu dance when he discovered gold.

"I told him to dance," Huston recalls, "but I had no idea that . . . I thought he would do a few prancing steps, but it was more than that—much more than that. It is magic, the way he did it. It's one of the best moments I've ever seen on film."

Sometimes an individual will be thrust into a role, with only the potential for playing it. A father will hand over the business to an inexperienced son. A youngster with unpolished skill will win a talent contest. An agent will get a contract for a novice with latent abilities. It is good fortune, but the fortunate individual is not up to playing the role well. Not yet.

"I have had the good fortune to be in the right place at the right time when good fortune has passed my way," says Julie Andrews. "What has often puzzled me is that there are an awful lot of people that are very disciplined and have had very fine training, probably even better than mine, and they haven't had the good fortune."

Julie Andrews looks back on a career filled with good fortune. She was a child prodigy, with an unusual singing voice—a powerful voice with a range of four octaves. When she was only twelve years old, she performed a difficult aria at a huge, sophisticated London revue. When she finished, this very innocent-looking twelve-year-old received such an ovation that it literally stopped the show.

Six years later, she was asked to appear on Broadway in an American production of an English show *The Boy Friend*, and was enormously successful. That led to *My Fair Lady*. But now the parts were becoming much more difficult. More was needed than native talent, no matter how prodigious.

Andrews says that *My Fair Lady* was one of the most difficult things she's ever done. During rehearsals, in fact, she began to falter. Moss Hart, the director, saw that she was floundering and dismissed the company for forty-eight hours. She remembers that experience well: "I really knew that I might be sent back to London because I simply couldn't cut it. It's fairly cutthroat on Broadway —you either do it or you don't, and you get sent home rather fast. . . . I knew it was going to be painful and that my inferiority complex was going to keep rising up and getting in the way."

But, she says, during that forty-eight hour period, the two of them slugged it out. "You couldn't say it was exactly taking a chance. I didn't have an alternative. But I was certainly committing to an enormous period of trying."

It worked. "I pulled through and found the character I was looking for. But I have to say it was absolutely thanks to Moss Hart's guidance. From then on, I think, I learned my craft." The Broadway production ran for three and a half years.

Andrews sees that experience as typical of her entire career: getting selected for a highly visible role, having an early success, and then working hard at learning how to do it well.

"I've always been successful—as I was in the opening in London as a child—and then had to learn what it was that made me successful. The same applied to Broadway. I was overnight successful, and then I learned my craft. Happily, the long run of *The Boy Friend* and the very long run of *My Fair Lady* taught me an enormous amount."

Isaac Asimov says he has had a lot of lucky breaks, but he has been able to take advantage of them. "The lucky break doesn't help you much if you don't take advantage of it. I honestly think that everybody has lucky breaks now and then, so that only what counts is taking advantage."

Tennis champion Arthur Ashe believes being in the right place is important, but not crucial. "If you are talented and if you have correct training and teaching, it's going to show, no matter what the breaks are. I mean, you get on the court and you're going to win. That's all there is to it."

J. B. Fuqua says he's had some lucky breaks, but adds: "I think you make a lot of your luck. You position yourself for things to happen that are favorable. If you want to feel the warmth of the sun, you stand where the sun shines, not on the north side in the shade."

Kristofferson says, "I've got to think that more important than the big break is the readiness—being ready for the opportunity when it occurs. If it occurs."

\*    \*    \*

High achievers are very aware of their environment, and what is more important, they use the environment purposefully. They are able to see what is happening. They process what they see in creative ways, and they exploit their environment for their own purposes.

From among the opportunities that high achievers perceive, they focus in on one or a few that suit their abilities and purposes. They think about the field they have chosen and look for opportunities in it. Then, when the breaks come, they are ready to act—and do.

# 10

# *Summing Up*

*I'm one of those lucky people who gets paid very well to do what I love doing.*

—Mario Andretti

*Don't stop the world. I don't want to get off, because I can't possibly have it as well as I've had it in this one.*

—Malcolm Forbes

*I've been enchanted. . . . I feel like a very lucky man.*

—Aaron Copland

*Life's choices always have a price. . . .*

—Lillian Vernon Katz

This chapter is about the prices high achievers pay to attain their goals, and about the way high achievers perceive those prices. As you'll see, high achievers do not seem to stop very often to take inventory. They spend little time casting backward glances, but when they do, for the most part, they reckon that the costs are not very great when measured against the benefits.

But that is getting ahead of the story. Let's look at the transactions these individuals have made—what they gave, what they received, and how they feel about the results.

## The Price of Achievement

"Life's choices always have a price," stated Lillian Vernon Katz. "Everybody pays them, whether in business or at home. Terrible prices sometimes." Those prices include friendships foregone, children neglected, and marriages that have unraveled under career pressures. Senator William Proxmire, for example, once referred to his first marriage as a "casualty of politics." It seems that high achievement often involves attending to tasks that do not make for domestic tranquility or stability.

Osborn Elliott concluded his 1959 study of heads of major companies thus: "Because his life is dominated by business, he spends lamentably little time with his family. Sociologists might be well advised to study the long-term effects on a nation when families in the leadership group are fatherless so much of the time." (1959:224)

Fatherless and *mother*less. Highly successful women in business and entertainment face the same kinds of demands that men do.

In the case of Loretta Lynn, her marriage is still intact, but the problems associated with long absences from her family have caused emotional stress and illness. Nine days after giving birth to twins, Lynn gave a concert. Four weeks later, she left for a six-week tour in Germany. "I cried every day I was gone," she remembers. "I never got to see them cut their first tooth, take their first step. I missed out on seeing them grow up. . . . That's when I really got sick," the Grammy winner said, recalling this difficult time in her life, "I looked around, and the kids were growing up, getting married and leaving."

Erskine Caldwell says that the price he has paid is that he has not been able to form close friendships: "I have not achieved any great friends because there's always something to impede, so I have avoided great friendships and great feelings of comradeship with other people. I suppose that might account for the fact that I have been married four times."

They may not see enough of their families and friends, but high-profile achievers often see too much of fans. Fans typically interrupt their conversations, meals, and work, even sneak into their residences and steal their belongings for souvenirs. Nor do they consider such behavior rude. It is the celebrity who is rude if he or she remonstrates. The fans are simply exercising their inalienable rights. Celebrities owe something to the public, so the thinking goes, and they should not have bothered to become famous if they object to this sort of thing. To a certain extent, many celebrities do, in fact, acknowledge a debt to their fans and extend themselves considerably trying to please them.

Some celebrities, however, may actually protest a bit too much. Complaining about fans and lack of privacy can be a none too subtle way of advertising their importance. One sometimes has the feeling that they would be dismayed if no one ever pestered them. But even the most accommodating of high achievers often find the process tiring.

Charles Schulz is a kindly man who makes a real effort to respond to the many requests that come to him. But some of the requests—and demands—tax his time and his temper. He described his trials by ordeal, when buses filled with camera-armed tourists pull up in front of his headquarters at One Snoopy Lane. "I can't drop everything and go out and autograph things for fifty people and pose for pictures. I mean, I've done it, but after a while, there becomes no meaning to the thing. . . . Unfortunately, you sometimes end up being mean to the good people. The presumptuous people are the ones that seem to get away with it." That's a common complaint.

And there is even physical danger.

Some of the high-achievers' stories are downright scary. Hank Aaron's is one of them. One would think that the happiest days of his life were those just before he broke Babe Ruth's home-run record. Not true. Those days were a nightmare. "The only place I could get any rest was at the ballpark," Aaron recalled. "The Braves fixed up a little room in the back." At hotels, he had to register under an assumed name. He no longer could eat a meal in a restaurant. "The commissioner put a bodyguard in every city I went," Aaron recalls, "and the Braves gave me one that was with me at all times."

Aaron received death threats. Scores of them. He couldn't open his mail. For a year and a half, it was screened by the FBI and the Postal Service. There were threats made on his children. "One night," Aaron remembers, "two FBI agents came in and said, 'We have reports that your daughter is supposed to be kidnapped.'"

Some of the threats came from bigots. They didn't want to see a black man eclipse a white man's record. Some of the threats came from true believers who saw Aaron as an iconoclast—as someone who was trying to destroy their idol and legend, in this case Babe Ruth.

However, a high achiever need not be a superstar trying to break a record in order to be at risk. Merely being rich or powerful justifies a call to the local bodyguard agency.

Prior to my interview with David Rockefeller, his assistants gave the camera crew strict instructions not to film any footage of his office suite that might help potential kidnappers or terrorists learn the layout of the building. Nor could the cameramen take any close-up footage of photographs of his wife and children, lest they become the targets of a hostage or kidnapping attempt.

In order to protect themselves from criminals, psychotics, and from the simply inconsiderate, many high-profile achievers devise elaborate strategies to isolate themselves from the outside world. Typically, there are tiers of gatekeepers and managers and guards who screen phone calls and visitors, open mail, and decide where the individual can and cannot go.

In the movie *Nashville*, the lead character—a country singer by the name of Barbara Jean, who resembles Loretta Lynn—is shot by an assassin in a bizarre final scene. That movie, Loretta Lynn's road manager admitted, made him fear for the safety of his kindhearted, unpolitical charge: "I watched for suspicious-looking violin cases for months after the movie was released. That never happened, but a nut with an eight-inch knife almost got to her on the stage during a performance."

My interview with Loretta Lynn took place in a plush twenty-fourth-floor suite at Harrah's in Reno, where she was performing twice nightly. Phone calls and visitors were strictly monitored by her manager and the hotel staff. As I listened to her describe the routines of her existence, it occurred to me—though perhaps not to her—that she had become a prisoner of her stardom. She was well paid and loved, but confined. When she is on tour, Lynn spends the day sleeping or traveling long miles on her customized bus. Then, the only people she sees are band members, back-up singers, the crew, well-wishers who manage to crowd into her dressing room, and, during the concert, the first few rows of spectators, whom she can glimpse through the glare of the spotlights.

She said she would like to be able to go to rummage sales and flea markets and restaurants, but cannot for fear of being besieged by autograph seekers. "I never go out," she stated. "We would never get to the next show."

Businessman J. B. Fuqua has experienced a different kind of isolation from Loretta Lynn's. His is a more subtle isolation, but still deeply felt. "I'm personally very wealthy, and that costs you a price. It costs you friends—people who, when my wife and I were younger, felt on the same level with us. Now, they don't, and they feel uncomfortable because they can't have the same things we have."

Fuqua observed that some highly successful individuals compensate by "taking up with other rich folks." But Fuqua has not felt comfortable doing that. "This is a problem many people don't talk about, but it's a price you pay for being rich in this country," Fuqua said. "It narrows your area of friendships."

Fuqua's is the classic dilemma of the nouveau riche, which is, of course, what many high achievers are. Old money and new money, like oil and water, don't mix well. Fuqua's many millions easily qualify him for the upper class, but he has not acquired the attitudes, interests, or the generations-long friendships those of the old-monied class inherit. "You pay a price, and I don't know what the answer to it is," said the multimillionaire.

Fuqua named another cost of high achievement— this one brought about by his single-mindedness. "I don't have outside interests." He explained that he had focused very narrowly on his business in order to achieve his goals—a strategy that has paid off at the bank. "As I've gotten older, I see it's a mistake I've made."

Dan Barry stated that the requirements of producing "Flash Gordon" for over three decades have taken him out of the mainstream of everyday life. "You have to accept a great deal of isolation. The price has been a lack of freedom to do as much as I'd like to have done."

The price Senate Majority Leader Robert Byrd has paid involves the conflicting demands of his office. He is, first of all, a United States senator, trying to reconcile the claims of the nation with those of his own state and the competing interests within that state. As Senate majority leader, Byrd has the additional problem of trying to cope with the needs of other senators. "The pressures are very great on the majority leader," he confessed. "I often find myself frustrated and under great tension."

Byrd paused and slumped down in his chair. Evidently it had been another long day filled with those kinds of problems. "One sometimes wonders why he continues to want to serve under the pressures." Then the West Virginia senator told how he dealt with his frustrations: "Winston Churchill turned to painting, and

I have turned to the violin. It allows me to get away from the world that I live in here."

For many high achievers, the price they think about most is not stress or loss of privacy or danger, but the loss of time. In fact, that is the only price Malcolm Forbes mentioned: "Unfortunately, time is what people really don't appreciate enough until they begin to run out of it." And Dan Barry: "The greatest price is the time consumed."

But few of the high achievers speak of their costs in self-pitying tones. After all, they know all along that they have other options. Nobody put a gun to Loretta Lynn's had and said, "Sing." She could have canceled the road trips to stay at home with her children. Nobody demanded that Hank Aaron break Babe Ruth's home-run record. Aaron could have dropped out of the race, leaving the old record intact. J. B. Fuqua could retire and spend the rest of his life developing interests he never pursued during his early years. And Senate Majority Leader Byrd could turn his mantle over to more than one colleague who would not mind inheriting Byrd's worries. The Senate majority leader's post is, after all, an elective office.

But they do not. Hank Aaron shrugs: "Records are made to be broken." Dan Barry says, "If I name it as a price, it sounds begrudging, but it's a *knowing* price."

Sometimes great success produces such profound changes that the high achiever cannot easily accommodate them. The results are unease, unhappiness, and even guilt. So, high achievement not only involves learning to be competent in some specialty, but also entails learning to accept the rewards that success brings.

Art Buchwald's work has brought him international recognition and wealth. He makes a lot of money—more than the President, he says, and less than Barbara Walters. At least eighteen honorary doctorates have been conferred upon this high school dropout. In fact, I have never been able to get an exact count from Buchwald. He told me that he has lost count.

But Buchwald's success has involved a substantial psychological cost. "I'm slightly manic-depressive, which I think all people are who do humor," Buchwald stated. "Humor is a defense. It's hostility."

During his fifties, Buchwald spent two and a half years in analysis. "I became very suicidal," he told me. "I mean, it was that serious, and that's when I went for help. I couldn't explain it. I had everything I wanted— everybody *thought* I had it made—and yet there was something going on in me."

Buchwald believes a great many successful people go through such a conflict. Having achieved all their fantasies and all their goals, they then realize that they're not happy. Buchwald learned, while in analysis, why he reacted to success the way he did. He felt embarrassed about being able to have all the things he had dreamed of as a youngster—because he didn't think he deserved it.

"When I was a kid, everybody told me I was going to end up in a bad way," Buchwald recalled. His elders apparently did not think Buchwald was very funny. In their eyes, he was a "wise-ass," a "troublemaker." He disrupted classes and was a regular visitor at the principal's office. "Having been told at an early age that I would wind up no good, that apparently stayed with me somewhere, and then when it all turned out all right, I still had those voices—people from my childhood who were saying that you don't deserve this and you're going to get in trouble."

When Buchwald came out of analysis, he realized that the elders were wrong. He really did deserve the fruits of his labor. "I figure I have it coming to me," he stated, looking at me confidently over his cigar. "I can deal with it now. I have a good time."

# Taking Inventory

Is the game worth the candle? The whole notion of costs and benefits—of prices paid and gains derived—implies that some kind of conclusion can be reached about whether the effort is worthwhile. So, is it?

When the high achievers are asked that question, it is astonishing how uniformly they answer the question in the affirmative. Measured in absolute terms, the costs for some of these individuals have been staggering—long, long days of hard work, vacations foregone, early years of poverty, initial rejection and obscurity, broken marriages. But the relative costs—the price measured against the benefits—are so great, by their reckoning, that many high achievers hesitate to even call them costs.

"I have to say I really don't think I've paid a price," stated *Cosmopolitan* editor Helen Gurley Brown. Then she ticked off a list of *seeming* costs—sacrifices she had not minded making.

That she has had no children is not a sacrifice, Brown stated, because she never wanted children anyway. Not having spent a lot of time partying brings her no regrets because she doesn't party very well. Spending the night boogeying is "unthinkable" to her, because she would have to spend the next day in bed recovering. *That*, she said, would be a great loss.

Nor does Brown miss not being able to spend long hours simply socializing. "I'm very goal-oriented, so it's very hard for me to just sit around and schmooze, even for an hour. To sit and talk and drink a few beers and watch the world go by—I just can't do that. If that's a good thing to be able to do, OK, but I don't miss it." Brown surveyed her turf and summed it up. "I'm healthy. I do what I love doing. I'm married to a good man. I can't think what the price has been."

The only price Isaac Asimov could think of was his

work-oriented life-style—a life style that some people might think is abnormal: "I don't travel. I don't take vacations. I don't go out fishing or camping or dancing or partying, or anything of the sort. And I don't miss it."

Architect Hugh Stubbins stated it bluntly: "I don't know if I've paid any price at all. That's the first question you've asked that's sort of thrown me.... I've worked so much, and had long hours, and I didn't have enough time for children and family, but other than that, I can't think of anything."

U.S. Supreme Court Justice Sandra Day O'Connor: "I don't think I paid a high price. I worked hard, but I enjoy working hard. I've not had time for pure relaxation as some people call it, but I don't think I have a great need to just sit on a beach with my feet up and relax. That isn't what I like to do."

Malcolm Forbes: "I can't think of anything that I would consider a big price. I am not loaded with regrets." Forbes used the word "fortunate" and "lucky" to describe his condition, and spoke with pleasure about being in business with his children, whom he is openly fond of.

Kris Kristofferson struck the same note: "I have so few regrets.... I can't think of anything I've paid."

Kristofferson, you recall, gave up a secure career in the military and afterward lived for many months in a slum tenement in Nashville, where he worked as a janitor. Yet he summed it all up thus: "I mean, I feel so lucky to be where I am right now.... What regrets?"

Actress Janet Leigh, when asked what price she had paid, repeated the question, paused for a long moment, and answered: "What price have I paid? God, I thought I was being paid."

Asked if she considered herself a success, Emmylou Harris did not hesitate a moment: "Yes, but I would probably be singing even if I weren't successful at it.

Fortunately, I can do music that I love and make a living at it, and live fairly well, and I am incredibly lucky because of that."

Richard Petty described his career thus: "I've built everything I've got around racing. Don't tell my sponsors, but if I was working at a regular job, I'd drive a race car on weekends for nothing." The winningest racer in stock-car history explained that, unlike some people who work all week long in order to go hunting or fishing, he works all week long on his car and then races it on the weekend. "I can do it as a hobby. I can do it to kill time, and I can do it to make a living. What else could you ask for?"

Loretta Lynn may be a virtual prisoner in her hotel suite or on the bus, but she finds an emotional and almost spiritual release in what she does. From the earliest days of her career, she has found music to be an outlet for her feelings. "I could sing the things I would have liked to have said and never could say."

Gradually, over a period of several years, her singing has brought her another benefit. Through performing, Loretta Lynn has begun to realize that she is in control, not someone controlled. "I know when I walk out on that stage, I am in control at that time," the most famous coal miner's daughter in history told me. "I know then that I can do anything I put my mind to doing."

Charles Schulz says he puts up with the hassles of being a celebrity because he appreciates being able to do what he does for a living. "This is a good job, and I'm very grateful for all the things that have happened to me. I try to return this goodness in whatever way that I can, without it becoming intolerable. . . ."

"How long has it been a good job?"

"I've always enjoyed it. . . . It's what I wanted to do. I think it's as good a job as a person can have. It offers extreme satisfaction. It offers an outlet for every creative thought which I have, and it seems to bring people a certain amount of small happiness."

Not long before his death, I sat with Eric Hoffer in his plain one-room efficiency apartment, located in a high rise near the San Francisco harbor. Nothing about the place—absolutely nothing—hinted that one of the nation's most gifted men resided here. There were a few pieces of inexpensive furniture, a narrow bed, a stereo that his neighbor across the hall said he sometimes played "very loud," a tiny kitchen, a walk-in closet. That was it, except for a big window that looked down toward the waterfront where the self-taught longshoreman had spent so much of his life.

The burly man whose hour-long interview with Eric Severeid had jammed the CBS switchboard, and whose book *The True Believer* had sold untold millions of copies, was almost a shadow of his former self, so frail that talking quickly tired him.

Hoffer told me that his "girl" had asked him what he wanted written on his tombstone. "I told her to write, 'He received much more than he deserved.' I've always felt I owed much more than I have given."

Aaron Copland stated that he did not have the vaguest notion what he might have been, had he not been permitted to be a composer. When asked if he was content with his choice, the quiet, gentle man who gave us "Appalachian Spring" and "Fanfare for the Common Man" replied: "I've been *enchanted.* . . . I feel like a very lucky man."

What a remarkable word to sum up a career: *Enchanted.*

# Afterword

These individuals are not supermen or saints. Although many of them are known to be extraordinarily decent and considerate human beings, some had had emotional problems, other have been notably unsuccessful in their private lives, and several are noisy, brash, or inconsiderate.

However, in the shimmering light of success, even those characteristics sometimes take on the quality of strengths rather than weaknesses. Charles de Gaulle, in an admittedly self-serving statement, said: "Every man of action has a strong dose of egotism, pride, hardness and cunning. But all those things will be forgiven him, indeed, they will be regarded as high qualities, if he can make of them the means to achieve great ends." (Taylor 1982:58)

The high achievers—despite their weaknesses and limitations—do enough things right to gain recognition in their respective fields. They are authors who get published, racers who win races, architects whose buildings dominate our cities' skylines, actors who get awards, performers who draw crowds, businessmen who have built companies and fortunes, scientists whose discoveries have changed our world.

All of these remarkable accomplishments are well within human reach. What this human-ness means is that there are practical lessons here for any highly motivated, bright individual who is willing to work smart and hard.

Many of the factors that make for success are not career-specific. When one hears high achievers from many different fields giving almost word-for-word answers to the same questions, the conclusion seems obvious that these are general principles of high achievement. They are just as valid for an entrepreuner as for a scientist or a politician.

Here, in summary, are those principles—high achievement factors, I call them. The caveat is that these probably are not the only high achievement factors. Others need to be explored, like fear of failure—which was only touched on here—patriotism, sublimation, and racial or ethnic consciousness. But these are the ones that the high achievers I interviewed mentioned again and again.

## 1.  *High Achievers Discover Their Vocation and Their Specialty*

They find something they love doing, something at which they can become really proficient. Helen Gurley Brown calls these *specialties*. Writers speak of the experience as *finding your voice*.

What is striking is that many high achievers talk about their work the same way some people describe their hobbies or vocations. Here is a Linus Pauling saying that he received a Nobel Laureate for "having fun," Jacques Cousteau saying that he has spent his life "playing," and "Bear" Bryant saying "coaching is my hobby." We should not be surprised, then, that people who derive so much satisfaction from their work do it well—and never watch the clock to see how much time remains until quitting time.

## 2.  *High Achievers Develop a Competency*

There is no long-term success without developing one's interest, or specialty, into a real competence. In fact, competence is so crucial to high achievement that it can be considered not simply an achievement factor but the foundation upon which all high achievement is built. It is the one achievement factor that comes closest to being a necessary and sufficient cause—a *sine qua non*. There are any number of individuals who have great ideas, massive egos, and huge needs. They dream great dreams. But they never acquire a mastery of anything, and they are never known as high achievers.

If such a mastery of something is so essential, how is it best attained? Here is the advice high achievers give:

*Love what you do.* Competency begins with an attitude, the high achievers agree. Whenever someone loves their work, they do it well, Malcolm Forbes says. And unless someone does something well, they aren't going to be successful. It's as simple as that.

*Passion* is the word Oscar de la Renta uses. Joe Rogers uses the word *commitment*. But they are describing the same basic idea—that one must care deeply about one's work in order to be successful at it.

High achievers emphasize the importance of loving one's work—because that love enables one to do the irksome tasks that are inherent in any occupation. Some of the duties associated with even the happiest career are boring, stressful, or tiring. That cannot be said too strongly, the high achievers say. But love or passion or a feeling of commitment transform nitty-gritty work into competency. And competency is the down payment on success.

*Attain depth of knowledge and skill.* A minimum of ten years of diligent effort is required to become expert in any difficult field, Nobel Laureate Herbert A. Simon believes. A growing body of research indicates that there is no way to become world class until the requisite patterns are stored in memory. That takes years of diligent application.

*Work hard.* These individuals seem to have a boundless capacity for work. Typically, they enjoy what they are doing so much that they literally splurge their time and energy on their chosen tasks. They work long and hard, but they rarely expect pity for it. They enjoy doing what they do so much that they do not think of the heavy investment of time and effort as a price. Norman Vincent Peale names "restless energy" as one of the qualities that has enabled him to attain his goals. "I have worked hard, energetically, every day since I got out of the cradle," says the eighty-eight-year-old clergyman.

*Practice excellence.* Mel Kranzberg uses the phrase "the *habit* of excellence" to describe how he approaches his work. U.S. Supreme Court Justice Sandra Day O'-Connor says she tries to do the very best she can at whatever task she undertakes. "To do a hard job and do it well is satisfying."

### 3. High Achievers Value and Manage What Everybody Starts Out With: Time

They are aware that they live in a very time-conscious society and that they must learn to cope with its demands. Had these interviews been conducted during the Middle Ages, or even in third-world countries today, time-consciousness probably would not have ranked high on such a list. When I was a Fulbright professor in Pakistan several years ago, a successful businessman in that country stated: "Time has no value here."

But time has enormous value in twentieth-century America. There are literally tens of thousands of occupational situations where time is of the utmost importance. Those who do not learn to value time and carefully manage its use in such areas flounder. Admittedly, time consciousness and time management are more critical considerations in some fields than others. But none of the high achievers treats time as a limitless resource.

High achievers devise little strategies to conserve time, like taking along a magazine or book to read in the taxi or at the doctor's office. Malcolm Forbes takes a pad and pen with him to write down ideas; Steve Allen uses a small tape recorder. Many of them have gatekeepers to screen their phone calls and letters and visitors. Norman Vincent Peale rates himself an eight on time consciousness, but says he is not particularly strong on time management. He says his "well-organized" wife and two efficient secretaries help him compensate for his deficiencies.

Even though they may be driven by the clock or the calendar, many of the high achievers have schedules that permit them to lavish time on activities that they love. Sometimes that means doing an extraordinary amount of work, if work is their only love. But others schedule time for tennis and concerts and reading and family life with the same kind of care that they schedule business appointments. "I am miserly with time in some areas so that I can be profligate with it in others," says Stanley Marcus.

## 4. *High Achievers Are Persistent*

They are not easily stopped—if they feel they are on the right track. Linus Pauling told me, "If I differ from other scientists, it is that I form my own opinions and stick to them. This sticking to them may be something that differentiates me from a good number of others."

Architect John Portman, as a student, was told by Frank Lloyd Wright to "go seek Emerson." Portman followed that advice, and in Ralph Waldo Emerson's essay "Self-Reliance" discovered the counsel: Trust thyself. Great men have always done so.

Psychologist B. F. Skinner stated that his pigeons and his mice provided him with sufficient reinforcement to persist with his ideas even though they were extremely unpopular in many scientific circles, and still are. Skinner became convinced that his experiments worked and that his interpretations were correct, and he has steadfastly stuck by them ever since.

Several of the high achievers believe in a kind of interchangeability of factors. Coach Bobby Cremins says, "I lose my confidence sometimes, and that's where the courage part comes in." Erskine Caldwell said something similar: "I'm only halfway self-confident. I'd be around a five or a six on a ten-point scale. If you have determination, you're going to use that determination to take the place of confidence."

High achievers may be persistent, but their styles vary. Some choose frontal attacks for their ideas and stay at it until the job is done or they return bloodied from the fray. Others choose compromise, attaining a bit of what they want with each transaction. Still others pull back from an undertaking—if they feel the times are wrong—moving to another project temporarily, then returning. That is what Jacques Cousteau has done throughout his career. Cousteau has had an agenda composed of many projects—a television series on the Amazon and one on Haiti, and the development of a windship—and one by one, as the means have become available, he has completed them.

Says Norman Vincent Peale, "I never let go of something that I desperately want to do or that I believe ought to be done." He says if he can't do it "head-on," he will look for a "circuitous" way to do it. Peale sums it up thus: "The idea is to do it—no matter what method you use."

## 5. *They Channel Their Needs and Wishes Into Their Work*

What people really want they often get. Trite as that sounds, it is true that individuals who are able to channel intense desire into focused, informed, and sustained effort often do attain significant goals.

The motives that high achievers mention most often are desire for recognition, especially recognition by people in their field, self-development, and self-fulfillment. Economic incentives are mentioned, but are usually ranked relatively low and even then are seen as symbolic of other needs, such as the need for security, or for power or status.

The desire for recognition is a powerful one. "I think recognition is probably the least acknowledged and one of the most powerful propulsions for those who succeed," says Malcolm Forbes. Sometimes the desire for recognition is a long-term one—a wish to do something that will endure after the high achiever is gone.

The need for self-esteem figures prominently in the high-achiever interviews. Many high achievers frankly admit that they have struggled with inferiority feelings during their entire careers. They generally regard inferiority feelings as negative, as dangerous. But some of the high achievers say that inferiority feelings, or fear of failure, in modest amounts, can be a spur to great effort.

A number of the high achievers speak of their work as fulfilling, as literally filling a void in their lives. They say that their lives would be incomplete without their work.

Psychologists describe a process known as sublimation, wherein an individual's energy is diverted from one goal or activity to another. That seems to occur a great deal in these careers. High achievers channel energy into their work. And when they describe the kind of rewards that their work gives them, they say it enables them to gain recognition, live well, make a contribution to society and, often, helps them gain a sense of self-actualization.

Overwhelmingly they say they enjoy what they do. "I'm happy to get up in the morning," say labor leader Joyce Dannon Miller. "I'm happy to come to work. I'd rather come to work than do anything else. I love it. . . . This doesn't mean that I don't have days of frustration, but basically I'm one of the few people in life that has never felt that I was working for money, but I was working because I liked what I was doing." For people like Miller, enjoyment of work is a closed loop—both cause and effect.

### 6. *High Achievers Develop the Ability to Focus*

Hank Aaron's observation that superstars concentrate more than average players applies to more than baseball. Superstars from many fields say essentially the same thing. They possess the ability to tune out static and distractions and give absolute attention to the task at hand.

Their concentration is so complete and intense that they sometimes lose a sense of time and whatever else might be going on around them. Csikszentmihalyi's research on the "flow state" provides a theoretical framework for understanding what happens. The high achiever creates a mental island composed of himself and the task at hand. For flow-state behavior to occur, the task must be neither too difficult nor too easy. Although high achievers sometimes test the limits of their ability and the situation, they learn to work within those limits.

Csikszentmihalyi believes the flow state is not simply for an elite few in our society, for champion ball-players and artists and performers and mountain climbers. He thinks it can also be attained by large numbers of highly motivated individuals—those who can develop the ability to concentrate on tasks that are neither too difficult nor too easy for them. The individual lets goals emerge in the situation and then strives to attain them.

Those who have experienced the flow state often have difficulty describing it or explaining it to others. But they feel delight, even ecstasy, when it happens. Hank Aaron says, "It feels good—like nobody can get you out." Cartoonist Dan Barry says it's "almost orgasmic." Loretta Lynn, Emmylou Harris, and Ray Charles all speak of the exhilaration on stage when they are in the flow and the audience is with them. "It's indescribable," said Emmylou Harris. "I hope I die on stage, maybe right after I receive a big standing ovation," said Chet Atkins. "I hope I fall over and that's it."

The logic behind focus, whether the focus is short-term or long-term, is a sense of priorities. Helen Gurley Brown believes the number-one secret of success is priorities.

The reason priorities are so important is that they make the other achievement factors meaningful and do-able. In the case of *time management*—one of the achievement factors—a sense of priorities helps determine how to use the hours in the day, what tasks need to be emphasized, and, long-term, how long to stay at one job. Even though high achievers may try to do the smallest task to the best of their ability, they know that they cannot—and should not—give every task equal priority or equal investments of energy. In the case of *persistence*—another of the achievement factors—priorities give a sense of whether continued efforts lead to a goal or if they are counterproductive.

## 7. *High Achievers Function Appropriately in Their Situations*

There is no denying the importance of being in the right place at the right time. Virtually all the high achievers say that, and a large number of them use the word *luck* to explain their accomplishments. They also mention the importance of mentors and discoverers and teachers. Obviously, our situations shape us profoundly, and, like our genes, define the limits of what we can do. Our situations even influence what we want to do.

But not absolutely. My impression, after being around a number of these individuals, is that they would have done well in some other field had they not succeeded in the ones they chose. Might-have-beens can never be proved conclusively. But I sense a restless energy about these people—one that seeks an outlet.

In the eighteenth century, Thomas Gray wrote the "Elegy Written In A Country Church-Yard," a poem that has been called one of the most eloquent statements in the English language. In it, Gray reflects on what the humble folk who lived and died in that obscure hamlet might have been had they lived elsewhere. In that grave-yard, Gray mused, lay the remains of latent Hampdens, Cromwells, and Miltons.

That is a lovely idea, and elegantly stated, but one that is off the mark. In all likelihood, the Hampdens, Cromwells, and Miltons left that village long ago and ended up in London, Paris, Rome, or in one of the colonies. For the most part, the people who stayed behind, and are buried in that obscure cemetery, were well suited to little challenges, to swimming in small ponds.

## 8.  *High Achievers Perceive Opportunities*

High achievers are open to what is happening around them. They are always learning, because they are inquisitive, questioning individuals. Janet Leigh compares herself to a sponge, soaking up information. They see applications and new uses for old ideas. They see new combinations and the way to put them to use. Because they have stored the requisite patterns in memory, they often see opportunities that others miss.

Many high achievers study what their peers and contemporaries have done in order to inform their own efforts. But they use these existing ideas selectively. Matisse, a pioneer of impressionist painting, used to tell his students: "I have simply wished to assert the reasoned and independent feeling of my own individuality within a total knowledge of tradition." (Hughes 1986:99)

Some of them will accept criticism, even welcome it, because they know that getting valid and timely feedback is absolutely vital to success. Francis Crick told me that *the* major consideration in scientific discovery was the input received from colleagues who are competent and candid. "When a close collaborator produces an idea, you try to destroy it," he said. "If it's any good, it will survive."

But not just any criticism. A good rule of thumb, the high achievers generally agree, is to take criticism only from people who are in a position to know what they are talking about.

And the criticism, or the advice, for that matter, must be convincing. I have come to the conclusion that the word that describes many high achievers is *persuadable* rather than teachable. Many of them are hardheaded. And as they get older, and more and more competent, they seem to turn less and less to others for input. They prefer their own eyes and ears, their own judgment.

Erskine Caldwell put it this way: "I'm really not interested in what someone else would advise me to do. I like to take my own advice.... I once wrote a novel; it was called *Tobacco Road*. [Maxwell] Perkins read the manuscript and wrote a note that said: 'We like your book and we're going to publish it, and it's all right the way it is. We're not going to change anything.' You see, to me that was the ultimate editorship. Anything better or worse than that I would never consider."

Breadth of knowledge is important to many of these high achievers. Not all of them, however, for, as we have seen, breadth is more essential in some careers than others. "Wide-ranging awareness is a requisite for my work," said Malcolm Forbes. But breadth of knowledge is often valuable even in occupations that do not seem to demand it. People in business and government, for instance, are forever finding significant ideas by reading, traveling, listening, keeping their eyes open. They speak of a "hunger" for knowledge. Many of them read voraciously for diversion, for general knowledge, and sometimes just for sheer delight—people like Emmylou Harris and Hank Aaron, who do not have to read to do their jobs.

### 9. *High Achievers Seize Opportunities*

High achievers do not see themselves as hapless creatures borne against their will by omnipotent forces over which they have no control. They recognize the existence and importance of trends and social forces, and they try to exploit them for their own purposes. They use their environment purposefully.

They seem always to be scanning the horizon for relevant information. What is more, they *use* the information. They are not like the proverbial bumbler who stumbles upon the truth, picks himself up, and continues his journey as though nothing happened.

They make creative use of what they find. Some of them seek to give their work their own special touch. Says Aaron Copland: "Either you have your own thing to say and it comes out in your own terms in a natural way without being too effortful, or you don't have your own style." Copland concedes that there are composers—good ones—who don't have any particular style of their own. "But most of the great ones you can recognize when you hear their music," says the celebrated composer.

They take risks. Obviously, some high achievers are more daring than others. Several, in fact, say they are cautious and logical rather than daring. They take risks, not gambles. As a rule, however, a principle from the world of investments applies to careers: investments without risks rarely pay high dividends.

"Any new undertaking has failure as a possibility,"

says Malcolm Forbes. That rule applies in business, entertainment, science, sports, or politics. "Any time you run for public office you are certainly taking risks," says Sandra Day O'Connor, describing her own career. Ted Turner's office is lined with the sailing trophies he has won, but he says, "I've lost a lot more races than I've won."

"I believe in experimenting," says Erskine Caldwell. "Now, if you experiment with anything, you are taking a risk because you are going beyond the known." Caldwell told me that he has always been willing to extend himself into the unknown in order to find out something new, something different.

"Science is an occupation for gamblers, says Nobel Laureate Herbert Simon. "Journeyman science can be done without much risk, but highly creative science almost always requires a calculated gamble. By its very nature, scientific discovery derives from exploring previously unexplored lands." (1987:13)

Coca-Cola chief Robert Goizueta sums up the attitude toward risks and gambles: "You just can't wait for somebody to make a path. You have to go in and make mistakes and create your own path. As the Spanish poet Antonio Machado says, 'Traveler, there is no path. Paths are made by walking.'"

# Biographical Notes

## Henry Louis "Hank" Aaron_____

Born February 5, 1934, in Mobile, Alabama. The son of a rivet-bucker for a shipbuilding company, Aaron attended Central High School in Mobile and graduated from the city's Josephine Allen Institute in 1951. His career in baseball began when he made the team of the semi-professional Mobile Black Bears during his junior year of high school. When he starred in a game against the touring Indianapolis Clowns, he was offered a chance to join the Clowns. He subsequently signed a contract with the Milwaukee Braves, playing for their Eau Claire, Wisconsin, and Jacksonville, Florida, farm teams. During his twenty-three year major-league career, he compiled some amazing statistics, including: playing in twenty-four major-league All-Star Games; most games, lifetime, 3,298; most runs batted in, lifetime, 2,297; most plate appearances, lifetime, 13,940; most long hits, lifetime, 1,477, and, of course, most home runs, lifetime, 755. In 1976, Aaron accepted his present position as corporate vice president of the Atlanta Braves, a position that involves player development and oversight of the Braves' minor-league organization.

## Ronald W. Allen

Born November 20, 1941, in Atlanta, Georgia. The son of a master photo-engraver, Allen attended public schools and graduated from Georgia Tech in 1964 with a B.S. degree in industrial engineering. He began his career with Delta Airlines in 1963, working part-time as a methods analyst. Allen advanced through the ranks, first as an administrative assistant in the personnel department; then as director, methods and training; and as assistant vice president, administration. In 1969, he was named a vice president and in 1983 became president and chief operating officer of the airline, which in 1987 was the nation's fourth largest airline. Allen was elected chairman and chief executive officer in July 1987.

## Stephen Valentine Patrick William Allen

Born December 26, 1921, in New York City, New York. The original host of *The Tonight Show* in the mid-1950s, in the late 1950s he hosted *The Steve Allen Show* during prime time on Sunday nights. Later, he was moderator and panelist on *What's My Line* and *I've Got a Secret*. Other shows include *The Steve Allen Comedy Hour*, and the Peabody Award–winning *Meeting of Minds*. In 1956, he played the title role in *The Benny Goodman Story*. He is author of more than a score of books and, by his own count, several thousand songs.

# Mario Gabriel Andretti

Born February 28, 1940, near Trieste, Italy. Beginning his career driving racing cars in Italy at the age of thirteen, Andretti emigrated to the United States with his family in 1955, settling in Nazareth, Pennsylvania. He subsequently dropped out of high school (he later earned a diploma through a correspondence course) and went to work in a garage. In 1965, Andretti captured the United States Auto Club national championship and in 1967 won the Daytona 500. In 1969, Andretti won the Indianapolis 500. A hotly disputed finish placed him first, then second behind Bobby Unser in the 1981 Indianapolis 500.

# Julie Andrews

Born Julia Elizabeth Wells on October 1, 1935 in Walton-on-Thames, England. She was the daughter of Edward C. Wells, a teacher of metalcraft and woodworking, and his wife Barbara, a pianist. After her mother's divorce and subsequent remarriage to Edward Andrews, a music-hall singer, Julie changed her name to "Julie" and took her stepfather's surname. The family toured the English provinces, and Julie studied with private tutors and studied voice with Mme. Stiles-Allen. Following her successful debut as a singer at London's Hippodrome in 1947, she appeared in the Broadway production of *The Boy Friend*, which ran for 485 performances. This was followed by *My Fair Lady*, 1956–60 (which became the unanimous choice of the New York Drama Critics Circle as best musical of the 1955–56 season), and *Camelot*, 1960–62. Her films include *Mary Poppins* (Academy Award for best actress, 1964), *The Americanization of Emily*, *Torn Curtain*, *The Sound of Music*, *Hawaii*, *Thor-*

*oughly Modern Millie, The Tamarind Seed, Victor/Victoria, The Man Who Loved Women.* She was the star of the TV series the "Julie Andrews Hour." Named World Film Favorite (female) 1967. She is married to Blake Edwards.

# Mary Kay Ash

Born in Hot Wells, Texas. Her present age is not reported; Ms. Ash says: "A woman who will tell her age will tell anything." Awards include the Horatio Alger Award and the Free Enterprise Award. She is chairman of the Board of Mary Kay Cosmetics, Inc., the company she founded in 1963. That company has grown from nine workers at its founding to over 150,000 salespersons today; retail sales in 1986 exceeded $600 million.

# Arthur Ashe, Jr.

Born July 10, 1943, in Richmond, Virginia. The first black man to hold the rank of top tennis player in the world, Ashe attended high school in Richmond, Virginia, and St. Louis, Missouri. After high school graduation, he accepted a tennis scholarship at UCLA, where he was coached by J. D. Morgan and Pancho Gonzalez, who lived near the campus. He won the junior indoor singles title in 1960 and 1961, and in 1963 was named to the Davis Cup team. He won the Wimbledon singles in 1975. Presently he resides in New York City, where he is a writer and consultant. His most recent book is entitled *A Hard Road to Glory: The History of the Afro-American Athlete.*

# Isaac Asimov _____

Born on January 2, 1920, in Petrovichi, Russia, he immigrated to this country at the age of three, and settled with his family in Brooklyn, New York, where they opened a candy store. He attended public schools and Columbia University, where he earned a B.S. degree in 1939 and an M.A. degree in chemistry in 1941. During World War II he worked as a chemist at the Naval Air Experiment Station in Philadelphia. At war's end, he returned to Columbia University, where he received the Ph.D. degree in chemistry. He joined the medical school faculty of Boston University as instructor in 1949. The author of hundreds of books and articles on a variety of topics, Asimov is regarded as one of the premier science-fiction writers of our time. His best-known work is the Foundation trilogy, which has been honored with the prestigious Hugo Award as the best all-time series.

# Chester Burton "Chet" Atkins _____

Born on his grandfather's fifty-acre farm near Luttrell, Tennessee, on June 20, 1924. The son of a music teacher and piano tuner, Atkins eventually became a regular performer on the *Tennessee Barn Dance* and subsequently the *Grand Ole Opry*. When RCA established a major studio in Nashville in 1957, Atkins was asked to head it. A discoverer and promoter of many of country music's top stars, Atkins has recorded 108 albums himself, and in 1973 was voted into the Country Music Hall of Fame. Atkins is the recipient of eight Grammys and is a ten-time winner of the Country Music Association's "Best Instrumentalist" award.

# Daniel Barry

Born in 1923 in Long Branch, New Jersey. Barry grew up in New York City, where as a youngster he won an art scholarship and studied at the Art Students League and the New School. He has won awards from the Freedom Foundation and a grant from the Fund for the Republic. He founded an art colony in Tyrol, Austria, and has had his work exhibited in galleries in the United States and abroad. Barry has produced the comic strip "Flash Gordon" since 1953.

# Frank Borman

Born on March 14, 1928, in Gary, Indiana, he graduated from the U.S. Military Academy in 1950 and in 1957 received a Master of Aerospace Engineering degree from the California Institute of Technology. As an astronaut he was command pilot on the fourteen-day orbital Gemini 7 flight, December 1965, including a rendezvous with Gemini 6. In December 1968 he was command pilot of Apollo 8, the first lunar orbital mission. Borman was senior vice president in charge of operations, Eastern Air Lines, Inc., from 1970 to 1974; he became president and chief executive officer in 1975 and served in that capacity until 1986. He is presently vice chairman of the board of Texas Air Corporation.

# Helen Gurley Brown

Born on February 18, 1922, in Green Forest, Arkansas. Most of her early life was spent in Little Rock, Arkansas, and in California. Beginning her career as a secretary in an advertising agency, Brown eventually became a copywriter. Her books include *Sex and the Single Girl*, *Sex and the Office*, and *Having It All*. Often named in the polls as one of the most influential women in the nation, Brown has been editor-in-chief of *Cosmopolitan* since 1965.

# Paul William "Bear" Bryant

Born on September 11, 1913, in Kingsland, Arkansas. Bryant grew up on the family farm in the hamlet of Moro Bottom, Arkansas, and in the nearby town of Fordyce, Arkansas. He was a lineman on high school teams and on the University of Alabama team, which defeated Stanford in the 1935 Rose Bowl. He coached at Vanderbilt University, the University of Maryland, the University of Kentucky, Texas A & M, and the University of Alabama. When he retired from the University of Alabama, after the 1982 season, he was then the winningest football coach in history (323 wins, 85 losses, and 17 ties). He received many Southeast Conference Coach of the Year titles and several National Coach of the Year awards. He died in 1983.

# Art(hur) Buchwald

Born on October 20, 1925, in Mount Vernon, New York, Buchwald grew up in New York City. After dropping out of high school, he served in the Marines from 1942–45, editing his outfit's newspaper. After his military experience, Buchwald studied for a time at the University of Southern California, Los Angeles. After moving to Paris in 1948, he became the Paris correspondent for *Variety*, and in 1949 began writing a column for the New York *Herald Tribune* called "Paris After Dark." He returned to the United States in 1962 and began his column, which today appears in some 550 newspapers worldwide. The author of several best-selling books, Buchwald is widely regarded as the nation's premier humorist.

## Robert Carlyle Byrd (Cornelius Calvin Sale, Jr.)

Born on November 20, 1917, in Wilkesboro, North Carolina. His mother died soon after his birth and he was reared by his aunt and uncle, Vlurma and Titus Dalton Byrd, in Stotesbury, West Virginia. He served in the West Virginia House and Senate, the U.S. House of Representatives, and the U.S. Senate since 1959. Byrd was elected Senate Democratic Leader in 1977 and has served in that post to the present, as Senate Majority Leader 1977–81 and from 1987 to the present. He holds the degree LL.B, J.D. *cum laude*, American University. Byrd is a recipient of the Horatio Alger Award (1983).

## Erskine Caldwell

Born December 17, 1903, in a three-room manse in the White Oak community near the village of Moreland, Coweta County, Georgia. His father was a Presbyterian minister and his mother was a teacher of English and Latin in seminaries and colleges for girls and young women in the Carolinas and Virginia. He attended Erskine College and the University of Virginia, but did not graduate. His best-known novels are *God's Little Acre* and *Tobacco Road*. *Call it Experience*, published in 1987, is the most recent of his autobiographical writings. Caldwell died April 11, 1987.

# Ray Charles (Robinson)

Born September 23, 1930, in Albany, Georgia, he lost his sight at the age of seven. His mother died when he was fifteen, and his father two years later. A versatile performer and recording artist, he was the first black to become a major success in country-and-western music. Many times a Grammy winner, his autobiography, *Brother Ray*, was published in 1978.

# Aaron Copland

Born November 14, 1900, in Brooklyn, New York. The son of a department-store merchant, he studied under several famous teachers in the United States and France, including Nadia Boulanger in Paris. He was the first composer to receive a Guggenheim Fellowship. Considered one of the most creative and influential American composers, his suite derived from his ballet *Appalachian Spring* won a Pulitzer Prize in 1944, and his dramatic score for *The Heiress* won an Academy Award.

# Jacques-Yves Cousteau

Born in 1911 in St. André-de-Cubzac, France. Co-inventory, with Emile Gagnan in 1943, of the aqualung. The undersea explorer, cinematographer, and environmentalist is the recipient of numerous awards, including the Legion d'Honneur for his aid to the Underground in World War II. He received Oscars for best documentary feature for *The Silent World* (1956) and *World Without Sun* (1965). Founder of the Cousteau Society.

# Robert Joseph "Bobby" Cremins, Jr.

Born on July 4, 1947, in the Bronx, New York, Cremins attended All Hallows High School in the Bronx. He attended the University of South Carolina, where he was a three-year starter under the legendary basketball coach Frank McGuire. He has been head coach at Appalachian State University, where his teams won three conference titles, and, since 1981, at Georgia Tech, where he has received numerous honors, including conference and national Coach of the Year awards.

# Francis Harry Compton Crick

Born June 8, 1916, in Northampton, England, Crick received his baccalaureate degree in physics with mathematics from University College, London, in 1937 and his Ph.D. in 1954 from Cambridge University. He and James Watson were awarded the Nobel Prize for Medicine in 1962 for their discovery in 1953 of the double helical structure of DNA—a discovery many regard as the most important in medical science in this century. Currently Crick is working on dream research at the Salk Institute for Biological Studies in San Diego.

# Malcolm S(tevenson) Forbes _____

Born August 19, 1919, in Brooklyn, New York. The son of a journalist who founded *Forbes* magazine in 1917, he received his B.A. degree in political science from Princeton University in 1941. Forbes served in the U.S. Army 1942–45 and received the Bronze Star and the Purple Heart. In 1947 he became associate publisher of *Forbes* magazine, and in 1954, after his father's death, became publisher and editor. After serving as state senator from 1951 to 1958, he ran unsuccessfully as Republican candidate for governor of New Jersey in 1957. An individual of wide-ranging interests, Forbes began motorcycle riding at the age of forty-eight, and when he was fifty-two he took up ballooning. He has been a regular contributor to the magazine that bears his name since he became associated with it four decades ago.

# John Brooks Fuqua (John Brooks Elam) __

Born in 1918, Fuqua was reared in Prince Edward County, Virginia, by his maternal grandparents, after his mother died and his father was unable to care for him. He joined the merchant marine after graduating from high school, where he became a skilled telegraph and radio operator. At age twenty-one he moved to Augusta, Georgia, and started radio station WGAC, thus becoming the youngest radio station manager in the nation. In 1953, Fuqua formed and headed Augusta's first television station. In 1965, he created Fuqua Industries, Inc., which today includes Snapper Power Equipment, Colorcraft Corporation, American Seating Company, etc. In 1984, he was awarded the Horatio Alger Award.

# Roberto C. Goizueta

Born on November 18, 1931, in Havana, Cuba. The son of a sugar plantation owner, he received his B.S. degree in chemical engineering from Yale University in 1953. Responding to a help-wanted advertisement for a chemist or chemical engineer in a Havana newspaper, Goizueta began his career with Coca-Cola in 1954. In 1961, he was transferred to Nassau as area chemist in the Caribbean Area Office of the Coca-Cola Export Corporation. In 1964, Goizueta was brought to the corporate headquarters in Atlanta, and in 1965, he was named assistant to the vice president for research and development. In 1966, he was elected vice president, engineering, and in 1975 executive vice president. In 1980, Goizueta was elected president and chief operating officer, and in 1981 became chairman of the board and chief executive officer, a post he presently holds.

# Patricia Roberts Harris

Born on May 31, 1924, in Mattoon, Illinois. The daughter of a railroad waiter, she grew up in Mattoon and in Chicago, where she graduated from high school. She attended Howard University, graduating in 1945. She then attended the University of Chicago for two years, studying industrial relations, and, after marrying Washington attorney William Beasley Harris, entered George Washington University Law School, where she graduated in 1960. Harris worked as an attorney with the Department of Justice, after which she became a faculty member and later associate dean of Howard University Law School. Later she was chosen U.S. Ambassador to Luxembourg, thus becoming this nation's first black woman ambassador. She was secretary of the Department of Housing and Urban Development (HUD) and the Department of Health, Education and Welfare (HEW). Harris died in 1985.


# Dennis Carl Hayes

Born on January 10, 1950, in Spartanburg, South Carolina. Studied physics at Georgia Tech. Hayes worked for National Data Corporation as a network management engineer. In 1977, he left that organization to form a new company in partnership with NDC colleague, Dale Heatherington. Today he heads Hayes Microcomputer Products, Inc., which builds and markets personal-computer modems and other sophisticated computer hardware. The Hayes modem is widely regarded as the standard of the PC modem field.


# Eric Hoffer

Born on July 25, 1902, in the Bronx in New York City. Blinded as a result of a fall when he was seven years old, and regaining his sight at the age of fifteen, Hoffer had a life-long passion for reading. The self-educated social critic and philosopher took odd jobs on the West Coast, including migrant farm work, and later became a dock-worker on the San Francisco waterfront. His books, *The True Believer*, *The Passionate State of Mind*, and *The Ordeal of Change*, were enormously successful. He was awarded the Presidential Medal of Freedom in 1983. He died in 1983.


# Henry (Harry) T. Hoffman

Born in Brooklyn, New York, Hoffman grew up in Free-port, Long Island. After graduating from Colgate University with a degree in history, Hoffman was a FBI agent from 1951 to 1954, a sales manager for Procter and Gamble from 1954 to 1959, and a marketing manager for Bell and Howell from 1959 to 1966. His career with books began when he became director of marketing for Demco, a library supply company, where he stayed two years. He was recruited to handle marketing at the Tennessee Book Company (later named Ingram Book Company), which he later headed and transformed into book publishing's biggest wholesaler. In 1979, Hoffman became president and chief executive officer of Waldenbooks, which has become the largest bookseller in the nation.


# Bob Hoskins

Born October 26, 1942, in Bury St. Edmonds, Norfolk, England, his father was a bookkeeper and his mother a schoolteacher. Hoskins was reared in London, and did not attend college. He has won acclaim for his stage performances, particularly that of Nathan Detroit in the National Theatre's (London) production of *Guys and Dolls*.

On film, he has appeared in *Zulu Dawn*, *The Honorary Consul*, *The Long Good Friday*, *The Cotton Club*, and *Mona Lisa*, for which he won best-actor awards at Cannes in 1986, a British Academy Award, and an Oscar nomination in 1987. Current and future work includes *Who Framed Roger Rabbit?*, *The Lonely Passion of Judith Hearne*, and *Raggedy Rawney*, a film he will direct.

## John Huston

Born on August 5, 1906, in Nevada, Missouri. The son of an actor, the legendary writer and director has produced numerous classic films, including *Sergeant York*, *The Man Who Would Be King*, *The Treasure of Sierra Madre*, *The African Queen*, *The Misfits*, *Key Largo*, *Wise Blood*, *Chinatown*, and *The Maltese Falcon*. Huston's numerous awards includes the New York Drama Critics Circle Award, the Screen Directors Guild Award, and an Oscar. His autobiography is entitled *An Open Book*.

## Lillian Vernon Katz

Born in Leipzig, Germany, in 1927, Katz lived briefly in Holland and fled to this country with her family at the age of ten. She studied psychology at New York University and dropped out after two years to start her successful Lillian Vernon catalog business in 1951. The corporation she heads, which is the leader in the gift-catalog business, mailed 91 million catalogs in 1987 in ten seasonal and specialized editions and employs fourteen hundred employees during the peak Christmas season.

# Melvin Kranzberg

Born on November 22, 1917, in St. Louis, Missouri, Kranzberg received his A.B. Degree from Amherst College and his M.A. and Ph.D. degrees from Harvard University. The recipient of numerous honorary degrees and awards, including the Jabotinsky Centennial Medal by the State of Israel, Kranzberg's major professional contribution has been the establishment and development of a new field of history: the history of technology. He is the principal founder of the Society for the History of Technology (SHOT), founding editor of its quarterly journal, *Technology & Culture* (1959–81), and its president (1983–84). Presently, he is Callaway Professor of the History of Technology at Georgia Tech.

# Kris Kristofferson

Born June 22, 1936, in Brownsville, Texas. The son of an Air Force officer, the musician and actor grew up in Brownsville, Texas, and in San Mateo, California. He attended Pomona College in California, where he was a football star, Golden Gloves boxer, member of the honor society, and the top-rated ROTC cadet. He won a Rhodes scholarship and after graduation went to Oxford University to study English literature. After an aborted career as an Army officer and helicopter pilot, Kristofferson chose to become a full-time songwriter and performer. His first big break came in 1969, when Roger Miller recorded "Me and Bobby McGee" and Janis Joplin made it a national hit. Other songs include "Sunday Mornin' Comin' Down," "Help Me Make It Through the Night," and "Why Me?" He has made several movies, the biggest to date *A Star is Born*, with Barbra Streisand.

# Janet Leigh (Jeanette Helen Morrison) _____

Born on July 6, 1927, in Merced, California. The only child
of employees of a ski lodge, Leigh grew up in Stockton,
California, where she attended public schools and the
College of the Pacific, majoring in music. Discovered by
Norma Shearer, Leigh's first film was *The Romance of
Rosy Ridge* in 1946. Since then Leigh has made more
than forty films, including *Psycho*, *The Manchurian Can-
didate*, *Touch of Evil*, *That Forsythe Woman*, and *Houdini*.
*There Really Was a Hollywood*, her autobiography, was
published in 1984. Her numerous honors include an
Oscar nomination and a Golden Globe Award.

# John Uhler "Jack" Lemmon _____

Born on February 8, 1925, in Boston. Lemmon graduated
from Phillips Academy, Andover, and Harvard University;
he served as an ensign in the U.S. Navy, 1945–46. His
movie credits include *Mister Roberts*, *Some Like It Hot*,
*The Apartment*, *Irma La Douce*, *Under the Yum Yum Tree*,
*Days of Wine and Roses*, *The Odd Couple*, *Save the Tiger*,
*Airport*, *The China Syndrome*, and *Missing*. His television
credits include "The Entertainer," and "'S Marvelous, 'S
Gershwin." Stage credits include *Tribute* and *Long Day's
Journey into Night*. Lemmon's numerous awards include
an Emmy (1972), a Tony nomination, the Broadway Drama
Guild Award (1979), two Cannes citations, three British,
one German, two Canadian, and two Italian Oscars, and
eight Academy Award nominations. He is the first man
ever to win Oscars as both best actor (1973) and as best
supporting actor (1975).

# Loretta Webb Lynn

Born on April 14, 1935, in Butcher Hollow, Kentucky. A Grammy winner and the recipient of numerous country music awards, Lynn has been named the Country Music Association's Female Vocalist of the Year as well as Entertainer of the Decade by the Academy of Country Music in 1980. Her autobiography, *Coal Miner's Daughter*, published in 1976, was a best-seller; the Academy Award-winning movie based on this book was released in 1979.

# Mark Hume McCormack

Born in Chicago, Illinois, on November 6, 1930. A graduate of William and Mary College and Yale Law School. A golfer since early youth, McCormack played on his college team and qualified for the U.S. Open and several U.S. and British amateur championship tournaments. In 1960, McCormack founded International Management Group (IMG) to represent sports celebrities. IMG has since diversified into other areas, but McCormack is still considered the founder of the sports-marketing industry and IMG the industry's premier firm. Clients include: Arnold Palmer, Wimbledon, Herschel Walker, Rolex, Martina Navratilova, Chris Evert Lloyd, Jackie Stewart, and Harvard University. His books: *What They Don't Teach You at Harvard Business School* and *What They Didn't Teach Me at Yale Law School*.

# (Harold) Stanley Marcus

Born on April 20, 1905, in Dallas, Texas. The son of the president of Neiman-Marcus Company, Marcus graduated from Forrest Avenue High School in Dallas and studied at Harvard University, where he graduated in 1925 and received his master's degree in business administration in 1926. Beginning his career as a salesperson in the apparel department, Marcus introduced a number of successful innovations at the Dallas-based store, including the fashion shows, the "Fortnights," the "his-and-hers" gifts in the Christmas catalogs, and the Neiman-Marcus Awards, presented annually to outstanding individuals in the field of fashion. The author of *Minding the Store* and *Quest for the Best*, Marcus retired in 1975 after fifty years in retailing and is now chairman emeritus of the Neiman-Marcus Company.

# Edith W. Martin

Born in Chicago, Illinois, in 1945, Martin received her B.A. degree from Lake Forest College, and her M.S. (1976) and Ph.D. (1980) degrees in information and computer science from Georgia Tech. Formerly deputy under-secretary of defense for research and advanced technology, Martin is one of the nation's highest-ranking women in high technology. She is presently vice president/technology of Boeing Electronics Company and is responsible for advanced electronics and the High Technology Center for all the Boeing Companies.

# Joyce Dannon Miller

Born in Chicago, Illinois, Miller received her baccalaureate degree in 1950 and an M.A. degree in 1951 from the University of Chicago. Miller is national president of the Coalition of Labor Union Women, vice president and director of social services of the Amalgamated Clothing and Textile Workers Union, AFL-CIO, the executive director of the Sidney Hillman Foundation, and the first woman ever to serve on the Executive Council of the AFL-CIO.

# Thomas H. Moorer

Born on February 9, 1912, in Mount Willing, Alabama. He entered the U.S. Naval Academy upon graduation from high school. Attained the rank of rear admiral in 1958, vice admiral in 1962, and admiral in 1964. He was named chief of naval operations in 1967 and chairman of the joint chiefs of staff for two consecutive two-year terms. Among his many decorations and awards are the Silver Star, the Purple Heart, Distinguished Flying Cross, and the Legion of Merit. Admiral Moorer retired from active duty on July 2, 1974.

# Arthur Murray (Teichman)

Born on April 4, 1895, in New York City, New York. The founder of a chain of dance schools, the famed dance instructor attracted national attention through his dance correspondence courses and his innovative use of radio and television. He and his wife, the former Kathryn

Kohnfelder, whom he married in 1925, and who appeared with him on his television series, now reside in Hawaii.

# Jack William Nicklaus

Born January 21, 1940, in Columbus, Ohio. The son of a pharmacist, he began to play golf at age ten and played in his first national tournament at age thirteen. Attended Ohio State University, but did not graduate. He has won the PGA five times, the U.S. Open four times, the British Open three times (runner-up seven times), and the Masters a record six times. Nicklaus has become widely known in the field of golf course design and architecture. He has been named PGA Player of the Year five times and Athlete of the Decade (1970–79).

# Sandra Day O'Connor

Born on March 26, 1930, on a 155,000-acre ranch in a remote part of Arizona and New Mexico, O'Connor attended public schools in El Paso, Texas. She graduated *magna cum laude* from Stanford University in 1950 and two years later was awarded the LL.B. degree, graduating third in a class that included Chief Justice William H. Rehnquist, who ranked first. She met her husband, John Jay O'Connor, at Stanford; he was in the class below hers. O'Connor was in private practice for several years; became assistant attorney general for Arizona in 1965; was appointed to the state senate in 1969 and won a seat in 1972, serving a total of five years; was elected a superior court judge in 1974; and was appointed in 1979 to the

Arizona Court of Appeals. In 1981, she was nominated by Ronald Reagan and confirmed as an associate justice of the United States Supreme Court—the first woman ever to occupy the position.

# Linus Carl Pauling

Born in 1901 in Portland, Oregon. He was educated at Oregon Agricultural College (now Oregon State University), where he graduated in 1922 with a major in chemical engineering, and at the California Institute of Technology, where he received his Ph.D. degree in 1925. Recognized as one of the most brilliant scientists of our time, he is the recipient of two Nobel Prizes—the Nobel Peace Prize for his opposition to nuclear testing in 1962 and the Nobel Prize for Chemistry in 1954. More recently, he has become heavily involved in research on Vitamin C. He heads the Linus Pauling Institute of Science and Medicine in Palo Alto, California.

# Norman Vincent Peale

Born May 31, 1898, in Bowersville, Ohio. The son of a Methodist minister, Peale earned his B.A. degree from Ohio Wesleyan in 1920. After a year pursuing journalism as a career, he decided to enter the ministry. Enrolling at Boston University in 1921, he was ordained into the Methodist Episcopal Church the following year, and graduated in 1924 with degrees in theology and social ethics. In 1927, he went to the University Methodist Church in Syracuse, New York, and five years later became pastor of Marble Collegiate Church in New York City, changing his denominational affiliation to the Reformed Church in America. For many years he has been regarded as perhaps the nation's most influential Protestant pastor. He founded the monthly religious magazine *Guideposts*. His books include: *The Art of Living*; *A Guide to Confident Living*, which was his first best-seller; *The Art of Real Happiness*; and *The Power of Positive Thinking*, which was number one on the *New York Times* best-seller list for three years. He received the Horatio Alger Award in 1952.

# Richard Lee Petty

Born on July 2, 1937, in Level Cross, North Carolina. The son of Lee Petty, a stock-car racer and owner of a small trucking business, he attended Randleman High School, where he made the all-conference football team as a guard. From age twelve until he was twenty-one, he was apprenticed to his father. In 1960, he posted his first Grand National victory in Charlotte, North Carolina. Petty was acknowledged the "king" of stock-car racing after the 1967 season, when he set a new NASCAR record of twenty victories—nine more than the previous record. In 1972, Petty broke the last of his father's major records, taking the Grand National title a fourth time. Petty was still active as a racer in 1987, finishing third in the Daytona 500.

# John Calvin Portman, Jr.

Born in 1924 in Walhalla, South Carolina, Portman grew up in Atlanta. After serving in the U.S. Navy during World

War II and attending the U.S. Naval Academy under a fleet appointment, Portman returned to Atlanta to study architecture, receiving a B.S. degree in that subject from Georgia Tech in 1950. His first major commercial success was Atlanta's Merchandise Mart in 1960, but it was his Hyatt Regency Hotel, with its atrium and exposed bubble elevators, that brought him international attention. Paul Gapp, architecture critic for the *Chicago Tribune*, once described Portman as "the most influential living American architect." His book *The Architect as Developer* (with Jonathan Barnett) describes his philosophy. His best-known structures are San Francisco's Embarcadero Center and Broadway's Marriott Marquis Hotel.

# Edward William Proxmire

Born November 11, 1915, in Lake Forest, Illinois. The son of a prominent surgeon, Proxmire received his B.A. degree in English from Yale in 1938 and an M.B.A. degree *cum laude* from Harvard University Graduate School of Business Administration in 1940. After a brief stint as a journalist, Proxmire began his political career when he was elected to the Wisconsin State Assembly in 1950. A U.S. Senator since 1957, Proxmire's major legislative accomplishments have been in the area of consumer protection. He sponsored the 1968 Consumer Credit Protection Act and the 1970 Fair Credit Reporting Act. Books include *Report from Wasteland: America's Military Industrial Complex*; *Uncle Sam: The Last of the Big-Time Spenders*; *Can Small Business Survive?*, and *You Can Do It*.

# Ronald Wilson Reagan

Born on February 6, 1911, in Tampico, Illinois. After graduating from Eureka College in 1932, Reagan became a sportscaster in Davenport, Iowa, and later in Des Moines. In 1937, he began a film career with Warner Brothers Studio, appearing in over 50 films that included roles in *Knute Rockne—All American* and *Kings Row*. In 1947, he became president of the Screen Actors Guild, and again in 1959. Reagan later became host of *General Electric Theater* (1954–62) and *Death Valley Days* (1962–65). He served as Governor of California from 1967 until 1975 and as President of the United States from 1981 to the present.

# Oscar de la Renta

Born July 22, 1932, in Santo Domingo, Dominican Republic. The son of an insurance salesman, he studied art in Madrid, and became interested in fashion illustrations. Subsequently trained in the European custom couture houses of Balenciaga and Lanvin-Castillo, he came to New York as a designer for Elizabeth Arden in 1963. Eventually he began to design under his own name, in a business partnership with Gerald Shaw. In June 1967, he won the "Winnie," presented by Coty to the designer having had the greatest influence on fashion for the past year. Has won two Coty awards.

# Xavier Roberts

Born on October 31, 1955, in Habersham County, Georgia. His father was killed in an automobile accident when

Roberts was five years old. He attended public schools in Cleveland, Georgia, and Truett-McConnell College but did not graduate. Roberts achieved success with his line of dolls, called "Little People" (and subsequently "Cabbage Patch Kids" by Coleco), which he marketed as "babies," united them with "parents." More recent products include the "Furskins Bears" and the "Bunnybees." In 1986, he opened a resort, the Villagio di Montagna, in the mountains of North Carolina, and Babyland on Fifth (New York City). Roberts is the chairman of Original Appalachian Artworks, Inc.


# David Rockefeller

Born on June 12, 1915, in New York City. The youngest of five sons born to John D. Rockefeller, Jr., David received his B.S. degree from Harvard University in 1936 and his Ph.D. in economics from the University of Chicago in 1940. His dissertation was published under the title *Unused Resources and Economic Waste*. He joined the Chase National Bank in 1946. When the bank merged with the Bank of Manhattan in 1955, Rockefeller was named executive vice president of the Chase Manhattan Bank; he was named president in 1960; chairman of the board 1961–81, and chief executive officer 1969–80. A generous patron of the arts, he was also active in developing Morningside Heights and the southern part of New York City. A former chairman of the Council on Foreign Relations, he was instrumental in the formation of the Trilateral Commission. His numerous honors and decorations include the Legion of Honor, France, the Order of Merit, Italy, the Order of the Southern Cross, Brazil, and the Order of the Crown, Belgium.

# Joseph Wilson Rogers, Jr.

Born on December 2, 1946, in Jackson, Tennessee. The son of the founder of the Waffle House chain, Rogers received his B.S. degree in industrial management from Georgia Tech in 1968 and the M.B.A. degree from Harvard in 1971. In 1973, Rogers became president and chief executive officer of the company his father founded in 1955. The company had 580 units in 1986.

# Andrew Aitken "Andy" Rooney

Born on January 14, 1919, in Albany, New York. Attended Colgate University until he was drafted into the Army in 1941. Wrote for *Stars and Stripes* during the war. He and Bud Hutton recalled their wartime experiences in *The Story of the Stars and Stripes*, published in 1946. After an unsuccessful attempt at free-lance writing, Rooney joined Arthur Godfrey, becoming a radio and television writer, and later wrote for other stars, including Victor Borge and Garry Moore. The author of widely read columns and the scriptwriter of numerous award-winning documentaries, Rooney began his career with CBS News in 1962 as a writer/producer. In 1978 he began the award-winning feature "A Few Minutes With Andy Rooney," on *60 Minutes*. He has won four Emmys, six Writers Guild Awards, the Peabody Award, and a host of other honors.

# David Dean Rusk

Born February 9, 1909, in Cherokee County, Georgia. Graduated from Davidson College with a B.A. in politics in 1931 *magna cum laude*. Won a Rhodes scholarship and attended Oxford University. Returning to this country, he taught political science at Mills College in Oakland, California, and studied law at the University of California, Berkeley. During World War II, Rusk served in the China-Burma-India theater, where he became deputy chief of staff to General Joseph Stilwell. He was discharged with the rank of colonel. From 1946 until 1952, Rusk served in the State Department, advancing to the rank of assistant secretary of state. From 1952 until 1961, Rusk served as president of the Rockefeller Foundation. Rusk served as secretary of state under two presidents, Kennedy and Johnson, and in 1970 became Sibley Professor of International Law at the University of Georgia.

# Charles Monroe Schulz

Born November 26, 1922, in Minneapolis, Minnesota. The son of a barber, Schulz attended public schools in St. Paul, Minnesota. After graduating from high school, he enrolled in a correspondence course given by Art Instruction, Inc., of Minneapolis. In 1943 he was drafted into the Army. In 1948 he sold his first cartoons to the *Saturday Evening Post*. Two years later, United Feature Syndicate liked his idea of a strip, which Schulz wanted to call "Li'l' Folks," and named it "Peanuts." He is the recipient of numerous awards, including an Oscar nomination for his feature film *A Boy Named Charlie Brown* and Emmys for "A Charlie Brown Christmas" and "A Charlie Brown Thanksgiving," the Peabody Award in 1966 for "A Charlie Brown Christmas," the 1978 International Cartoonist of the Year, and the Elzie Segar Award in 1980.

He has twice won the comic art form's highest honor, the Reuben, in 1955 and 1964.

## Robert (Lawson) Shaw

Born April 30, 1916, in Red Bluff, California. His father was a minister and his mother was a leading vocalist in church choirs. Shaw attended public schools and graduated from Pomona College in Claremont, California. He was associated with Fred Waring from 1938 until 1945, working with Fred Waring's Pennsylvanians. In 1941, he founded the Collegiate Chorale—a two hundred-voice volunteer chorus in New York City, out of which grew a number of professional choruses identified with the broadcasting networks and RCA Victor, and ultimately the Robert Shaw Chorale. In 1948, the Robert Shaw Chorale made its debut on NBC radio. Shaw was on the faculty of the Juilliard School of Music from 1946 to 1950. During these years, Shaw recorded in association with Arturo Toscanini, Leopold Stokowski, and Fritz Reiner. In 1953, Shaw became conductor of the San Diego Symphony; in 1955, he became associate conductor of the Cleveland Symphony Orchestra under George Szell and director of the Cleveland Orchestra Chorus. He became music director of the Atlanta Symphony Orchestra in 1967. Shaw has received seven Grammy awards and numerous academic honors.

## Herbert Alexander Simon

Born June 15, 1916, in Milwaukee, Wisconsin. The individual whom Carnegie-Mellon president Richard M.

Cyert once called "the one man in the world who comes closest to the ideal of Aristotle or a Renaissance man" received his B.A. degree from the University of Chicago in 1936 and his Ph.D. degree from the University of Chicago in 1943. Known for his research in economics, psychology, management, and the artifical simulation of human thought and problem-solving process with computers, Simon is the Richard King Mellon University Professor of Computer Science and Psychology at Carnegie-Mellon University. His numerous awards include the Nobel Prize in Economic Science in 1978.

# Burrhus Frederic Skinner

Born in 1904 in Susquehanna, Pennsylvania, Skinner received his B.A. degree (1926) from Hamilton College, Clinton, New York, where he majored in English language and literature, and his M.A. (1930) and Ph.D. (1931) degrees in psychology from Harvard University. He taught at the University of Minnesota, became chairman of the Department of Psychology, Indiana University, in 1945, and in 1948 he joined the Department of Psychology at Harvard as professor. His ideas have been enormously influential within the social sciences and in society at large. His numerous works include *The Behavior of Organisms*, *Verbal Behavior*, *Walden Two*, *Science and Human Behavior*, *Beyond Freedom and Dignity*, and his autobiography *Particulars of My Life* and *A Matter of Consequences*. Awards include the National Medal of Science (1968), the Gold Medal of the American Psychological Association (1971). Professor Emeritus at Harvard University since his official retirement in 1974.

# Gloria Steinem

Born March 25, 1936, in Toledo, Ohio. The daughter of an itinerant antique dealer and summer-resort operator, she received her B.A. degree from Smith College in 1956. After graduating from Smith, she went to India, where she studied at universities of Delhi and Calcutta. One of the major figures in the women's movement, Steinem was instrumental in founding *Ms.* magazine in 1972 and has been its editor ever since. Her latest publication is a biography of Marilyn Monroe, *Marilyn*.

# Hugh Asher Stubbins, Jr.

Born January 11, 1912. Stubbins grew up on a farm near Birmingham, Alabama. He received his undergraduate training at Georgia Tech and then went to Harvard University, where he received a Master of Architecture degree in 1935. From 1935 to 1938 he practiced in the firm of Royal Barry Wills in New England. Then he formed a partnership with Marc Peter in Boston, collaborating on work that won several prizes in national competitions. In 1940, Walter Gropius invited Stubbins to join the Harvard faculty. Stubbins remained at Harvard for twelve years, serving as chairman of the Department of Architecture for one year. Presently he is chairman of the board of The Stubbins Associates of Cambridge, Massachusetts. The firm is best known for the design of the Citicorp Center in New York City and Congress Hall in West Berlin. Current work includes the Ronald Reagan Presidential Library.

# Gloria (May Josephine) Swanson

Born in Chicago in 1899, the legendary movie queen began her five-decade film career in silent films in 1914. Once known as the "Queen of the Box Office," Swanson's numerous films include *Male and Female* (1918), *Sadie Thompson* (1928), *The Trespassers* (1929), and *Sunset Boulevard* (1950). Her autobiography is called *Swanson on Swanson* (1980). She died in 1983.

# Robert Edward "Ted" Turner

Born on November 19, 1938, in Cincinnati, Ohio. He attended public school in Cincinnati until he was nine years old, when the family moved to Savannah, Georgia, where his father had bought an advertising company that became known as Turner Advertising Company. Turner subsequently attended the Georgia Military Academy and the McCallie School in Chattanooga. He attended Brown University, but did not graduate. When his father committed suicide in 1963, Turner took charge of the company, eventually expanding into television with the purchase of Channel 17, a money-losing UHF station (WTCG). Expanding into cable, Turner has transformed his original television station into the "Super-Station," linked by satellite to a national cable network, acquired the Atlanta Braves baseball team and part ownership of the Atlanta Hawks basketball team, and created the Cable News Network. In 1977, Turner won the America's Cup.

# General Albert Coady Wedemeyer _____

Born July 9, 1897, in Omaha, Nebraska. Wedemeyer graduated from West Point in 1918. During World War II, he became the deputy chief of staff of the South East Asia Command under Lord Louis Mountbatten in 1943, and in 1944, when General Stilwell was recalled from the China-Burma-India theater, he assumed command of the China theater. A recipient of the Distinguished Service Medal in 1943 and the Presidential Medal of Freedom in 1985, Wedemeyer now resides on his cattle farm in Maryland.

# Thomas Lanier "Tennessee" Williams ____

Born on March 26, 1911, in Columbus, Mississippi. Williams moved to St. Louis, Missouri, when he was twelve years old and studied at the University of Missouri, Washington University, and the University of Iowa, from which he received his B.A. degree in 1938. His best-known plays include *The Glass Menagerie*, *A Streetcar Named Desire*, *Cat on a Hot Tin Roof*, and *Night of the Iguana*. He received four Drama Critics Awards and two Pulitzer Prizes. His screenplays include *The Rose Tattoo* and *Suddenly Last Summer*. He also wrote a novel, memoirs, a book of poetry, and collections of short stories. He died in Manhattan in 1983.

# The Interview Guide

Listed below are skills, aptitudes, attitudes, experiences, and events that high achievers frequently mention as contributing to their careers. How important have these been in your own career? (Use the following scale: 0—low, not present or unimportant; 10—high, very important.)

1.  Time consciousness

    _____

2.  Time management

    _____

3.  Flexibility—in other words, being willing to alter your agenda if something important comes up _____

4.  Focus—concentrating on one thing

    _____

5. Intensity _____

6. Breadth of knowledge

   _____

7. Competence—knowing
   or doing something very
   well _____

8. Small details

   _____

9. How important is the
   good teacher?

   _____

10. How important is the
    lucky break?

    _____

11. How important is being
    in the right place?

    _____

12. How important are
    economic incentives?
    At beginning of career?

    _____

    Today? _____

13. How important is a
    discoverer in your
    career? _____

14. How important is a
    mentor? _____

15. How teachable are you?

    _____

16. Are you a good listener?

    _____

17. How brave are you?

    _____

    (Follow-up question:
    Are you a risk-taker?)

    _____

18. How important is
    reading? _____

19. How important is
    travel? _____

20. How persistent are you?

    _____

21. How important is
    nerve, chutzpah?

    _____

22. How important is desire
    for recognition?

    _____

23. How self-confident are
    you? _____

24. How important is a
    feeling of inferiority?

    _____

25. How much do you enjoy
your work?

_____

26. How important is desire
for self-improvement?

_____

27. How important is the
challenge itself?

_____

28. How important is a
sense of playfulness?
Having fun?

_____

29. How important is
creativity? Innovation?

_____

30. How important is
discipline?

_____

31. If you had to choose
    three factors to explain
    your accomplishments,
    which have been the
    most important?

    _____

32. What is the greatest
    price you have paid to
    get where you are?

    _____

33. Which of these factors
    has required the most
    effort on your part?

    _____

34. Would you do it all
    over again?

    _____

# The Achievement Factors
# Selected Interviews

FACTORS:

Ranked from 0 to 10
or:  L (low)
      M (moderate)
      H (high)

| | Hank Aaron | Julie Andrews | Mary Kay Ash | Isaac Asimov | Helen Gurley Brown |
|---|---|---|---|---|---|
| Time consciousness | 10 | 6 | 9 | 10 | 9 |
| Time management | 10 | 7 | 9 | 8 | 9 |
| Flexibility | 10 | 7 | 9 | 3 | 6 |
| Focus | 10 | 9 | 9 | 5 | 8 |
| Intensity | 8 | 9 | 9 | 9 | 10 |
| Breadth of knowledge | 0 | 6 | 4 | 10 | 5 |
| Competence | 10 | 10 | 10 | 10 | 10 |
| Small details | 8 | 7 | 10 | 5 | 9 |
| How important is: | | | | | |
|   The good teacher | 10 | 8 | 10 | 1 | 0 |
|   The lucky break | 10 | 10 | 8 | 3 | 4 |
|   Being in the right place | 10 | 10 | | 8 | 6 |
|   A discoverer in your career | 10 | 7 | 0 | 10 | 7 |
|   A mentor | 10 | 7 | 10 | 1 | 0 |
|   Reading | 6 | 6 | 9 | 10 | 5 |
|   Travel | 0 | 8 | 0 | 0 | 3 |
|   Nerve, chutzpah | 6 | 5 | 9 | 7 | 5 |
|   Desire for recognition | 10 | 8 | 9 | 10 | 9 |
|   A feeling of inferiority | 0 | | 0 | 0 | 5 |
|   Desire for self-improvement | 7 | 10 | 8 | 8 | 10 |
|   The challenge itself | 10 | 8 | 10 | 6 | 7 |
|   A sense of playfulness | 0 | 9 | 4 | 9 | 5 |
|   Creativity | 0 | 10 | 8 | 10 | 5 |
|   Discipline | 10 | 10 | 10 | | 10 |
|   Economic incentives: | | | | | |
|     At beginning of career | 10 | 5 | 8 | 5 | |
|     Today | 7 | 5 | 4 | 0 | 7 |
| How teachable are you? | 7 | 6 | 8 | 5 | 9 |
| Are you a good listener? | 10 | 7 | 10 | 3 | 10 |
| How brave are you? | 6 | 8 | 10 | 8 | 5 |
| How persistent are you? | 10 | 9 | 9 | 10 | 10 |
| How self-confident are you? | 10 | 4 | 10 | 10 | 4 |
| How much do you enjoy your work? | 10 | 9 | 10 | 10 | 10 |

| Erskine Caldwell | Malcolm Forbes | Harry Hoffman | Kris Kristofferson | Janet Leigh | Jack Lemmon | Stanley Marcus | Sandra Day O'Connor | Norman Vincent Peale | Robert Shaw | RATE YOURSELF |
|---|---|---|---|---|---|---|---|---|---|---|
| 10 | 9 | 10 | 8 | 8 | 8 | 9 | 10 | 8 | 9 | |
| | 8 | 10 | 4 | 10 | 8 | 7 | 10 | 7 | 9 | |
| 9 | 8 | 10 | 10 | 5 | 10 | 8 | | 10 | 4 | |
| | 9 | 9 | 10 | 9 | 10 | 4 | 10 | 10 | 9 | |
| 9 | 9 | 10 | 10 | 5 | 10 | 9 | 6 | 10 | 9 | |
| | 8 | 7 | 10 | 4 | 7 | 6 | M | 8 | 5 | |
| 9 | H | 10 | 10 | H | 10 | | | | 9 | |
| 9 | 6 | 7 | 10 | 9 | 8 | 9 | 10 | 7 | 8 | |
| 1 | 9 | 9 | 10 | 10 | 9 | 10 | H | 10 | 8 | |
| | 10 | 9 | 6 | 10 | 4 | 10 | 10 | | 7 | |
| | 10 | 9 | 10 | | 4 | | | | 7 | |
| 0 | | 9 | 8 | 10 | 4 | 0 | M | 5 | 8 | |
| 5 | 0 | | 10 | 10 | 0 | 0 | 1 | 7 | 7 | |
| | 10 | 9 | 10 | 10 | 9 | 10 | 10 | 10 | 7 | |
| | | | 10 | 5 | 7 | 10 | L | 10 | 7 | |
| 3 | 8 | 9 | 10 | 3 | 9 | 8 | H | 8 | 3 | |
| 9 | | 10 | 10 | 8 | 8 | 5 | M | 4 | 7 | |
| 5 | 0 | | 0 | 6 | 8 | | M | | 8 | |
| 10 | 1 | 8 | 10 | 10 | 10 | | | 10 | 9 | |
| 9 | 9 | 10 | 10 | 9 | 10 | 10 | 10 | 10 | 8 | |
| 2 | 7 | 10 | 10 | 10 | 10 | 9 | L | 7 | 5 | |
| 10 | 9 | 10 | 10 | 10 | 10 | 10 | M | 5 | 9 | |
| 10 | 6 | 5 | 0 | 10 | 10 | | H | 10 | 8 | |
| | | 4 | | | | | | | 1 | |
| 5 | | | 0 | 4 | 3 | 7 | L | 4 | 5 | |
| 5 | 5 | 5 | 10 | 9 | 8 | 8 | H | 10 | 8 | |
| 5 | 4 | 9 | 10 | 9 | 10 | 5 | H | 10 | 8 | |
| 9 | | 7 | 10 | 3 | 10 | 6 | | 10 | 9 | |
| 10 | 8 | 10 | 10 | 5 | 10 | 10 | M | 10 | 9 | |
| 5 | 8 | 10 | 10 | 5 | 8 | 9 | H | 8 | 2 | |
| 10 | | 10 | 10 | 10 | 10 | 10 | 10 | 10 | 9 | |

# References

**Asimov, Isaac**
1980 *In Joy Still Felt: The Autobiography of Isaac Asimov, 1954–1978.* Garden City, New York: Doubleday & Company, Inc.

**Barrett, James T.**
1986 *Contemporary Classics in the Life Sciences.* Philadelphia: ISI Press, Volume 1: Cell Biology (Contemporary Classics in Science).

**Barzun, Jacques, and Henry F. Graff**
1962 *The Modern Researcher.* New York: Harcourt, Brace, and World.

**Bass, Bernard M.**
1981 *Stogdill's Handbook of Leadership: A Survey of Theory and Research.* New York: The Free Press.

**Beilenson, Evelyn L., and Ann Tenenbaum**
1986 *Wit and Wisdom of Famous American Women.* White Plains, New York: Peter Pauper Press.

**Bernard, Bruce**
  1985 *Vincent By Himself: A Selection of Van Gogh's Paintings and Drawings Together with Extracts from His Letters.* Boston: Little, Brown and Company, A New York Graphic Society Book.

**Bloom, Benjamin S.**
  1985 *Developing Talent in Young People.* New York: Ballantine Books.

**Brown, Helen Gurley**
  1983 *Having It All.* New York: Pocket Books.

**Burns, James MacGregor**
  1978 *Leadership.* New York: Harper and Row.

**Cawthon, Raad**
  1986 "High Flying Mind of Ted Turner," *The Atlanta Journal and Constitution,* June 29.

**Charles, Ray, and David Ritz**
  1978 *Brother Ray.* New York: The Dial Press.

**Clemens, Samuel Langhorne (Mark Twain)**
  1917 (1874) *Life on the Mississippi.* New York: Harper & Brothers Publishers.

**Collier, Peter, and David Horowitz**
  1976 *The Rockefellers: An American Dynasty.* New York: Signet Books, New American Library.

**Copland, Aaron, and Vivian Perlis**
  1984 *Copland: 1900 Through 1942.* New York: St. Martin's/Marek.

**Csikszentmihalyi, Mihaly**
  1982 in Ronald Gross, editor, *Invitation to Lifelong Learning.* Chicago: Follett Publishing Company.

**Current Biography: Who's News and Why: 1952**
  1953 Anna Rothe and Evelyn Lohr, editors, New York: The H.W. Wilson Co.

**Current Biography Yearbook 1967**
 1967, 1968, Charles Moritz, editor. New York: The H.W. Wilson Co.

**Elliott, Osborn**
 1959 *Men at the Top.* New York: Harper and Row.

**Emerson, Ralph Waldo**
 1947 in Saxe Commins and Robert N. Linscott, *The World's Great Thinkers. Man and Man: The Social Philosophers.* "Self-Reliance." New York: Random House, pp. 383–408.

**Florman, Samuel C.**
 1986 "Toward Liberal Learning for Engineers," in *Technology Review*, February, March.

**Franklin, Benjamin**
 1964 Leonard W. Labaree, editor, *The Autobiography of Benjamin Franklin.* New Haven, Conn.: Yale University Press.

**Galbraith, John Kenneth**
 1977 *The Age of Uncertainty.* Boston: Houghton Mifflin Company.

**Gallup, George Jr., and Alec M. Gallup**
 1986 *The Great American Success Story: Factors That Affect Achievement.* Homewood, Ill.: Dow Jones-Irwin.

**Goleman, Daniel**
 1985 *Vital Lies, Simple Truths.* New York: Simon Schuster.

**Hemingway, Ernest**
 1984 *A Moveable Feast.* London: Panther Books.

**Hughes, Robert**
 1986 "Inventing a Sensory Utopia," *Time*, November.

**Huston, John**
 1980 *An Open Book.* New York: Alfred A. Knopf.

**Iacocca, Lee, with William Novak**
1984 *Iacocca: An Autobiography.* New York: Bantam Books.

**Judson, Horace Freeland**
1979 *The Eighth Day of Creation: Makers of the Revolution in Biology.* New York: Simon and Schuster.

**Koestler, Arthur**
1964 *The Act of Creation.* New York: The Macmillan Co.

**Lamb, Robert**
1982 "Erskine Caldwell," *The Atlanta Journal and Constitution.* January 31, 1982.

**Lubin, Albert J.**
1972 *Stranger on the Earth: A Psychological Biography of Vincent Van Gogh.* New York: Holt, Rinehart and Winston.

**Lynn, Loretta, with George Vecsey**
1976 *Loretta Lynn: Coal Miner's Daughter.* New York: Warner Books.

**McClelland, David C.**
1961 *The Achieving Society.* Princeton, New Jersey: D. Van Nostrand Company.

**McCormack, Mark H.**
1984 *What They Don't Teach You at Harvard Business School.* New York: Bantam Books.

**Maccoby, Michael**
1981 *The Leader.* New York: Simon and Schuster.

**Marcus, Stanley**
1974 *Minding the Store.* Boston: Little, Brown and Company.
1979 *Quest for the Best.* New York: Viking Press.

**Maslow, A. H.**

1954 *Motivation and Personality.* New York: Harper and Row.

1968 *Toward a Psychology of Being.* New York: Van Nostrand Reinhold Company.

**Michener, James**

1984 "Keys of the Past Open Doors to the Future: Liberal Arts Decline is Not Gain for Technology," in *The Atlanta Journal/The Atlanta Constitution*, October 21.

**Murray, Kathryn, with Betty Hannah Hoffman**

1960 *My Husband, Arthur Murray.* New York: Simon and Schuster.

**Pollock, John**

1985 *To All the Nations: The Billy Graham Story.* Minneapolis, Minn.: The Billy Graham Evangelistic Association and Harper and Row.

**Salk, Jonas**

1985 *Anatomy of Reality: Merging of Institution and Reason.* New York: Praeger.

**Samuelson, Paul A.**

1986 "On the Prowl in an 'Enchanted Forest.'" *The New York Times*, October 12, 1986.

**Schonberg, Harold C.**

1986 "Barry Tuckwell vs the Treacherous French Horn," in *Connoisseur.* September.

**Schulz, Charles M.**

1976 *Peanuts Jubilee: My Life and Art with Charlie Brown and Others.* New York: Ballantine Books.

**Simon, Herbert A.**

1979 *Models of Thought.* New Haven, Conn.: Yale University Press.

1985 Centennial National Lecture Series (unpublished transcript), Georgia Tech, Atlanta.

1987 "How Creative Managers Create," in *The Library Management Quarterly*, Vol. 10, No. 1.

Sinderman, Carl J.
1985 *The Joy of Science: Excellence and its Rewards.* New York: Plenum Press.

Skinner, B. F.
1983 *A Matter of Consequences.* New York: Alfred A. Knopf.

Stieglitz, Harold
1985 *Chief Executives View Their Jobs.* New York: The Conference Board.

Stoppard, Tom
1982, 1983 *The Real Thing.* London: Faber and Faber.

Swanson, Gloria
1980 *Swanson on Swanson.* New York: Random House.

Thomas, Benjamin Platt
1952 *Abraham Lincoln: A Biography.* New York: Knopf.

Taylor, Nick
1982 "The American Hero as Media Mogul," *Atlanta* magazine, September.

Theodorson, George A., and Achilles G. Theodorson
1969 *Modern Dictionary of Sociology.* New York: Thomas Y. Crowell Co.

Vaughan, Roger
1978 *Ted Turner: The Man Behind the Mouth.* Boston: Sail Books.

Wallace, Robert Keith, and Herbert Benson
1972 "The Physiology of Meditation," in Timothy J. Teyler, *Altered States of Awareness: Readings From Scientific American.* Washington, D.C. Scientific American.

**Watson, James D.**

1968 *The Double Helix: A Personal Account of the Discovery of the Structure of DNA.* New York: Atheneum

**Williams, Christian**

1981 *Lead, Follow, or Get Out of the Way: The Story of Ted Turner.* New York: Times Books.

**Wind, Herbert Warren**

1983 "The Sporting Scene: Mostly About Nicklaus," in *The New Yorker*, May 30.

# Index